Kids on YouTube

KIDS ON YOUTUBE

Technical Identities and Digital Literacies

Patricia G. Lange

Walnut Creek, CA

Left Coast Press, Inc.
1630 North Main Street, #400
Walnut Creek, CA 94596
www.LCoastPress.com

ISBN 978-1-61132-935-3 hardcover
ISBN 978-1-61132-936-0 paperback
ISBN 978-61132-937-7 institutional eBook
ISBN 978-61132-938-4 consumer eBook

Library of Congress Cataloging in Publication Data
Lange, Patricia G.
Kids on youtube : technical identities and digital literacies / Patricia G Lange.
    pages cm
    Includes bibliographical references and index.
    ISBN 978-1-61132-935-3 (hardback) -- ISBN 978-1-61132-936-0 (paperback) --
ISBN 978-1-61132-937-7 (institutional ebook) -- ISBN 978-61132-938-4 (consumer
eBook)
    1. Internet and children. 2. Internet--Social aspects. I. Title.
    HQ784.I58L364 2014
    004.67'8083--dc23
                                        2013041743

Printed in the United States of America

The paper used in this publication meets the minimum requirements of American
National Standard for Information Sciences—Permanence of Paper for Printed Library
Materials, ANSI/NISO Z39.48–1992.

Book Design by Lisa Devenish
Cover design by Piper Wallis

CONTENTS
<<<◀ ■ ▶>>>

ACKNOWLEDGMENTS

First and foremost, I would like to thank my parents Jay and Lilia Gonzalez. This book would not have been possible without their generous support. I would also like to thank my husband Andrew Lange, and my children Catherine and Alexander for their patience during the time-consuming processes of field-work, research, and writing. I cannot thank them enough for their understanding as I traveled across the United States to attend YouTube meet-ups, watched seemingly countless videos on YouTube, and sequestered myself away to write. Thanks also to my sister Leah Gonzalez Jarlsberg, with whom I had fun analyzing films when growing up, and my brother Michael Gonzalez, whose technical expertise I enjoy learning about and admire greatly. Special thanks also to the Lange clan—especially Janet, Jay, Colin, Tessa, and Jonathan—for their enthusiastic support. For their enduring friendship and encouragement I would like to thank Brian Cheu, Eric Share, Matthew Carhart, Christopher Cooke, Jan Cooke, Kevin Carter, Lisa Taylor, Sally Rayn, Deanne Pérez-Granados, and Lisa Naulls.

I am deeply grateful to The John D. and Catherine T. MacArthur Foundation for supporting my research and the project Kids' Informal Learning with Digital Media: An Ethnographic Investigation of Innovative Knowledge Cultures. I would like to thank to Mizuko Ito and the late Peter Lyman for their inspiration in researching informal learning through digital media, as well as the Annenberg Center for Communication and the School for Cinematic Arts at the University of Southern California (USC). Thanks also to everyone on the digital youth research team at USC and the University of California, Berkeley. I am especially grateful to Barrie Thorne, Michael Carter, Diane Harley, Heather Horst, danah boyd, and Becky Herr-Stephenson. I would also like to thank Virginia Kuhn, Holly Willis, Steve Anderson, Gabriel Peters-Lazaro, Mike Jones, and all the staff at the Institute for Multimedia Literacy at USC for providing support and a stimulating environment to discuss my ideas. I am very grateful also to the Department of Anthropology at USC, and would like to thank Nancy Lutkehaus, Lanita Jacobs, and Jennifer Cool for providing a strong base of anthropological support.

For intellectual inspiration, I would like to thank Conrad Kottak, Bruce Mannheim, Ruth Behar, Lesley Milroy, Webb Keane, the late Sharon Stephens, Gwen Dewar, Adrienne Young, M. Bianet Castellanos, Daniel Bass, and the late Christopher O'Leary.

My odyssey into anthropology began while I was a technology analyst at SRI International. I appreciated the opportunity to work with Charline Poirier on studying virtual reality systems. For provocative discussions during an ethnographic research project on computer use in homes in Celebration, Florida, I would like to thank David Millen and ATT Labs.

I would like to thank Jan English-Lueck and Chuck Darrah for their contributions to the field and for their generous support. As a lecturer at San José State University, I was particularly grateful for the opportunity to teach students about culture through film. I also appreciated the support of everyone from the Silicon Valley EthnoBreakfast Club and the consistently helpful exchanges that we have had over the years. Thanks to Diane Schiano for keeping this group alive. I am especially grateful to Bonnie Nardi, Gitti Jordan, Charlotte Linde, Jeanette Blomberg, Melissa Cefkin, Anne McClard, Roxana Wales, Brinda Dalal, and Elizabeth Churchill. I appreciated the opportunity to engage in stimulating conversations with anthropologists and social scientists working in technical cultures.

Many scholars have provided inspiration during this challenging process. I am deeply grateful for the encouragement that I received from Henry Jenkins at USC. Thanks to USC students in communication and anthropology for their feedback on my work. I would also like to thank scholars who shared their insights on online video and digital cultures including Jean Burgess, Joshua Green, Howard Rheingold, Michael Wesch, and Mindy Faber.

Most especially, I would like to thank the people of YouTube and the first-generation video bloggers who contributed their time and insights to this study. Although I cannot name everyone here, I am grateful that they shared their experiences, which provided important information about what it means to share the self through media. I would like to thank pioneering video bloggers including Ryanne Hodson, Jay Dedman, the "Field" family, Markus Sandy, Alicia Shay, Michael Verdi, Zadi Diaz, Steve Woolf, Roxanne Darling, Mike Ambs, and all the first-generation video bloggers who encouraged me to participate in video blogging spaces, both online and off.

I would like to thank California College of the Arts for providing a stimulating intellectual home. Finally, I would like to express my gratitude to the anonymous reviewers and to my editor, Jennifer Collier Jennings, who helped bring this book into its final form. I will be forever grateful for your guidance and support.

CHAPTER 1

Introduction: Ways with Video

Every day, kids are sharing their lives through video. The most popular video-sharing site is YouTube, which streams more than 4 billion videos daily (Oreskovic 2012; PR Newswire 2013). With 1 billion users visiting every month, more than 100 hours of video are uploaded to the site every minute (Warman 2013). As kids increasingly engage in this vastly popular activity, society is debating the question, Are kids actually learning anything by making so many videos?

YouTube's catalogue is so vast that it can seem like a different phenomenon depending on how one uses it (Lange 2008a). Most people think of YouTube as simply a repository of disturbing or funny videos of things like skate boarding dogs. Indeed, the site's earliest beginnings stemmed from its founders' desire to share videos of interest to them. At that time, casually sharing videos online was difficult given videos' high bandwidth. The company was founded in February 2005 by Chad Hurley, Steve Chen, and Jared Karim, who met when working at PayPal, an online payment service (Hopkins 2006). The site's first test video had the look and feel of a grassroots effort. Entitled *Me at the zoo,* the 20-second video depicted Karim in front of an elephant exhibit simply commenting on the animals' trunks (Pham 2010). In its initial years, the site garnered interest in part because of the wide variety of videos it displayed, including both amateur and professional fare, and in part because it allowed participants to interact and comment on videos. Numerous thriving sub-communities formed, including one that was oriented around connecting with other YouTubers who enjoyed making more communicative videos.

After YouTube was acquired by Google for 1.7 billion in 2006 (Hopkins 2006), ongoing desires for profitability lead to increased use of advertising mechanisms and deals with media companies to show more videos made by professionals. I observed that the look and feel of the site changed frequently, and eventually morphed from being a more social media platform with links to friends and commentary, to emphasize more commercial fare and individualized consumption of the professional media that the corporate entity of YouTube chose to feature.

The site's vast catalogue makes it a kind of Rorschach mirror that reflects each viewer's own desires, fantasies, and fears. Typically when I tell someone I am researching YouTube, they describe the particular video or genre that they find most amusing or frightening. A parent might ask if I have seen videos made by cyberbullies; a college student might ask if I've seen the latest video of a popular 20-something celebrity who had just hit the big time. Politicians are also part of the action; many have seen their campaigns derailed or their issues boosted by participating on YouTube, thus underscoring its importance to the civic landscape (Schwab 2008). Others pointed out the vast array of tutorials YouTube offers on everything from making cakes to tackling a complicated piano piece. Many people have observed, "You can learn anything on YouTube."

YouTube is much more than a place to go and see viral videos. Although kids have fun simply watching YouTube, many choose to make their own videos. In so doing, they develop new media literacies that kids and scholars believe will help them communicate and participate more fully in an increasingly networked world. New digital communication media invite us to reconsider the skills, knowledge sets, and tools that future generations need to master to be able to participate fully as networked citizens and self-actualized individuals. While some parents and educators see what happens on YouTube as frivolity, in fact, kids are exhibiting an awareness that they must have the skills to use new technical tools in order to self-actualize and achieve visible personhood among heterogeneous, networked publics.

When young people express themselves through video and socialize with family and friends, they are building on a long tradition of media sharing in the United States. Having an online presence and sharing one's message through media are key aspects of being a socially connected young person. Sites such as YouTube enable children and families to broadcast their message in ways that yield both opportunities and complications for their personhood, technical identities, and self-actualization. On the one hand, kids have exciting opportunities to learn digital skills by choosing preferred media and tackling personally exciting projects. They learn many technical and participatory media skills when they make and distribute videos online. Such activities are changing the definition of literacy. On the other hand, making videos presents participatory and ethical challenges, as people create and share media that may circulate in perpetuity to unpredictable publics. Knowing what to share is an important aspect of media literacy.

Skeptics need only examine the crucial role that social media played in the U.S. presidential elections of 2008 and 2012 to appreciate the importance of online expression for achieving tangible success in one of the world's most visible seats of power (Knight 2012; Wortham 2012). Social media skills are becoming widely perceived as crucial for participating in everyday civic processes, discussing issues, and influencing voter outcomes. But such skills are not developed overnight. Media skills are built up through the micro-interactions that individuals have when creating personally interesting media, receiving feedback, and learning to craft the self and broadcast one's message.

In many ways, Shirley Brice Heath's (1983) classic work on people's "ways with words" serves as an important inspiration for this research. Years ago, Heath investigated how people learned to read, write, and communicate in everyday contexts at home and in school. She examined what kids read and how they learned to communicate during play, religious activities, and casually on the family's front porch. She explored in great detail the effects of community interaction patterns on the development of working-class kids' literacies. In some cases, home-based basic reading and writing practices did not prepare kids well for school, and what was learned in school was not always integrated back into family life. She found that language use was greatly influenced by the values and social roles that people engaged in with their families and communities. Such factors were crucial in "determining an individual's access to goods, services, and estimations of position and power in the community" (Heath 1983:11). Heath describes severe disconnects between the literacy practices at school and at home. The importance of language development outside of school depended a great deal on its perceived usefulness in everyday communication and socialization.

A new disconnect is now being observed with video—except the trajectory is going in the opposite direction. Instead of seeing people struggle to understand the everyday value of things taught in school, many young people are now developing important skills outside of the classroom, yet these skills are not yet consistently recognized as important in formal institutions. Although the situation varies cross-culturally and is changing, parents and educators do not always value social media and video. Conversely, many kids and teens are learning important digital skills outside of the classroom, a trend which fuels an unrealistic mythos that informal learning outside of classrooms is guaranteed and natural for all young people who are growing up with suites of digital technologies. Kids are assumed to be inherently fluent at using all media to the same degree. These trends yield popular binary discourses that either characterize youth as frittering their time away on sites like YouTube, or as natural-born technologists who learn nothing from peers, families, or teachers. Neither extreme is helpful for understanding media experiences.

Although informal learning environments like YouTube enable exciting learning opportunities for people to make media together and gain crucial feedback, not everyone does it alone, and people's learning opportunities vary. This book enhances our understanding of media experiences by developing these central arguments:

- Despite the mythos that technically oriented kids are mostly self-taught, the meaning of that term varies greatly, and includes intensely social forms of learning when making media with friends and family.

- Many children and teens wish to project an identity of being technically savvy, and the dynamics of technical identity negotiations have a direct influence on how and what kids learn.

- Digital inequities persist, even when kids in the same peer group have access to people and tools.

- Asymmetries of ability remain entrenched because people have different mediated dispositions and interests with regard to digital tools.

In the future, people who lack crucial self-expression skills across media may find themselves at a disadvantage to those who are acquiring these skills, whether inside or outside of classrooms. Yet informal learning opportunities present challenges. This book describes successful informal learning interactions, while also investigating the circumstances under which people who have physical access to technical and social tools struggle to master digital media skills.

Interpersonal dynamics and self-perceptions of identity shape learning opportunities. Kids sometimes compete and jockey for status among their peers in techno-cultural and techno-social hierarchies. They vie to appear technically savvy and superior to their friends and family. This competition means that learning is not always straightforward, even among well-intentioned friends. Kids also have different commitments to media; some achieve mastery as advanced amateurs, and others are content to stay casual. While exciting opportunities exist to learn in environments like YouTube, people's learning opportunities are not isometric.

People's "ways with video" quietly shape their individual learning opportunities, especially with regard to their perception of constructing, maintaining, and negotiating a technologized identity. Discourses about "digital youth," "digital generations," "net generations," and similar terms often orient toward kids who are growing up with an ever-increasing suite of digital tools (Ito et al. 2010; Palfrey and Gasser 2008; Prensky 2006; Tapscott 2009). Discourses about "digital youth" acknowledge and honor the abilities of young people as they develop the skills necessary to communicate through technology. This book shares with these prior works an excitement about how such tools and access to networked publics offer fascinating growth opportunities to youth.

At the same time, if terms such as "digital youth" are taken to an extreme and analyzed in homogenous terms, people may assume that all kids of a certain age are equally knowledgeable about and are willing to use all types of digital tools. Yet, studies show that kids engage with technologies in very different ways, ranging from the social to the intensely geeked-out (Ito et al. 2010). In addition, not all young people have the same access to technologized media. Scholars have observed "participation gaps" (Jenkins et al. 2006), which often exhibit familiar socio-cultural inequities based on sex, gender, ethnicity, and class. It is difficult to grapple with advanced new media, for example, if you cannot afford a reasonably fast and reliable Internet connection. As new media become available, basic technical and infrastructural needs commensurately increase. Public access points such as libraries and community centers may not provide adequate platforms for advanced media manipulation. Such gaps reveal that not all children in the same age cohort have equal access to new media ecologies.

Many policy makers and technology advocates argue that if only each child had a computer, gaps in technical literacy skills would be eradicated. Having a robust computer is a good first step, but subtle participatory gaps, such as competition for relative technical identity, also influence what is learned within informal learning environments. This book contributes to our understanding of these more subtle but equally important digital inequities.

Children in the same age cohort may have widely different mediated dispositions, or tendencies toward certain activities with regard to the type of media or devices they use, and the online milieu within which they feel most comfortable. Such differences in approach to technology have been observed elsewhere, including formal technology classes. Some kids have associated computer use with being a "geek" and thus eschewed intensive engagements with technology (Holloway and Valentine 2003). Sometimes kids exhibit different trajectories with regard to how they enter into digital spaces (Ito et al. 2010). While some kids have preferred to engage in online spaces through "friendship-driven" social media sites such as Facebook, others gravitate toward a more focused interest in developing "geeked out" skills in niche areas, including making YouTube videos. Although it is possible for children to transition from modest engagements to developing deep skill sets, such a pattern is not necessarily a blue print for all kids' informal, extracurricular engagement with digital technologies of communication and play. Youth who enjoy geeking out are still perceived by many other kids as existing "at the margins of teens' social worlds" (Ito et al. 2010:16).

By attending closely to kids' perceptions of technology and its uses, this book contributes to the project of new media literacy studies, which acknowledges the ideological and socially constructed definitions of what a particular cultural group sees as "literacy"—including which sets of knowledge and skills are necessary to succeed (Hull and Schultz 2002; Ito et al. 2010; Jenkins et al. 2006; Mahiri 2004). Literacy discourses are normatively constructed and are often emotional. Discourses about media literacies are often infused with concerns by adults, parents, and educators who are anxious about new technologies, and largely see themselves as marginalized from kids' techno-cultural worlds. Although definitions in technical environments are moving targets, media literacy can be defined as "the ability to access, analyze, evaluate, and create messages in a variety of forms" (Aufderheide and Firestone 1993). Digital media literacy does not ignore prior forms of literacy such as reading and writing, but rather extends traditional definitions to include skills such as digital video production that are required to navigate new media environments (Buckingham 2003; Jenkins et al. 2006).

Despite the mythos in technical cultures that the best way to learn is to be "self-taught" through hands-on "tinkering," in fact, technical learning has a profoundly social quality (Bakardjieva 2005:102). What is meant by cognitive forms of "learning" and identifying the precise moment of the acquisition of new information or skills is beyond the scope of the present work. What is of vital interest is understanding how and when kids perceive that they can experience actionable learning opportunities, and whether they feel they can capitalize on such opportunities in their everyday video-making efforts. A learning opportunity in media is any situation in which participants perceive a possibility to change the status of their technical knowledge, production capabilities, participatory abilities, or self-expressive skills. This book argues that perceptions of learning opportunities' effectiveness in peer-to-peer settings was deeply intertwined with how people perceived their technical identities in relation to other people. Sometimes the perceived asymmetry of technological knowledge among a group of video making peers was so high and time pressures so great to keep pace with video production schedules that video makers did not have the resources or energy to bring all of their friends up to speed. This kind of asymmetrical learning was not intentionally harmful or selfish, but emerged because people had different goals and dispositions with regard to how much time and energy they realistically wanted to spend on learning video skills.

If kids often learn by "observing and communicating with people engaged in the same interests and in the same struggles for status and recognition that they are," then it is imperative to analyze informal social processes of using digital media (Ito et al. 2010:22). This book investigates new media literacy dynamics by ethnographically exploring the intersection between informal learning, technical identities, and lived experiences of video production and participation on YouTube. Central questions include: How do youth use video to express the self? How do they achieve a technical identity, and do these identity negotiations help them capitalize on learning opportunities to achieve digital media literacies? Under what circumstances do things go smoothly and when do complications ensue? What are the roots of these complications and how might ethnography reveal them?

The book draws on a two-year ethnographic study of U.S. kids and adults on YouTube that I conducted from 2006 to 2008. Because many young people generally referred to themselves as "kids" rather than "children" in ethnographic interviews, terms such as "kids" and "youth" will be used interchangeably throughout the book. The ethnography included interviews with 110 adults, including parents of young children, and 40 young people who participated on YouTube. Interviews were conducted with 22 kids, aged 9 to 17, and 18 young adults, aged 18 to 26. The study also draws on participant-observation methods, and analyses of artifacts such as videos and text comments to understand everyday video making practices. Online observations of interaction were collected as people discussed videos on the site through text and video comments. Observations were also recorded at in-person, You-Tube meet-ups where people gathered to socialize, have fun, and make media with friends and family.

The ethnography also included a participatory component. I established my own video blogs called *AnthroVlog* (one on YouTube and another on a separate site off of YouTube) and posted one video per week to viscerally understand what it meant to display one's work-in-progress for the world to judge. The project is comparative in that I studied YouTubers, as well as early video bloggers who maintained websites off of YouTube. The videos posted to *AnthroVlog* on YouTube received a combined total of more than 1 million views. This level of viewership prompted a request from the site to apply for YouTube partner status, an invitation which I have so far declined to pursue. Additional details about the ethnographic approach are in the Appendix.

In mapping the ethnographic terrain, one inevitably grapples with the kind of videos and video makers that should be studied. Rather than choosing between pre-professionals and vernacular video making, the ethnography explored a diverse array of videos that will be referred to as personally expressive media. Many study participants were early adopters of YouTube. They strove to hone their craft and become media professionals. Many advanced amateurs also posted casual, everyday media of themselves and their friends hanging out. Conversely, several casual video makers saw their videos take off, and they began to monetize their work and change career plans. Such trends problematize strict delineations of videos and video makers as either professional or vernacular. As a result of the study's open-ended approach, the ethnography includes a diverse set of videos, from live-action versions of computer games to deeply felt video blogs about civic engagement to casual footage of teens having fun on a hike. While many of the youth in the study strove to prepare for a media career, others were more interested in connecting with people who shared similar interests.

The aim of the study was to investigate the interrelationship between video self-expression, learning opportunities, and technologized aspects of identity. To grapple with these issues, the ethnography draws on three main concepts: personally expressive media; performances of technical affiliation; and phenomenologies of the mediated moment. Studying people's interpretive experiences of specific mediated moments challenges the crude categorizations of "creator" and "viewer," and opens a path to exploring how the creation of personally expressive media helped shape informal learning encounters.

Personally Expressive Media

In researching the subtle dynamics of informal learning, an ethnographer is faced with an important challenge. Should one study advanced amateurs and pre-professionals, or should one focus on everyday video making such as posting videos of a fun time at a coffee shop? Which category will yield the greatest insights for understanding how people build technical and participatory skills in informal learning environments? Any discussion about what is happening on YouTube must be considered within a larger context of past traditions of making media. Are things being posted to YouTube the same or different, for example, to what Chalfen (1987) called the "home mode" of photographs and video?

Studying YouTube means acknowledging and dealing with a complicated variety of videos. Such diversity problematizes prior categorizations that strictly delineate amateurs from professionals. Such binaries have been theoretically problematized in other areas of amateurism and media (Buckingham et al., 2007; Burgess and Green, 2009b; Moran, 2002; Stebbins, 1977; Toffler, 1980). For example, Stebbins (1977) argued that a system of professionals, amateurs, and publics exists such that amateurs are distinguished from the publics who view and appreciate their work. Further, many prior categorizations were essentially synchronic. A video made for fun, targeted for a family or a few friends, is assumed by scholars to forever hold the same status. But YouTube's publicity complicates this assumption, given its context of potential commercialization. People may put up a video for fun and see their view count rise to the point where the corporate entity of YouTube might invite them to become a partner. YouTube partners agree to have ads placed within or next to their videos. In return, they receive a share of advertising revenue that results from the ads. Over time partners may develop a more advanced amateur or even professional status on the site.

Rather than adjudicating categories of videos or video makers that eventually may change commercial and/or social status, the study uses the broader term of personally expressive media. YouTube became popular in part because different kinds of works existed alongside each other, giving the site immense variety (Burgess and Green 2009a). The press tends to focus on high-profile, wacky videos such as those depicting piano playing cats. Such videos may certainly help people explore how to operate cameras and discover content that captures an audience. However, YouTube videos are rarely explored for their opportunities for skill development. More wacky videos are chosen by professional media to speciously illustrate that all vernacular media lacks technical merit. They are used to emphasize corporate media professionalism. This book is concerned with how a variety of works—both pre-professional and vernacular—reveal various dimensions of digital media skill development.

What emerged from the ethnography of such a diverse body of videos is a category productively termed "personally expressive media," which includes any mediated artifact or set of media that enables a creator to communicate aspects of the self. Personally expressive media covers a wide terrain that does not pre-judge the intent or ultimate commodification (successful or unsuccessful) of a work. On YouTube, some people wish to commercialize their work while others do not. Some participants wish to reach only a few close friends with their media, while others seek connection to broad audiences to achieve personal fame or accomplish forms of civic engagement. What unites these media makers is a wish to communicate personal ideas, feelings, or experiences through video. An advanced amateur video made by committee may not be particularly personally expressive for anyone; an intimate video made by a professional may be quite personally expressive.

Many people see YouTube videos as "home mode" work because the videos were made at home or with a few friends in public or semi-public places such as parks, cafes, and schools. Yet, what is seen on YouTube today covers a vaster and more complex terrain than what anthropologist Richard Chalfen originally meant when he used the term "home mode." Studying families in the United States in the 1970s to early 1980s, Chalfen referred to the "home mode" as a "pattern of interpersonal and small group communication centered around the home" (Chalfen 1987:8). Encompassing photography, film, and video, home mode media was shared by families and close intimates. Video makers knew their subjects and their audiences, who could identify most of the people in the images. They rarely branched out farther than close kin groups, and generally did not include people at the office, gym, or even schools.

Chalfen (1987:8) distinguished the home mode from media that were produced for "mass distribution to large, heterogeneous, anonymous audiences." Deliberately bracketing out professional and advanced amateur media makers (such as people who would join local camera clubs) from his study, Chalfen did not study photographers, filmmakers, critics, scholars, or anyone else with training in visual media production. This intellectual move addressed crucial gaps in the analytical record; scholars had ignored this sector of media production, despite its widespread popularity (Camper 1986). When scholars did address home media, they were often dismissed as banal, uncreative, and technically limited by widespread commercialization of inexpensive equipment (Pini 2009; Zimmerman 1995).

More recent studies recognize the importance of honoring the stylistics and aesthetic contributions such works have made to the cultural production of images (Moran 2002; Pini 2009). For example, as Moran (2002) argues, stylistics such as fast zooms and shaky camera images are often used routinely in mainstream, narrative films as tropes of authentic voices as expressed through home video recording. Studies have also analyzed the profound meanings such media have on individuals and social groups, especially with regard to how media sharing affirms family values and strengthens friendships by uniting people who are separated across space and time (Buckingham et al. 2011; Pini 2009).

What constitutes the "home mode" has changed significantly. Home mode media on YouTube depict diverse groups of kin, non-kin communities, and "families we choose" (Weston 1992). Home mode media are no longer binarily contrasted to professional work but rather lie on a continuum between relatively private and more public practices aimed at wider audiences (Buckingham et al. 2011). What is depicted in the home mode is no longer limited to Chalfen's description of themes of personal progress and family continuity through recording special events such as birthdays or the arrival of a new car. Home mode video also now includes a range of creative, delightful, and sometimes disturbing content. In fact, a great deal of content on YouTube is embarrassing, disturbing, and violent, and often involves unwilling media subjects (Strangelove 2010).

Whereas home mode video of the past functioned as memory aids, contemporary video on YouTube exhibits a more interactive and experiential character between the people who are making media together. It is not unusual to see young people post videos of spontaneous, ephemeral, and even banal experiences, such as going to a coffee shop. Although watching this footage may one day serve as a sentimental memory aid for the participants, such video is more about the experience of creating a video together that is fun. Themes in the home mode video idiom have also expanded considerably to include more artistic, playful, and even unpleasant experiences and reflections on life.

Notably, Chalfen (1987) bracketed out of the home mode category anything that was shared in a mass way. However difficult it is for scholars or members of the public to see video of people recording themselves at a ball game or on a hike as anything but home mode, it is important to examine the meanings and viewership of such work. Sometimes home mode footage is posted innocently to facilitate easy video sharing with family and friends. This footage may gain mass viewership. At many other times, people on YouTube post footage of their home-based activities to deliberately gain widespread viewership. Footage intended for mass audiences, even if recorded at home, would no longer qualify under Chalfen's rubric.

Youth whom I interviewed echoed the sentiments of kids in other online studies who often assumed that if it was not "interesting" to people, viewers would simply not watch (Stern 2008). At other times, kids hoped to gain a broad audience by recording aspects of their everyday lives. Sites such as YouTube operate within a networked ecology of numerous communities of interest, or groups of individuals who deeply share passions for particular activities such as playing computer games, watching reality television, talking about contemporary problems, or making videos (Ito et al. 2010). A seemingly banal video about individual reactions to a video game can receive thousands of views from other gaming enthusiasts. People in the study reported feeling delighted when their personal humor seemed to resonate with other viewers, and their popular videos with modest production values propelled them into a new status of video making. One participant even changed his major and career plans when his YouTube videos took off in a serious way.

Most scholars who use terms such as "amateur," "pre-professional," or "home mode" do so in a synchronic way, meaning that a video will begin and end its viewing life in one category. However, YouTube's dynamics challenge such synchronic assumptions. Footage may begin with one intent, but might be reused, repurposed, remixed, or rebroadcast to be perceived by audiences in quite different interpretive contexts. For example, what do we call videos of a child's antics that receive millions of views and in which the mother becomes a YouTube partner? Receiving millions of views constitutes a significant audience. Niche cable television comedy programs such as *The Daily Show* and *The Colbert Report*, for example, receive about one million views per episode (de Moraes 2013). Of course, YouTube view tallies may be inflated with automated view counters (Gayle 2012). Some videos may have started life as "home mode," but on YouTube they became something different. Whether or not any video begins "innocently" as a home mode work (and some intimate videos are born with an intention of widespread circulation and monetization), it is possible for such work to change status, become watched on a global scale, and become folded into a commodified, advertisement-fueled context.

Researchers now struggle to characterize what it is they are seeing on the 'Tube, especially when one considers the diverse range of videos that kids are creating and sharing. Terms all seem to have advantages and disadvantages. Because the term connotes the ordinary and the everyday, using the term "vernacular video" is a logical move. But such a term seems to bracket out pre-professional participants' work, and many participants in my YouTube study were former, current, or pre-professionals who were formally trained in and quite experienced in making media.

Van Dijck (2007) uses the term "homecasting" to characterize contemporary forms of video sharing. Homecasting is defined as "the use of video-sharing websites to download and upload prerecorded, rerecorded, tinkered, and self-produced audiovisual content via personal computers from the home and to anybody's home" (van Dijck 2007:4). Of course some videos may be recorded as they are being broadcast, as well. The term homecasting emphasizes the media distribution mechanism rather than the media itself, which may never make it online, may not be recorded at home, or may be deleted from the airwaves in the future. "Homecasting" is oriented around "snippets" or the three to six minute fragmentary videos that are commonly found on YouTube, but may not be what advanced amateurs are oriented around. Videos that are "homecast" in this rubric are ultimately only the work of non-professionals, even if, as van Dijck (2007:13) suggests, they "imitate the begin-middle-end form of a polished audiovisual production." But why must the term "imitate" be used? Here again, the amateur work seems to be characterized by its relative position to the professional. Although it receives respect, it seems to be viewed as merely "mimicry" of more polished professional work. Yet to exhibit a well-formulated structure of story telling or documentary does not necessarily constitute mimicry. Amid binary discourses, it is important to remember that professional work is not always high art, and amateur video can be quite polished and compelling.

Personally expressive media refers to works in which video makers communicate personal, artistic, political, or other messages and content of interest to them. It is an intentionally broad category that avoids presupposing the existence of any particular content or theme; it may be planned or unplanned "home mode" content that centers on friends and family. Alternatively, it may include videos that are highly structured shows with narrative formats and popular content targeted to wide audiences. It may even receive compensation and through its popularity, help change a video maker's social status. The term personally expressive media does not assume any particular audience size, which may be intentionally or unintentionally large or small. Whether a particular artifact is genuinely personally expressive for all parties in a video team is an empirical and interpretive question. It is quite possible for people to help their friends make a video in a way that realizes their friends' feelings and vision more than their own, and thus is not particularly personally expressive to all contributors in the same way.

Studying a broad category such as personally expressive media reveals different levels of intensity in media making, and sheds insight on the dynamics of informal learning between peers and within families. By studying personally expressive media, it became clear that kids and adults often exhibit different dispositions with regard to the kind of media they generally prefer to make. Some preferred more visually oriented media, while others felt more comfortable communicating through text, voice, or social media. Mediated dispositions refer to the types of media, communicative channels, and devices that people generally prefer to use to communicate. Exhibiting a mediated center of gravity means that although kids may use many different communicative forms or devices at one time or another, their preferences may be tangibly manifested in visible weightings towards specific media content, skills, and tools. In contrast to discourses about digital generations, the kids whom I studied did not display an equal interest and level of intensity of engagement with all forms of digital communication.

Mediated dispositions were intimately intertwined with people's self-perceptions about their technical identities. An important dynamic affecting learning opportunities had to do with how people created personally expressive media while performing technical identities within individual mediated moments of experience. For some kids, appearing to be a technical person was very important, and showcasing such identifications through the process of making personally expressive media ultimately impacted the range and depth of their perceived learning opportunities.

Performing Technical Affiliation

Learning in public presents a prideful conundrum. On the one hand, people can learn much by posting videos and receiving feedback and encouragement on their work. Even relatively advanced media makers can learn by sharing their videos. For example, a video maker who made popular tutorials on technical special effects said in an ethnographic interview that he learned to make better tutorials in part through viewers' feedback. On the other hand, showing one's work-in-progress reveals to the world potential areas of improvement. It may challenge one's sense of self to hear harsh criticisms about one's work and technical abilities. If one wishes to propose a technical identity of competence, one might be reluctant to show one's work and potentially expose "mistakes." Study participants sometimes reported being embarrassed and removing old videos from YouTube. How people choose to present the self in a technical way is an important subject of this book.

When creators post a video, they often transmit—whether intentionally or not—important information about their technical ability. For example, a well-executed video from a technical perspective potentially indexes a person who has the technical skills to make polished videos. However, viewers beware. Making videos is often a communal process and an individual's skills may not always be "read" from a single artifact. In addition, people may claim to have greater skill than is apparent in a single video (Lange 2012). Watching videos should be considered a touchstone or first step in exploring an individual video maker's abilities.

Technical identity work sometimes takes the form of sharing interests expressed in video content. As discussed in Chapter 3, when a teenaged girl geeks out by talking about her favorite game console, she is performing affiliation to particular types of technologized activities. In another example, a girl geek might post a *machinima* video, a technologized genre in which a video is created by recording activities in a game. Such a genre displays certain technical abilities because it requires multiple and interwoven literacies that include both gaming and video in order to envision original stories and use images from one technologized genre to create artifacts in another. However, negotiating technical identity is about much more than the video content. The choices one makes about where to post a video, whether to respect or subvert a site's technical parameters, and how to handle commentary and feedback from viewers are also mechanisms for establishing a favorable, technically situated understanding of the self.

To deal with the question of how learning opportunities are influenced by technologized identity performances, this book uses a rubric called "performing technical affiliation," which refers to displaying in words and actions certain beliefs, values, or practices that are assumed to be associated with particular techno-cultural groups (Lange 2003, 2011). Such performances help interlocutors move through processes of identification so that relative levels of expertise may be interactively established. This rubric is influenced by Goffman's (1959) performative lens, but ultimately focuses on how identifications interactively interweave on- and offline, and attends closely to how a performance's uptake is negotiated according to audience and context (Brubaker and Cooper 2000; Jacoby and Gonzales 1991).

Many studies of online visual participation (that focus on posting photographs, videos, or websites) take a (questionably executed) Goffmanesque analysis of performative identity display that avoids consideration of interactive, identification processes. Goffman (1959:15) defined a performance as "all the activity of a given participant on a given occasion which serves to influence in any way *any of the other participants*" (emphasis added). Many studies that crudely apply Goffman's framework only analyze what people "display" when they post personally expressive content online in public settings. But Goffman discussed signals—exhibited in person—that are "given off," which may not be intentional but nevertheless provide identity clues. It is simplistic to assume that online identity display is completely controlled, when in fact, signals are also inadvertently given off about identity online.

What is also crucial is the audience "uptake" that technical identity performances receive. Technical identities of both creator and audience are negotiated during an interaction, in that viewers may ratify or reject a particular proposed performance of technical competence (Jacoby and Gonzales 1991). In this way, "audiences indulging in others' self images, or for that matter responding skeptically to them, are actively (though not necessarily knowingly) committing their own self-action" (Battaglia 1995:5). When people share a technical video, viewers who comment positively may ratify it as technically proficient. Such comments set up a relation of technical expertise for both the creator and viewer, who both propose to be capable of creating and judging a video's technical merit. More robust performative models of identity include an acknowledgment of the active participation of an audience and the interaction between performers and audiences. Such interactions illustrate that identity negotiations have emergent, contextual, and relative qualities.

Goffman's theories are often (mis)applied in almost facile ways when studying online identity display. Often scholars equate what happens online with Goffman's idea of a "front" or onstage area that helps a performer to convey certain identities or roles. For instance, a study of family websites emphasized the "control" that online display supposedly guarantees, in contrast to the less controlled identity-making that purportedly occurs during in-person interactions (Pauwels 2008). Although acknowledging that online participants may give off unwanted identity signals, the study asserted that, "Website owners have much greater control over how they present themselves. They can carefully construct a desired identity and leave out aspects they consider unwanted or possibly damaging" (Pauwels 2008:44).

While a certain amount of control is arguably in evidence online, one cannot always be sure about who has control when it comes to group media-making. Also, mere displays of identity cannot control people's interpretations; viewers may not ratify the impression that video makers aim to project.

A prior study, for example, showed how women quickly saw through the ruse of men pretending to be women online (Herring 1996). Robust performance models include a notion of an interactive audience. It is not enough to assume that broadcasting an aspect of technical identity will guarantee that all viewers will interpret this display in the same way. One may think one is broadcasting a strong technical identity, but in fact, relatively more technical audience members may see the person as a technical novice.

Given the multiple steps in recording, posting, and sharing videos on commercial websites whose owners have their own agendas, it is important to ask what we mean by control, and to what extent individual video makers have control at any point in the media production or sharing process. For example, when we are speaking of a "family" website and the "control" that *families* have to carefully craft "their" identity, we may rightly ask, who exactly is in control? As this study illustrates, sometimes family negotiations occur about what constitutes appropriate media making, and not all parties to a mediated interaction may have equal ability to influence how their identities are publicly displayed or interpreted. If a mother posts her children's baby pictures, not everyone has equal "control" over that image. It is an image that is personally expressive for the mother, but the babies cannot control how they are being portrayed or that their images are broadcast globally. If YouTube uses such an image to make more money than the person sharing the video, who is in "control"? If a video is removed without the video maker's permission because it contains the copyrighted song *Happy Birthday*, can we really speak of media makers' total control over display of their work? Of course, babies cannot argue about their distributed image, but teenagers can. We will see in Chapter 6 that when parents post their teenagers' images during private home moments, community debates may ensue about what is appropriate to post. These interactions and negotiations are crucial for forming and transmitting digital literacies to future generations of media makers.

This book draws on an interactive performance model that extends Goffman's rubric, to examine the special case of technical identity performance and how interactive uptake remains a crucial part of its success (or failure). In contrast to many applications of Goffman's model that contrast online (onstage) to offline (offstage), this book argues that identification processes weave on- and offline and are not simply static, binary, and separate, even though researchers continue to talk about identity as bifurcated on- and offline. The concept of performance is not equated with "masks" and fakery, or the special case that Goffman called the "cynical" performance. People may engage in a technical performance that is sincere, in which they believe what they are saying and doing. They may believe they are broadcasting a technologized identity through their choice of content and media production, even though not all audience members may view them that way.

A performance is only as successful as its uptake. Posting a video that responds to a technical comment or argues a technical point with a commenter is merely an opening bid into an interactive process of what Brubaker and Cooper (2000) call "identification." Identification includes how one characterizes oneself, and how "one is identified by others" in various contexts. In this model, "Self-identification takes place in dialectical interplay with external identification, and the two need not converge" (Brubaker and Cooper 2000:15). Identification is not static but is a process that depends upon factors such as context, audience, intent, and self-conception. Technical identities are typically relative; a non-technical parent may see their child as a technical wizard, but ultimately their children's abilities may be confined to specific skill sets, and kids may lack particular knowledge for future success. Kids do not always display the abundant technical skills that parents assume they have (Livingstone 2009:36). Conversely, techno-geniuses may not be appreciated as such by less technical parents and peers.

Technology as a variable is often not discussed in children's use of media. When technology is discussed it is often assumed to dovetail with traditional identity variables. For example, many studies are rightly concerned with challenging the stereotype that females are discouraged from exhibiting technical interests while males are technologically dominant (Kearney 2006, 2011). Yet technologization patterns are not always gendered in pre-assumed ways. Crucial differences of technical ability and interest often exist within gendered groups (Bakardjieva 2005; Holloway and Valentine 2003; Lange 2003). For example, in several studies, some males displayed cultural and personal predispositions to push the envelope in technology while other males in the same cohort did not (Holloway and Valentine 2003). Similarly, not all boys in my ethnographic study achieved equal technical prowess. In contrast, some girls embraced an explicit geek identity. Technical affiliations should be studied as identity variables in their own right, rather than being assumed to be "readable" from other traditional aspects of identity such as gender.

Consider the experience of two male teens, Clyde and Ben, who are discussed in detail in Chapter 2. In an interview, Clyde told me that his friend and video-making partner Ben had jokingly said he did not need Clyde to make videos. This was a performance of technical identity, one which attempted to establish a techno-social hierarchy between them. In this dyadic micro-hierarchy, Ben portrayed himself as more knowledgeable than Clyde. As Bauman (1977) has suggested with regard to everyday verbal performances in conversation, at root they are often about establishing particular social orders. Clyde responded to Ben's criticisms by establishing a separate, secret YouTube account in which he planned to learn how to make better videos and one day reveal his successful new YouTube identity to Ben. Their rivalry was a playful competition of competence and expertise about what constituted appropriate sets of knowledge in making videos, and who had the ability to execute such knowledge.

By setting up a separate account to learn on his own, Clyde created a learning opportunity to make personally expressive media that provided a safe space to gain technical competence outside of the critical eye of his video making partner. For them, technical identity negotiation started offline, but moved online as Clyde established a secret account, with the goal of one day becoming an expert and revealing his success—both on- and offline—to Ben and other YouTubers. Clyde attempted to craft a technologized, successful video-making identity in part by reacting to Ben and creating separate learning opportunities. In this instance, technical identity, digital literacies, and appropriate learning opportunities exhibited an interwoven dynamic that is of central concern to this book.

Although its point of departure is the website of YouTube, this book is not only concerned with video artifacts, but also offers a behind-the-scenes look at how participants were engaged in interactive moves that tried to establish relative technical expertise vis-à-vis one's video-making peers, friends, family, and audiences. Many studies of online identity performance are limited to analyses of single videos. Rarely do researchers consider the influence of the website in which such videos are embedded. Further, they tend to consider single texts, rather than analyzing a whole body of work by a video maker, or even simply exploring the contextualizing text description that accompanies such works. Yet, analyzing interactive processes of expertise benefits from exploring media-making experiences and processes of technical identification, rather than only analyzing the final public artifacts. The moment of posting a video is but one instance in a phenomenological chain of mediated acts and decisions that shape situated forms of informal learning.

Phenomenologies of the Mediated Moment

In traditional media studies, the unit of analysis is typically a single video or "text." But it is important to consider how a text is contextually embedded and displayed on a particular site. I have heard scholars refer to any online video as a "YouTube video," as if the context of its posting had no bearing on its interpretation. Yet sites have specific features and participatory connotations, as the YouTube phenomenon illustrates (Burgess and Green 2009a). For some participants, posting videos on YouTube versus their own video blogging website was a crucial and meaningful decision. Although this book analyzes mediated identity work within artifacts, it also seeks to examine the contexts, social interactions, and co-constructed meanings of interactive media creation and sharing. It is concerned with the study of experiences, or phenomenologies of micro-media moments, and how they influence technical identity work and informal learning.

Most media scholarship relies on crude categories of "production" and "viewership" to analyze how media is created and shared. Yet, many small instances along this chain are crucial for shaping the creation and interpretation of mediated learning. The act of posting a video is constituted from a series of sub-tasks that are in turn comprised of many micro technical decisions and social interactions. For example, when a person posts a video, they first need to make a video, which includes many sub-tasks such as recording the material, editing a video, and deciding where to post it. But within each of these tasks are other sub-tasks. In recording, for instance, choices must be made about the subject matter, how it will be framed, who will operate the camera, and what jobs participants have when making media collaboratively. Each of these tasks is constituted from a series of smaller, yet potentially very significant actions and decisions.

Many of the individual steps that comprise making a video help craft a social order and influence learning opportunities between co-creators and viewers. For example, as discussed in Chapter 3, the interpersonal dynamics between Lola and Ashley, a mother-daughter video-making team, turned out to be important for how Ashley learned. Lola said in an interview that she encouraged her daughter Ashley to do most of the editing, in order to develop her abilities. Crafting a video is a process, in which participants' social experience, relationships, and decisions shape the learning environment that provides opportunities to improve. In this case, a mother made it a priority to help her daughter develop her technical and self-expressive skills. Such a learning opportunity might have taken a different shape if Ashley had interacted with another video-making partner who jockeyed for technical identity with her, and did not give her the room to develop her skills. Relational identities and goals in specific moments are significant for helping someone to improve.

This book explores subtle dimensions of individual mediated moments as people craft personally expressive media. A mediated moment is an experience that involves some aspect of recording, manipulating, distributing, or viewing a mediated artifact. In phenomenological approaches to social science or interpretive analysis, one conundrum involves determining the appropriate level of analysis (such as "making a video") for study, and deciding where to draw the line when investigating the level of detail needed to understand particular tasks. Making a video may be too crude a category for understanding how learning opportunities are crafted. But what about script writing, filming, and editing? How far must these categories be broken down to achieve understanding? The mediated moments examined in this book are those that participants identified as important or meaningful, in part because they formed inflection points that offered the possibility to change a media maker's identifications, learning opportunities, or negotiation of digital literacies.

This book investigates the meanings and ramifications of mediated moments as participants describe their experiences of them, and it analyzes the effects of these micro-decisions and negotiations on identity formation and digital literacies. When adults post media, they are providing models to their children for what they code as appropriate and important for online participation. With all the attention that has been given to "digital youth," it is important to remember that children on YouTube entered a video world that was created by adults (Herring 2008). They were young adults, perhaps, but it was adults who set the tone and technical parameters for how YouTube participation would work (Herring 2008; Livingstone 2009).

Mediated moments are inflected, as are all experiential moments, with crucially important temporalities. When a group of friends make a video because it would be funny to share on YouTube, their present mediated moments of creation are inflected with the anticipation of future delight of viewers, including themselves. In this way, "the meaning of an action is different depending upon the point in time from which it is observed" (Schutz 1967:65). Having fun with friends and making a video set in the present is light-hearted fun, but takes on a different emotional patina when the same video is viewed years later when everyone has grown up and gone to college, and the teens know they will not be able to make videos together. When we speak of a mediated moment, we are trying to understand how various intersecting temporalities of the past, present, and future shape the experiences of conceptualizing, creating, and sharing media.

Media meanings are co-productive between creators and interpretants. A mediated artifact or set of mediated interactions that have become recorded often invite publics to comment and therefore engage in discourses about the meaning of specific media as well as the ethics of making a particular kind of artifact. Media meanings are not only co-productive with other people, but also with future versions of a self that may bring alternative future interpretations to it, depending upon prior experiences (Sobchack 1999). Sometimes those interpretations include a sense of embarrassment when a video does not map to a creator's current perceived level of technical ability, and so the video is deleted from YouTube, sometimes producing distress in commenters who had taken considerable time to view and post text comments to the video (Lange 2010). The status of so-called "texts" and their interpretations and meanings shift over time. Using a phenomenological approach provides a rich path to rethinking how media research is conducted and how temporalities influence media making.

My study was filled with examples of how people chose to represent themselves and others through media, which is a taken-for-granted exercise for many people in the United States. Maintaining personhood now involves being mediated. In fact, it is not uncommon to find the identities of people who are no longer alive used in social ways. Consider that deceased anthropologists such as Franz Boas, Leslie White, and Mary Douglas all have their own Facebook page! Whether or not these individuals would ever have chosen to be on Facebook, other anthropologists may experience delight in connecting to a fantasized social representation of their intellectual idols. Being a person in many cultural and social circles in the United States includes having a mediated presence. Having a mediated social presence in turn requires appropriate navigation of one's digital footprint, which is becoming almost impossible to protect given commercial and governmental information-sharing environments.

Considering the phenomenologies of the mediated moment helps identify opportunities of informal learning and identity negotiation. Terms such as "creator" and "viewer" are rather lumpen and need to be broken down phenomenologically. For example, most video creators must view their work at some point. Video interpretations may change across viewings. Consider the case of teen-aged Crystal, who recorded a video of herself lip synching and dancing to a song. During editing, the video seemed appropriate for YouTube. After it was posted, she noticed that her dress seemed inappropriately low cut. Fearing that she might risk attracting unwanted sexual attention, she removed the video. Through this exercise she enacted an interpretive representational ideology about how young females should share their online image. The mediated moments of recording and viewing/editing did not reveal problems. It was only when she saw the video later, in its context of being posted to the specific site of YouTube that she identified a potential problem. If we wish to understand the relationship between presentation of the self and negotiation of appropriate digital and participatory literacies, we need to consider more finely how individual mediated moments are played out. Understanding kids' informal learning benefits from multi-method ethnographies that go behind the text, and examine the subtleties of mediated moments. By doing so, we can begin to disentangle the threads of meaning and digital literacies that kids negotiate when hanging out and making videos with their friends and family.

The Plan of this Book

This book begins with a discussion of the most common forms of video making encountered in my ethnographic study, which involved kids making videos with peers. Chapters 2 to 4 provide analyses and case studies of kids making videos with friends or on their own. As previously indicated, the book focuses on the everyday video making of mostly advance amateurs who were early adopters of YouTube, as well as some kids and teens who were more socially oriented. Many kids made videos with their friends, especially comedy sketch and spoof videos, a common pattern in online video making among youth (Willett 2009). Chapter 2 describes the fascinating variety of videos that kids made. Moving beyond analyzing single videos, the chapter analyzes kids' entire oeuvres on YouTube. Such an analysis quickly reveals that "digital youth" have mediated centers of gravity and do not exhibit equal fluency in all media modes and content themes. Similar to other studies on amateurism, kids tended to specialize in video content, digital skills, and distribution choices. These specializations profoundly impacted kids' perceived peer-to-peer, informal learning opportunities and negotiation of digital literacies. In some cases these specializations introduced kids to new forms of technical and self-expressive skills; in other cases, the choice to specialize did not encourage immediate development of new knowledge and abilities.

Chapter 3 focuses on girls on YouTube. Most of the girls in the study were early adopters who considered themselves technical, and engaged in "geeked out" behaviors on the 'Tube. Prior studies of girls' media making tend to explore how technology is used to express other identity variables, such as how media helps girls' express gender or ethnicity. The goal of the Chapter 3 is to understand girls' self-perceptions as technically savvy individuals. In interviews, girls portrayed themselves as technical through their narratives about the tasks they accomplished and the tools they used when making videos. Girls also expressed a technologized identity through their choice of video form and content. In addition to examining videos, the chapter also considers interactional choices between girls and viewers through comment systems. As with boys, technical identities were relational, and were often expressed in terms of how they compared to someone who proposed an identity of being more or less technical than themselves.

Although civic engagement videos formed only a small part of the video corpus, the videos that did appear were quite compelling and demonstrate the promise for video making as a path to increasing kids' civic participation. The videos analyzed in Chapter 4 not only show kids' future potential, but also highlight kids' current ability to thoughtfully discuss important matters of local and global interest. With themes ranging, for example, from improving neighborhood parks to tackling the effects of global conflict, the videos show a sensitivity, insightfulness, and tolerance that civic engagement scholars say is crucial for stimulating and maintaining a thriving democracy. Kids' civic videos need to be recognized as much as their work on creative fiction and spoofs. Chapter 4 argues that kids are following a more socially reticulated model of civic engagement that does not orient around issues but around sociality and connecting through shared interests such as making media.

Chapters 5 and 6 address the ramifications of making media with families. Attending YouTube meet-ups provides an opportunity to see how friends and family make media together and play offline, and facilitates conversations with parents of small children. Parents often provide crucial behavioral role models with regard to creating video and interacting online. The media often portrays kids as feckless geeks in contrast to parental media novices, but such a stereotypical and ageist dichotomy is not the recognizable pattern for kids who are growing up in technologized households.

Chapter 5 on video lifestyles illustrates how some very public family media making has become a common way of life for some kids. Although parents in my study showed different comfort levels with regard to issues of safety, many parents believed that digital and participatory skills were important for their kids' self-expression. Voices behind the camera have also changed since early home movie making, which was reportedly dominated by fathers (Zimmerman 1995). Chapter 5 examines how moms are taking up cameras to express their perspective on family life. In addition, the chapter shows how parents exhibit a sense of fun when making videos, and include pranks and forms of humor that are prevalent in technical cultures. Pranking and humorous videos also provide opportunities to learn about appropriate participation in technology-oriented, video-making groups. The chapter discusses how parents involve children not only to have fun and improve skills, but also as a path toward parents' professionalism and families' economic improvement.

Family media making is not without tensions, and increasing numbers of media makers find themselves struggling with questions of representation and phenomenological media choices when recording, editing, and distributing personally expressive media that contains images of loved ones. Chapter 6, which is on representational ideologies, carves out terrain from the larger theoretical rubric of media ideologies (Gershon 2010a) by discussing these issues and outlining tensions involved in public self-expression. It explores how kids negotiate their participation in their own and their parents' media worlds. Given people's different mediated dispositions, participants often have different approaches as to what constitutes appropriate representational ideologies when creating personally expressive media. Rather than provide proscriptive rules, the chapter aims to be co-productive with readers who are invited to consider their own media-making practices. Readers and media makers may participate in a collective discourse that acknowledges the cultural and individual need for self-expressive media while creating respectful environments for those who hold different dispositions with regard to crafting and distributing human images.

Chapter 7 ties together themes from prior chapters, and explores what is meant by the oft-used term "being self-taught." It traces multiple lines of input that children receive when formulating their ideas about how to learn to make videos, participate publicly online, and construct a technologized identity. When kids reflect on their learning experiences, they create learning narratives, or personal stories that describe how they learned to use a device, accomplish a task, or adopt particular attitudes and literacies that code certain information as worth knowing. Their learning narratives tend to focus on being self-taught, which is commensurate with the normative mythos of how technical people should learn by themselves without manuals or teachers. In fact, their learning narratives reveal that they often learn through the interactive processes and experiences of media making with friends and family. They also learn by observing behaviors that they see modeled by adults online and in person. Being "self-taught" is a taken-for-granted term in discourses of digital youth. Yet, its broad variety of meanings among study participants suggests that the term should be viewed as a mere starting point for exploring phenomenologies of informal learning.

The book concludes by tracing the connections between what it means to be technical in video-making milieus and how media literacies are negotiated in practice. Being technical is a relative term, and what constitutes technical identities changes according to cultural, social, and technical contexts. The idea of being technical remains at the core of many participants' identities on YouTube and among first-generation video bloggers outside of YouTube who passionately advocate a democratization of the lens. Kids are learning many lessons by working through contemporary forms of mediated personhood with friends and family. This book seeks to explore how learning is alternately facilitated and complicated by micro-level, interpersonal dynamics that will likely persist long after the ideal of physical access is globally achieved, if it ever can be. The hope is that by analyzing informal learning patterns, we will learn how kids craft technologized identities and co-define media literacies when they collaboratively create and share their videos on YouTube.

CHAPTER 2

《《◀ ■ ▶》》

Video-Mediated Friendships:
Specialization and Relational Expertise

Wacky viral videos of piano-playing cats, laughing babies, and boys wielding toy lasers in their garage are typical associations people have with YouTube. Many people visit the site after someone has given them a link to a popular video (Madden 2007). One girl whom I interviewed said that her father sent her a link to a video in which a man played guitar with a spoon. Separated by distance, people sharing media can feel closer by experiencing similar forms of mediated humor. Although many people watch YouTube, not everyone posts a video, or even rates or comments on videos. Many people are content to share the more viral forms.

Nevertheless, creating and sharing visual works are on the rise; most Americans have tried posting original videos or photos or reposting existing video or photographs (Brenner 2013). YouTube's strengths include its variety, and its ability to attract many kinds of participants, from the rank newbie to professional media companies. This book focuses on people who not only have posted videos, but who have expressed an interest in technical aspects of making videos, using computers, and participating online. That the supporting research is weighted this way is not surprising, given that many of the people interviewed were early adopters. Some had even discovered the site before it was open on a wide scale to the general public. It is the experiences of these technically oriented early adopters that are the subject of this chapter.

Mass media often characterizes YouTube's viral videos as a foil to claim that professional media is superior in form and content. But one need only turn on the television to be disavowed of the notion that all professional media qualifies as high art, and all professional news is rigorously researched. Such a binary opposition between amateurs and professionals obscures the experiences of video makers with abilities that range from beginners to advanced amateurs to pre-professionals. An important part of the YouTube story—and one that is rarely told—includes understanding the dedicated kid- and teen-based video teams that have worked hard to contribute to YouTube's success. Whether or not they are financially compensated, these video makers are competing within and contributing to an online attention economy (Goldhaber 1996) that provides online content to people seeking to be entertained or informed.

Discourses of "digital youth" and "digital generations" prompt expectations about young people's general abilities with regard to technology. If all kids are so facile with technology, it is reasonable to assume that every video maker's body of work would be highly eclectic, and video makers would be fluid in their video-making roles. When I began my study of YouTube, I imagined that young people would take turns operating the camera, writing scripts, and acting in the videos in a relatively balanced way.

My ethnographic investigation challenged my initial assumptions about digital youth. I discovered that not all kids were equally interested in making videos at all. Further, when they did make videos, whether they were advanced amateurs or casual creators, they tended to specialize in several ways. They specialized in terms of the video content they filmed, the style of video they preferred, the tasks they contributed to making videos, and the site on which they chose to broadcast their video-mediated message. For example, not everyone sought to become the team's director. Although many kids experimented with an impressive array of styles, in the end most people exhibited mediated dispositions and preferences for making certain genres or using particular devices and media. These internal media dispositions often manifested in visible mediated centers of gravity in kids' video oeuvres. Some people tended to video blog and face a camera while discussing their ideas, while others broadcast well-crafted narrative comedy videos and spoofs. Individuals displayed specific talents, skills, and preferences; the video making was often designed to expediently capitalize on contributors' pre-dispositions and known abilities rather than provide intensive hands-on training to bring everyone up to speed on all tasks.

Over time, many kids who intermingled with serious video makers benefited greatly and learned much about video. They reported not only developing technical knowledge about video craft, but also improving their personal confidence and expanding their self-presentation skills. Kids and youth learned by watching other people's video tutorials on YouTube or through the feedback they received on the videos they posted. By pursuing their organic interests and passions, kids extended their skills and participatory knowledge. By specializing in different tasks, they could accelerate the process of achieving something collectively, and begin to see how a more complex work might take shape.

Yet in other instances, kids jockeyed for techno-social position both within and outside of their peer-based, video-making groups. Even when such identifications were not intentionally competitive, disparities in technical ability between kids could complicate individuals' perceived learning opportunities. Kids sometimes specialized in ways that compromised their ability to break out of their comfort zones and move beyond personal, mediated dispositions. Sometimes gaps in ability were perceived to be so wide that more advanced kids did not know where to begin to bring someone up to speed. This chapter analyzes how the dynamics of specialization and mediated dispositions influenced what was learned, and what was deemed possible to learn within particular video-making peer groups. It discusses kids' video landscapes, the tasks they completed, and their distribution choices. It explores how interpersonal friendships and identity dynamics subtly impacted development of digital media literacies.

The Dynamics of Specialization

Specializing in an activity often connotes developing a particular expertise in it (Scott and Shafer 2001). Researchers studying serious leisure activities originally argued that over time, amateurs tend to move on a continuum from more general and less-intense interest to more specialized and high-intensity involvement (Bryan 1979, 2000). Aspects of specialization include types of equipment used, distinctive orientations toward an activity, time spent focused on the activity, and development of particular skills (Bryan 1979). For instance, a study of popular musicians that included both professionals and students found that even when they had the ability to play guitar, bass guitar, and drums, musicians routinely specialized in particular instruments (Green 2002:10).

However, more recent investigations in amateurism have questioned the widespread applicability of the assumed progressive aspect of specialization in leisure activities. Scott and Shafer (2001:322) conducted a survey of studies on serious leisure activities and found that participants often varied widely in the "desire" they displayed to "develop their abilities and acquire knowledge." Most importantly, specialization was not always progressive, but rather could be categorical. In other words, people tended to remain in a particular category of participation over time. For example, in the social worlds of contract bridge, participants did not always move from being social players to becoming competitive tournament bridge players, which required in-depth knowledge about the game (Scott and Godbey 1994). Participation was categorically different according to level of competitive desire. Both types were highly social, but with different emphases and levels of participatory intensity.

Perhaps even more profoundly, some scholars have argued that amateur specialization is a way of handling the eventuality of one's death (Becker 1973; Bryan 1979:54). It is by specializing in particular activities—including leisure pursuits such as video-making—that one feels a sense of individual identity in comparison to other people during one's life course. Recreationists and those who pursue "careers" or enduring commitments to paid or unpaid leisure activities "find their 'specialness' in the high degree of manipulation and control they bring to an activity and the status from their leisure world reference group that such performance brings" (Bryan 1979:55). Specialization can take many forms, including an emphasis on the technical or social dimensions of an activity. If one wishes to feel "special," one must find ways to "specialize" by displaying or performing relative difference with regard to a chosen activity. Yet, how do kids on YouTube specialize, and what are the results of that specialization?

Media disposition is defined as preferring to make certain kinds of media or engaging in certain media activities. Not all participants in my study displayed positive dispositions toward making or posting YouTube videos publicly. For example, 18-year-old Sharon (a researcher-chosen pseudonym) stated, "I don't really like the idea of anyone in the world being able to watch me do something." A 12-year-old white girl from the west coast of the United States referred to here as Akmalla (her chosen online pseudonym) noted that she "loved" YouTube and considered herself a YouTube "fanatic." Yet, it became clear over the course of her interview that her true passion was playing online role-playing games in which she adopted characters and created impressive interactional stories through text with other players. Indeed, during the interview she said she had not yet posted a YouTube video. Several years later, I noted, she had only one video uploaded. Not every young person in the study felt comfortable displaying video recordings of themselves to the world.

Nevertheless, all but one of the 40 young people studied posted at least one video to the site. A few people made videos by themselves, but most kids and youth made videos together. The discussion in this book focuses on the output from 29 channel accounts, each of which represents the efforts of one or several people making videos together. Each account displays a "channel page" on YouTube. A channel page is similar to a social media profile page. It contains a list of account holders' uploaded videos, as well as volunteered information (such as likes and dislikes). It also displays YouTube-generated statistics such video views. Kids sometimes created videos with parents, and the experiences of very young children and families making videos are detailed in Chapters 5 and 6. Chapters 2 to 4 analyze the videos that kids made with each other, and the pleasures and tensions that surfaced.

Content

What kinds of videos do kids make? Why do they choose these genres? How do technical identity proposals influence videos' execution and the learning opportunities that result? While many YouTube studies focus on acontextual analyses of single videos, this chapter examines a video maker's oeuvre as a whole. It draws on data from my ethnographic study to understand the broader meanings of participants' behind-the-scenes experiences of video making.

Video popularity is defined here as the percentage of accounts that exhibited at least one of a particular genre of video. The most popular types of kids' videos that I encountered were video blogs (15 out of 28 accounts included at least one). In video blogs, people addressed the camera and disclosed observations or thoughts about their lives. It is not surprising to see so many video blogs in the study. First, this finding resembles YouTube patterns exhibited at the time of the research; another study found that just over half of the uploaded videos from a large-scale sample came from user-created sources (Burgess and Green 2009a:43). Of those, many (nearly 40%) were video blogs. Second, my study partly targeted participants who created video blogs, as that genre was of personal interest to me. Finally, an important goal of the study was to identify participants aged 10 to 18 and to analyze their digital experiences. Genres such as personal video blogs in which kids filmed themselves assisted in visually identifying and recruiting appropriate study participants. Additional details about recruitment are found in the Appendix.

Three other popular genres in my study included: 1) comedy sketch videos (11 accounts posted at least one); 2) "hanging out" videos (11 accounts), in which people recorded everyday interaction with friends and siblings; and 3) "event" videos (10 accounts), in which kids recorded events such as sporting activities, games, school functions, and car shows. Comedy sketch videos appeared to have a higher weighting for kids than observed in a prior general study of YouTube content in which all types of scripted material, including sketch comedy, animation, and machinima, comprised only about 8% of the sample (Burgess and Green 2009a:43).

Genre identification is always interpretive, as multiple categories may appear in a single video. For example, how should a video be categorized when kids are hanging out at a baseball game? Should this be considered a "hanging out" video or an "event" video? Although it certainly may be both, the answer for my study depended on the central focus of the video, including its themes and emotional timbre. A camera trained mostly on youth talking at a baseball game would be categorized as a "hanging out" video. In contrast, a video in which the camera mostly captures exciting action on the field would qualify as an "event" video.

The next most frequent types of videos were promotional or demonstration videos (8 accounts posted at least one). For example, a participant might post a video that describes or promotes another video from their own collection, to gain more visibility for that video. Other genres included: animation and special effects (7 accounts), parodies (5 accounts) and music or lip synching (4 accounts). Genres appearing in 3 accounts included political or civic themes (which are discussed in Chapter 4), school projects, interviews with other people, travel videos, and people filming themselves doing an activity such as painting or applying make-up. Also appearing were short films, direct messaging of other participants, stunts, inspirational videos, clips of media (such as television shows), pranks, tutorials, and unboxing videos (in which a new product is opened and discussed or reviewed). One young adult posted a video that was part of a job interview. In two other accounts, uploaders posted phatic videos that were focused on testing their YouTube channel, or providing an image of themselves for their YouTube channel page.

Specialization in Novices and Pre-Professionals

Prior trends in leisure activities might predict that over time, participants would increase their productivity and intensity in video making, and would likely specialize in creating particular video genres. Further, this specialization would lead to increased knowledge and skills. But did kids and youth tend to specialize in terms of video content? If so, what was the result of such specialization? The answer depends upon how one defines specialization. If specialization means selecting one genre and only making that kind, then such an extreme definition would apply to no one whom I interviewed. Most kids and youth posted videos in various genres. This was true of both the pre-professionals and those who remained novices throughout the study.

Nevertheless, whether they considered themselves pre-professionals or just sought to have fun, kids seemed to have a disposition for making particular genres. One interesting case is that of a white, mother-daughter team from the east coast of the United States, who asked that I refer to them as Lola and Ashley. Sixteen-year-old Ashley was a pre-professional who intended on going to film school. She described her parents as very technical in terms of computers. Having posted more than 2,000 videos, Lola and Ashley often reviewed and commented on so-called reality television shows and competitions (including programs such as *Survivor, Dancing with the Stars, The Bachelor*, and many others). A random sample of their collection showed that 60% were chat show videos that used the format of movie review programs. They also posted more personal work, but even those videos arguably were designed to promote their specialized talk show videos.

A strong preference for technologized videos was evident in the account of a white, 19-year-old named MysteryGuitarMan or "MGM" (he asked to be referred to by his YouTube account name). In a random sample of more than 168 of his videos, 80% were special effects videos in which he performed music or achieved comedic effects by technically manipulating video form. MGM said he learned much about programming from his father, and noted that he often helped peers at school with computer problems.

A year after our first interview, MGM told me that he edited for a living, and that YouTube had "definitely changed the course of his life." Originally, he was a biology major in a pre-medical program, but he aspired to be a film-maker after finding success on YouTube. His story echoes that of several You-Tubers whom I interviewed, who said that early on they made videos for fun, and it was only after they received widespread attention that they considered professionalizing. A random sample of MGM's account also revealed that not all of his videos were centered on special effects; 10% were music videos in which he performed a song, and 10% were video blogs, including one in which he elaborately proposed to his eventual fiancée.

Such weightings were also observed among participants who had not de-clared an overt goal of professionalizing their work. An example is a 15-year-old white girl on the east coast of the United States who requested that I refer to her using the pseudonym of Elizabeth. She said her mother had just started getting into computers and was a technical writer for a software company. Her father was also knowledgeable about computers. Elizabeth posted 15 videos, 40% of which were hanging out videos and 32% were video blogs. She also experimented with animation, comedy sketch, event videos, and parodies. If hanging out and video blogs are subsumed under a more general category of personal experiences, the total of 72% would make her account seem rather specialized.

Similarly, a white, 19-year-old teenager named Amelia (she requested I use her real name) said she taught herself how to make videos and preferred more personal genres. She posted 19 videos which concentrated on video blogs (74%) in which she addressed the camera with personal thoughts. She also posted videos on travel (11%), hanging out (5%), painting (5%), and one school project (5%). Amelia's video blogs are compelling as she describes her everyday life. As discussed in Chapter 4, video blogs with important social messages could be a launching point for a public voice that dealt with impor-tant civic matters. For example, in one video, Amelia said she was fired over religious views that her employer did not share. Being personal with one's ex-periences in video blogs could often tap into profound and widespread civic and political issues, such as job discrimination.

Although most people included multiple genres, both pre-professionals and novices tended to post regular types of content. Individuals typically displayed a mediated center of gravity, or tangible instantiation of media dispositions. Such preferences often included choosing particular kinds of technical tools to create media. Most of the 29 channel accounts examined in this chapter displayed a distinct mediated center of gravity, where certain genres were more represented than others. Additional research would be required to understand how and why kids develop particular mediated dispositions. It is at root helpful to recognize and reveal mediated predilections, in part so that the phenomenology of kids' mediated lives can be better understood.

Relative specialization in terms of video content offered advantages. Kids' mediated predispositions often enabled them to learn more about video craft. Kids explored making videos and presenting the self in ways that developed organically from their own interests. In addition, developing specializations sometimes gave kids' techno-cultural status among their viewers, who began recognizing their work and following it on YouTube. This pattern follows Stebbins' (1980) model of the professional-amateur-public system, in which amateurs become recognized by the publics they serve for their abilities and talents. For example, a white, 17-year-old teen from the east coast of the United States whose preferred pseudonym was "Skittles," aspired to be a professional comedian. He characterized himself as "somewhat technical" in comparison to his parents whom he said were not technical. A random sample of his 58 videos revealed that approximately 80% were comedy sketch videos. His account also included one parody and one animation video. He used his account to showcase his comedic talents and build a following for his future professional work. He used his real name on his account, he said, so that his material, upcoming appearances, and open mic nights at comedy clubs might be searchable online.

As discussed in Chapter 3, which is on girl geeks, Anesha, an African American 18-year-old participant from the west coast of the United States (who wished to be referred to by her real name) demonstrated a passion for making *machinima*, a genre in which creators manipulate characters and backgrounds in a game to create original action and stories. Anesha was a pre-professional who saw herself as having a specialty in editing, an important quality for constructing narratives. She characterized her mother as more computer literate than her father, but noted that neither of them had experience with video. Being technical in one area does not guarantee fluency in other areas. Creating *machinima* videos both drew on and helped develop her interests in technical forms of video making.

However, specialization alone did not necessarily promote a desire to develop additional skills. For example, 15-year-old Elizabeth specialized in video blogs and hanging out videos. Her specialization concerned more personal forms of video making. When I asked her about her future plans with regards to making videos, she responded in a chat interview, "Well, I don't know how much longer I'll make videos. They take up time that I don't have to spare." Specializing in a certain kind of video, even one of organic interest to her, did not spur additional interest to learn more about video making. Something that "takes up too much time" does not reveal a disposition toward that activity nor encourage additional learning from that genre. In terms of content, specialization only sometimes led to interest in pursuing deepened technical engagement with video.

Tutorials

Mediated centers of gravity are dynamic; they may change over time. Early in my study, MysteryGuitarMan made comedic videos. Later, he specialized in music and special effects videos. Originally from Brazil but living in the United States, MysteryGuitarMan began his YouTube career by parodying famous YouTubers, making instructional videos, and spoofing hot trends on the site. For example, mobile video blogging was (and still is) a popular YouTube genre. A camera might be mounted on a car's dashboard and trained on the driver, who records comments when traveling on everyday commutes or when visiting new places. In one video, MGM spoofed this trend by awkwardly and comically video blogging while riding a bicycle.

A more recent glance at MGM's collection shows a shift from spoofs of video blogs and popular YouTubers to a concentration (80%) on special effects and music videos. Even his more personal videos are technically manipulated. In one video blog, he elaborately proposed to his girlfriend by taking her to a movie theater running a film that he had created for the proposal, complete with professional actors. More indicative of his later oeuvre were videos on special affects and music. For example, one video depicts him playing the overture of Mozart's opera *Die Zauberflöte* by blowing into beer bottles. The image shows a split screen of six squares in which he is depicted blowing into the bottles. Some screens are lit and highlighted as he blows, while others are darkened as he waves his hands around or over the bottles. This combination of music and special effects editing appeared to be a special emphasis for MysteryGuitarMan.

Notably, his special effects videos situate him as relatively more expert than the viewers who asked him for help in learning about special effects and editing techniques. Asking MGM for help reifies a techno-cultural hierarchy of relative expertise in which MGM is constructed as more expert than those who need his assistance. Such hierarchies may shift over time; as people learn how to manipulate videos, they in turn may help others. A tutorial maker is often perceived as knowing more than the viewers who watch them to gain information. However, a relatively more knowledgeable viewer may gain something quite different from the experience; some experts may watch tutorials to critique or supplement the information within a video (Müller 2009:135). Whatever the trajectory of knowledge, tutorial videos offer ways to negotiate relative hierarchies of expertise.

Early in his YouTube career, MysteryGuitarMan noticed a demand for instructional videos. In his perception, video bloggers did not use edits in the sophisticated way that he used them in his popular, techno-visual videos. He believed that making instructional videos would help him gain attention and help YouTubers learn how to improve their technique. One of the earliest videos he posted was an instructional video on Windows Movie Maker, an editing program. After posting this tutorial he said his subscribers doubled to 500. At the time of the research, subscribers were viewers who chose to be alerted at no cost when a video maker posted new videos. The tutorials' popularity challenges the academic discourse that YouTubers are disinterested in improvement. In fact, a "discourse of quality" is present on YouTube, evidenced in part through the many tutorials and comments that participants make and discuss (Müller 2009).

Like other participants whom I spoke to, MysteryGuitarMan learned through other sources on YouTube, including instructional videos created by a 26-year-old man from Spain who wished to be referred to in the study by his YouTube name of Therapix. Although the study focused on U.S. kids and youth, Therapix was asked to participate due to his strong influence and popularity among young YouTubers in the United States. Therapix specialized in instructional videos, such as showing people how to use green screens and add images and special effects to videos.

Therapix was the only participant in the study to specialize in tutorials. As discussed in Chapter 7, tutorials have been defined in many ways. The present discussion defines them as "step-by-step sets of instructions on how to achieve a certain outcome" (Perkel and Herr-Stephenson 2008:7). Therapix's account name highlights his specialization. He told me in a chat interview that his YouTube name was a combination of "therapy," which connotes treatments or healing, and "pictures." A snapshot of Therapix's 12-video account long after the interview revealed five tutorials (42%), four event videos (33%), one demonstration of a technical device, one contest-oriented video, and one special effects video. Although he posted several different genres, his public, mediated center of gravity and his YouTube reputation were weighted towards tutorials.

Therapix described himself as a "geek" (but not a nerd, since he said he had a thriving social life). He said his mother was technical but noted that his father was not as up to speed. His computer use was heavy, and he characterized himself as unable to "live" without gadgets such as a cell phone, iPod, and portable gaming device. Like several other participants, he initially used

YouTube as an ancillary storage space, and because it was easy for his friends to find his videos. After "playing around" with a camera and consulting web resources, he gained enough knowledge and confidence to make a video tutorial on how to create an animated "light saber" or laser sword, modeled after those used in the popular *Star Wars* films.

Clearly, his efforts were successful; he garnered more than 9,000 subscribers by March 2012, and his videos saw a combined total of more than 3.9 million views. These numbers are impressive for non-professional accounts, which might receive a few hundred views for each video. MGM stated that most filmmaking tutorials on YouTube were "boring" because they just used a screen capture program while someone provided instruction. Yet such was not the case with Therapix's work, as MysteryGuitarMan explained:

> [Therapix] actually uses, like, the blue screen behind them and he actually makes the video editing, like, wicked awesome. He's showing the uh, final effect of what he's gonna do with filmmaking, you know? Yeah, so you can actually see what your videos could look like, you know?

MysteryGuitarMan argues that it is not enough to post an instructional video; audiences demand high quality and particular tutorial features, such as previewing the final output of a technique and exhibiting "wicked awesome" editing. MGM's description depicts two levels of learning: the first is that of less expert YouTube participants seeking specialized instructional videos to improve; the second is of relative experts such as MGM and Therapix using sources within and outside of YouTube to learn how to make useful tutorials to serve the publics who request them.

By creating tutorials, Therapix not only helped others, he also learned how to make well-received tutorial videos. Tutorials are one example of multi-direction social chains of learning. Therapix said he learned much from making tutorials for others, including how to create "tv shows." Therapix learned to make videos by playing with a camera and "Googling" or searching for information using online search engines to identify helpful web sources. In turn, popular video makers such as MysteryGuitarMan and others benefited from learning about videos through Therapix's tutorials. Similarly, as Therapix taught others about special effects, the feedback and questions he received taught him to be conscious of and attend to the form of a tutorial as a visual and interactive artifact with its own conventions and standards of excellence. Making tutorials helped Therapix to see that they required quite a bit of work, because, he said, it was incumbent on the tutorial maker to make them "clear" and "fun to watch." Further, the tutorial should make techniques look "easy" to understand and replicate. Through making tutorials, Therapix learned that the process requires advanced planning, information, appropriate soundtracks, and patience for rendering the video.

Tutorials are an important genre on YouTube that deserve study in their own right. As MGM noted, it is possible to find someone demonstrating or providing overt instruction on myriad topics including playing instruments, making repairs, cooking, applying make-up, and making videos. To create tutorials, Therapix said he drew on numerous sources including consulting a French post-production forum that displayed text and picture tutorials, and also allowed participants to ask for help. Participants often discussed special effects on television or films, and they debated how professionals accomplished these effects. As discussed in Chapter 7, Therapix's narrative illustrates that being "self taught" often requires drawing on socially encoded forms of information—such as web resources, forums, and discussions about video making—that others have consolidated and packaged for distribution in ways that code them as useful. Artifacts are socially encoded in that someone has deemed the information within them to be important for someone else to know. The artifact mediates an asynchronous social encounter between mentor and novice. Such socially encoded forms of information greatly supplemented the individual trial-and-error approaches encountered in my study when YouTubers sought to learn how to use technologized devices and software.

The study also showed that content specialization did not guarantee skill acquisition. For example, people who created video blogs did not necessarily learn about technologized aspects of video making such as incorporating special effects. Participants who exhibited a mediated center of gravity for technologized special effects videos did not necessarily learn how to make a good video blog with articulate arguments that connected to larger issues of civic engagement. However, specializations could broaden one's abilities. Whatever content they chose, participants often not only learned technical video making skills, but also learned characteristics of compelling content in their preferred genre. Even relatively advanced video makers improved their craft. Tutorial makers learned to make better tutorials through their interaction with YouTube publics. Clearly many kids and youth learned about video by making personally interesting videos. Specialization in content allowed kids to learn about video and develop particular passions, but what they learned was often influenced by the type of content that they were pre-disposed to explore.

Skills

In addition to genre and content, many kids whom I interviewed developed a specialization or relied on a pre-disposition for certain kinds of video-making tasks, including operating the camera, writing, acting, directing, editing, and video promotion. In general, the study found that some kids benefited greatly from being involved in group video-projects in which more experienced participants could introduce others to video-making processes and skills. Group video making also helped kids gain an appreciation of how videos and underlying narratives are put together. On the other hand, kids also performed technical affiliations and displayed different levels of relative expertise that sometimes complicated a peripheral participant's ability to experiment with or gain deeper understanding of technical and communicative skills.

For many kids, experimenting with video often began with the arrival of a socio-material object, namely, a video camera. Several participants reported that they began making videos, experimenting, and developing skills after receiving a video camera from a family member or close friend. Therapix received a MiniDV camera from his gadget-loving uncle, who seemed intent on having the latest models. A popular 19-year-old Australian participant, who asked that I refer to her by her real name of Caitlin, started by recording "random things" on her grandmother's digital camera. Eighteen-year-old Anesha began making videos after receiving a digital camera with a video setting from her parents for Christmas. These stories illustrate how parents sometimes initiate kids' video activities through socially encoding a particular device as an appropriate possession for them.

Despite the binary the rhetoric dividing school and informal learning environments, kids sometimes became interested in participating on YouTube as a result of a school assignment. For instance, Anesha got started on YouTube after her history teacher assigned a project requiring visuals. Anesha made a slide show video that synchronized images to song lyrics that referred to historical events. She said that, given her difficulties with the class, it was enjoyable to engage with the material by using her video editing skills. Ashley, a 16-year-old who made videos about reality television shows said she became interested in making videos through a school English project, in which she was tasked with retelling a Peruvian folktale. Selecting a video option for the assignment, Ashley involved her family to help her improvise scenes for the video. In some instances, kids in the study said that they owed their initial inspiration or early experimentation with video to teachers who encouraged them to use the medium to meet the requirements of in-class assignments.

Most kids described in this book made videos with friends, a pattern observed in other studies of young people's online video (Willett 2009). For example, Fred, an 18-year-old study participant made videos with his younger brother, 16-year-old Stuart (both researcher-chosen pseudonyms), and other friends. Fred began making videos at around aged five, by using his father's camera. When they began, their father recorded them making skits. Later, Fred said he purchased better equipment and found himself moving beyond video-making as a mere "hobby." Fred's group, which I will refer to using the researcher-selected pseudonym of "Clubhouse Productions" also eventually broadcast their work on television. Fred's father and uncle had produced a television show for a local cable access station, and Fred and his friends took over their slot and broadcast their own shows. Such a pattern resembles traditional Hollywood production lineages in which opportunities are often "handed down" through personal contacts in the industry (Cole and Dale 1993:28; Kearney 2006:193).

The most common video-making story involved bringing a camera to a gathering, such as a sleepover or even when hanging out. Making videos together was a way of having fun with friends, including those co-located in the same schools and neighborhoods (Lange 2007d). A prototypical description came from a white 14-year-old named Max (a researcher-chosen pseudonym) from the east coast of the United States, who already aspired to be a professional filmmaker. He stated:

> Almost all my videos, except for a couple of the recent ones, they haven't really been planned. We just, like – my friends would come over and we would say, "Hey, let's make a movie." And they'd say, "All right. About what?" Like, like for example, the Dora video. And I was like, "Oh. Let's go out in the woods and make like uh, make like, an explorer movie and, like, someone can, like, jump out of the trees and, like, mess around or whatever." And someone was like, "Kinda like Dora the Explorer." And then another one of my friends would say, "Oh, yeah. Let's make a Dora the Explorer video."

For Max, one idea might lead to another as friends picked up a camera and improvised. Max opened his YouTube account together with a close friend. Their videos all included a logo with the name of their production company, which helped display professionally desired identities and aspirations. Max said that he was usually the director and spokesperson in his video-making group, but if others had ideas to direct, the group was flexible. However, later in the interview, Max also stated that among his school peers, he was known as being far more expert at making videos. In his prior middle school, he was considered the "video guy." His relative expertise helped define his social identity in a central way. Max explained:

> In my middle school, that's [who I was]. Oh, Max, the video guy, the one that makes all the videos and, like, if anyone had a question on, like, "Well, I'm trying to make a slideshow and I'm trying to use Windows Movie Maker, how do I do this, this, this," they would call me or, "How do I edit audio?" and they would call me and stuff like that. So, I'd get a lot of questions for my friends or, like, people that actually liked my videos and stuff.

When asked whether he helped his friends and peers at school, Max stated, "Yeah. I try and help them as much as I can. A lot of them are hard to um, to help just because they don't really, like, understand, like, a lot of computer stuff, but [I] try to—I help."

Max's narrative exhibits a highly asymmetrical degree of perceived relative expertise in the technical field of making videos among his peers. If all "digital youth" made videos to the same degree, few would need basic assistance, such as needing help to make a slideshow. Further, those few who did need assistance would obtain it easily from a large pool. Yet, this is not the scenario that Max describes. Although he initially characterizes his immediate movie-making group as more fluid with regards to taking on different skills and roles, he also portrays his school peers as knowing far less than he does. He characterizes them as being so remedial that it was difficult for him to mentor them. Processes of informal learning may falter if the gap between mentor and mentee is perceived to be so wide that they do not share basic vocabulary and concepts for a learning encounter to be productive.

A similar experience was described by 15-year-old Frank (a researcher-chosen pseudonym), who characterized himself as very technical. Frank posted several videos to YouTube, yet he identified web design as his "forte." He had a web hosting and design business in which he helped family members, people he met online, friends from school, and other referrals to create and fix websites. Even though Frank's oeuvre was impressively eclectic, about a third of his videos were soap opera parodies. Many of his videos show him interacting with friends and engaging in comedic activities such as creating an explosion by throwing a bottle filled with dry ice. In his interview I asked him whether he had particular preferences with regard to skills such as directing versus editing. He did not characterize video roles as particularly fluid among his friends. Rather, their relative difference in expertise necessitated more work for Frank. He stated:

> I don't really have any preferences. Whenever I've done any videos or anything with my friends, they don't really know how to do any of those, so I usually end up doing all of it. So sometimes, I like to do directing, sometimes I do editing, but I usually end up doing everything.

Two 14-year-old white boys, Liam and Edward (researcher-chosen pseudonyms), who were close friends, made many videos together. Liam and Edward were the core drivers and made the major decisions in their video-making endeavors, but other friends helped with certain tasks or projects. Intermittent or less-intense contributors resemble what Lave and Wenger (1991) called "peripheral members" who engage in "communities of practice." In communities of practice, people engage in an activity that includes routines, conventions, and shared histories. Wenger (1998:100) observed that being a peripheral member carries varying connotations such as taking fewer risks, requiring special assistance, or participating with less intensity than full participants. However, to be a peripheral participant, one must at least engage with other members and have access to the negotiation of the activity. For Lave and Wenger (1991:36), peripherality was empowering to the extent that members could develop expertise and gain greater access to the core activities. Peripherality could also be disempowering if members were continually prevented from gaining access to full participation. The concept of peripherality is a dynamic one; participants' skills and specializations might change over time.

Like other video makers, Liam and Edward drew on "networks of sociability" to make media (Clawson 1999:106). Such "structures of acquaintanceship" are often sex-segregated with a weighting toward one sex or the other (Clawson 1999:106). It was not uncommon to see groups of mostly males or mostly females making videos, although I did interview individuals from a few mixed groups in the study.

In his interview, Liam said that he and Edward did "all the editing and the web site" work and all the others in the videos were actors who were given a script that he and Edward had written. Liam said that it would be "cool" to get more people involved in "editing and stuff." Edward said that they were open to ideas and certainly their friends contributed input. The script was often more of a "guideline." However, over time, Liam and Edward learned that videos would "turn out better" if they had some kind of pre-planned script to guide action. People learned from experience as well as from external tutorials and mentorship. Although Liam and Edward were open to increased participation, the practical reality was that after everyone "went home" after recording, they often did the editing. Additional research would be required to understand what combination of disposition, desire, and social expectations influenced perceived learning opportunities. Perhaps Liam and Edward's friends made their own videos later; future studies might pursue under what circumstances kids took charge of their own media.

Displaying dispositions with regards to particular skills was not limited to male groups. For example, a 13-year-old white girl named Jordan (her chosen pseudonym) from the west coast of the United States made videos with her sisters. Jordan noted that although her dad was "excellent" with computers, her mother was not particularly knowledgeable. However, neither of her parents worked extensively with video. Jordan made beautiful photographic slide show videos and sang songs with her sisters. She did most of the directing, and she said she told people "what to say and do." Although her sisters might give her ideas, she typically did the editing. She said her older sisters could make their own videos, and that her younger sister was also very good at editing. Although Jordan painted a slightly more fluid picture of skill sets and roles than did Liam and Edward, she nevertheless said she typically handled most of the directing, lighting, and editing.

Both males and females mentioned feelings of social marginalization through making videos and participating on YouTube. Such marginalization would not occur if digital generations were equally enthusiastic about all media. For instance, 19-year-old Caitlin from Australia said she nearly lost friends over her mediated interests.

> *Patricia*:   How did you "nearly lose friends" over your [YouTube] site?
>
> *Caitlin*:   They just didn't see the point of YouTube. I was told that I was wasting my life and a lot of them didn't want a part in it. Then I was just so busy doing internet things that I fell out of touch with my best friend and didn't tell her I was going to the U.S. until the day before. So she was pissed off, understandably. But we're all good now that I realized that it's JUST the internet.

According to scholars in serious leisure studies, feelings of marginalization between advanced amateurs and the general public, as well as between amateurs and immediate family and friends are common. As Stebbins (1992:121) stated, "The amateurs' friends, relatives, workmates, and neighbours on the one hand, are often in the dark about what they do and why they tend to pursue their activity with such passion." Conversely, professionals and advanced amateurs are better positioned to understand their goals and drive.

Possessing different skill sets—and the benefits and tensions they produced—were evident in the pre-professional video-making group of Clubhouse Productions. For all of its members, making a movie was a way to have fun; for a select few, however, it also helped them realize a pre-professional desire to improve their craft and gain a wide audience. Clubhouse Productions was composed of mostly white teens on the west coast of the United States. Many of them became close at social functions held for home-schooled families. The core group began with 18-year-old Fred and his 16-year-old brother Stuart. Two other core members were 17-year-old Jones (his chosen pseudonym) and 17-year-old Jack (his preferred pseudonym). More peripheral participants were 18-year-old James (a researcher-chosen pseudonym) and 19-year-old Qwerty (his chosen pseudonym). Peripherality exhibited gradations; some friends were regular contributing members while others (who were not interviewed for the study) were pulled in for specific projects.

Whereas Fred, Jones, and Jack expressed definite interest in a media-based career, others envisioned different paths. Fred said he could imagine becoming a filmmaker, but he was also quite interested in music. Jones envisioned being a director, either of live action or animated films. He said he had always been attracted to artistic pursuits. Jack thought that he might be an actor or radio talk show host, given his self-characterization as quite "talkative." Qwerty planned on majoring in computer science and mathematics and envisioned a career in artificial intelligence. His chosen pseudonym is a playful performance of technical identity; it evokes a computer-associated, technologized device, the "qwerty keyboard." Qwerty had martial arts training and contributed moves for action and fight scenes. James participated mostly by being an "actor" in the group. He said that he was often "type cast" in the group as a "lunatic character" when the project called for one. He felt that the group did not see him as a particularly good actor, and he was involved in his own technical projects and videos.

Clubhouse Productions included advanced amateur and novice video makers, which affected their production dynamic. All participants whom I interviewed identified Fred and Stuart as the most technically savvy and the most earnest about making videos. Qwerty called Fred and Stuart the "heart and soul" of the videos. Interviewees portrayed their skills and roles as highly asymmetrical. Jones told me that although he sometimes co-directed, he usually wrote and acted. In contrast, he said that Stuart and Fred usually directed, operated the camera, and edited. Stuart said that although he worked the camera, he was reluctant to label himself as the group's "cinematographer." In fact, Fred usually set up the shot, and then stepped into the scene while Stuart ran the camera. Phenomenologically breaking down video recording into smaller levels of analysis reveals more details about specific roles and about the processes of video making. Stuart portrays an important relative difference in ability between himself and Fred, in that Fred "set up" the shots, while Stuart worked a device. Jack summed up their dynamic:

> Well, um when it comes down to it, I'm mostly an actor, I would say. Um, and, you know, because Fred and Stuart are really, they're really good with the camera. They really are good at, you know – editing and cinematography and everything and writing. And so, I help write, you know, when I can, and I help write, you know, a script. It's kind of like we all have our own kind of specialty in script writing in certain areas, and we all just kind of, you know, whichever direction we want the script to go, we'll have somebody write that. So we all are writers and we all are actors, but Stuart and Fred kind of run a lot of stuff.

Jack notes that even when they engaged in the same task such as writing, the group had particular "specialties" with regard to the material they contributed. Jack's observation invites future fine-tuned exploration of the phenomenologies of the mediated moment in informal learning studies, in which a larger task such as "writing" is broken down to reveal important details about the group's video-making dynamic. His narrative suggests that mediated dispositions and specialties continue to appear, even when larger tasks are broken down. Writing and acting appeared to be more fluid activities than were directing, operating the camera, editing, and decision making, which typically fell to Fred and Stuart.

The group began by making improvisational, comedic videos that often drew on aspects of their personalities. Indeed, one of their most popular videos—referred to here by the pseudonym *Stuart's Lunch*—fictitiously exaggerates their asymmetrical skills and dispositions toward video making. The story of this video is that the boys are making a video for an online site. Each participant essentially plays a caricature of themselves as they show how the group makes videos. Fred plays a "director" character, while Jack and Jones play "actor" characters. The plot of the video-within-the-video is never made explicit and is unimportant for the story, which is ultimately a meta statement about their video making process. Although it is an exaggeration, Fred explained that *Stuart's Lunch* emphasized his comparatively higher dedication to video-making and was based on the group's actual interpersonal dynamics. Fred stated:

> I can get into a mood where you know I take things a lot more seriously than I should and um so I can be a bit more stern with making movies and just wanting to get it done, and I have a vision. I take whatever the project is a bit more seriously than my friends do. So they, of course, don't share some of the ideas that I do so they really can't relate to what I'm talking about. And to them it's just a fun thing to do with friends during the day. "Let's go to Fred and Stuart's house and maybe they'll have a movie for us to make." [Yeah], really, a lot of it is me kind of telling them to mellow out and start doing what we're supposed to be doing or else nothing will happen.

As with Max's and Frank's narratives, Fred portrays such a wide gap between himself and the other participants that they have trouble "relating" to what is he talking about. Certainly individuals may exaggerate their prowess in ethnographic interviews; such interactions also offer a way to perform technical identity. Still, other members of Clubhouse Productions confirmed these asymmetrical sets of expertise. These differences in desire and disposition produced occasional tension, even within a mostly male group. Ultimately these conflicts dismantle gendered assumptions that all males have guaranteed socio-cultural advantages with regard to technology. In fact, males within the same socio-economic group sometimes display highly asymmetrical forms of skill and desire to learn about technologized activities such as making videos. Although gendered discrepancies clearly require investigation, technical identity performance and competencies cannot simply be "read" or predicted from other traditional identity variables such as gender.

As *Stuart's Lunch* opens, the "director" character, played by Fred, says in voiceover that he is frustrated that online videos are often bad yet receive many views. As he says this, a video is playing in the background on an online site. In this video, a young child repetitively jumps up and down on a bed. Notably, this video is actual home movie footage of a younger Stuart jumping on his bed. The home movie footage is reimagined and repurposed to seem like just another bad video that the group sees on YouTube. This repurposing of the home video, or what Moran (2002) calls the "video in the text," is an important aesthetic that contributes to the narrative through the stance that the video makers portray through its juxtaposition within a larger story. The repurposed footage is cast to seem like random YouTube material in a way that underscores the group's current, comparative expertise. Home movie footage of supposedly other YouTubers (which they portray using footage from their own actual childhood) is simple and mundane; their video making exhibits clever editing and a compelling narrative. The frustrations over popular, wacky, viral videos likely resonate with other advanced amateurs who attend closely to quality yet may not receive as many views as did the famous video of a baby biting his sibling's finger. At the outset, Fred's narrative creates a hierarchy of relative expertise vis-à-vis those of other online video makers. He portrays himself and his group as more knowledgeable about what constitutes video quality than other YouTubers. Over the course of the video, he further sets himself apart from other members, creating an internal technical hierarchy.

In *Stuart's Lunch*, Fred, the director character, mentions that he "dreads" the next day of filming. In several of the subsequent shots, Fred attempts to direct the actors, who are portrayed by Jones and Jack. They often lose focus, joke around, and rough house. The characters portrayed by Jones and Jack seem to focus on having fun and hanging out with close friends, rather than doing the "work" of making the video. As a result, scenes are filmed multiple times, until the Jones and Jack characters feel too bored to continue. In voiceover, Fred as the director character says he wishes his friends would "shut up" and work until the project is complete. Here again, the narrative depicts the director character (portrayed by Fred) as relatively more expert and desirous of results than his friends.

After repeated problems, Fred, as the director character, becomes exasperated with his friends' lack of focus. The actors portray versions of themselves breaking character, meaning that they begin acting like their normal selves rather than as characters in the video-within-the-video. In one instance, Jack and Jones start laughing and cannot complete their lines. In an effective manipulation of form, the video plays in slow motion as Jack and Jones continue to laugh out of control. Such a technique is often used in professional filmmaking to index different states of mind between characters. While Jones and Jack laugh in "slow motion," Fred is building to a boiling point. His friends' laughter becomes intolerable and is depicted as frustratingly surreal to Fred. Next we see an odd-angle shot of Fred, a trope which is used in narrative films to index a character's frustration or disorientation to their observable reality.

Finally, Fred the director achieves a moment of inspiration and the camera zooms in on him; he states that he is determined to complete the project. Although it is a group effort, the exaggerated fictional story depicts Fred as in control. He tells his actors to shut up. He commands the "Jack character" to look at a laser in Fred's hands and say his line while following the moving light with his eyes. This simple but straightforward tactical instruction proves successful; Jack is suddenly serious and delivers his line. He follows the laser with his eyes, thus achieving the desired eye line effect apparently required for the video-within-the-video being filmed. Fred indicates they got the shot; Jack's performance appears focused and convincing.

The next few shots depict Fred alone at his computer editing the video-within-the-video using a program that appears to be Final Cut Pro. It is a more sophisticated editing system than programs such as iMovie or Windows Movie Maker, which often come bundled with desktop computers. Traditionally associated with independent filmmakers, Final Cut Pro is also used by professionals (O'Brien 2013). The shot of Fred using this technology displays his technical affiliation to the program as appropriate, and indexes him as relatively more expert than those who would use less complex editing systems. The film helps Fred perform a technical identity of being knowledgeable about more sophisticated editing programs than YouTubers who are limited to using basic editing tools.

Finally, the video depicts Fred uploading the video-within-the-video to a fictional site called "MyTube," an obvious parodic mash-up of the social networking site of MySpace, and YouTube. In the video, MyTube's administrators reject the video for upload. An error message explains that it was rejected due to "inadequate entertainment value." Further, the message states that the uploader's privileges have been temporarily suspended for six weeks. The error screen provides links to other recommended "hilarious, random videos" for viewing. Fred, as the director character, is thoroughly disgusted and runs from the room. Again, Fred is depicted as knowing what constitutes quality, but is rejected by unknown administrators who unfairly promote popular yet vacuous content. The video sets up a tone of relational expertise in which Fred is situated as higher on the hierarchy of video craft than are the fictional "MyTube" content editors.

Stuart's Lunch was a highly successful video. It received a college film-festival prize and the filmmakers were awarded new mini digital video cameras. Although Fred called the social dynamics in the film "slightly exaggerated," he said that it actually depicted some of the tensions that he experienced when making videos with his close friends. However, it is important to note that the team made many popular YouTube videos and even won a festival prize. Jack and Jones and other team members were clearly capable of focusing and producing work that garnered attention among their fans and experts. To overemphasize Jone's and Jack's loose social video-making dynamic is to under appreciate what they contributed to the team and to prize-winning work. Indeed, Fred was appreciative of team members' participation and their willingness to depict exaggerated aspects of their personal dynamic and personality traits so publicly. These personally expressive social dynamics made compelling viewing and were crucial for the video's success. The team's closeness, tensions, and bonding through videos shone through in many of their comedic videos and improvisations.

Ruby's (1991) distinction between "cooperative" and "collaborative" filmmaking is useful for understanding the social dynamics of video-making groups. Although he was speaking about documentaries, the differences between cooperative and collaborative filmmaking show how peripheral and full participant roles may influence a video's construction and outcome. In cooperative works, filmmakers retain control although they solicit the input and assistance of the subjects whom they record. For Ruby (1991:55), "Cooperative ventures turn into collaborations when filmmakers and subjects mutually determine the content and shape of the film." Ruby (1991:55) observed that, "For a production to be truly collaborative the parties involved must be equal in their competencies or have achieved an equitable division of labor. Involvement in the decision-making process must occur at all significant junctures."

In many ways, the video-making groups discussed in this chapter exhibited more of a cooperative dynamic between full and peripheral participants. Participation might be more collaborative when core members made videos together. As more peripheral participants joined a project, it became more cooperative, with control resting among a few team members. How personally expressive the media was depended upon how much control participants exercised. Media arguably became less *personally* expressive for those peripheral members who did not achieve "equal competencies" or "equitable divisions of labor" that facilitated creative control.

Not all peripheral participants had access to the core activities or to the decision making, nor did they exhibit a desire to do so. Nevertheless, having a group of video makers with various dispositions and desires helped several members learn how to make videos and present the self in public ways. In some cases, participants learned about the basic technical aspects of making video and about narrative construction of stories and character development. For example, Jack noted that he learned about the 180 degree rule and about how camera placement can illustrate a character's personal qualities or intentions. In continuity editing, the 180 degree rule states that a camera should be placed on one side of an imaginary line that is discernable and consistent across a set of shots in a scene (Bordwell and Thompson 1997:285). In this way, audiences can discern actions as they occur within a spatial orientation. Jack mentioned learning about the semiotics of camera angles, or the position in which a subject is framed (Bordwell and Thompson 1997:236). For example, a character filmed from below can appear to be powerful, menacing, or evil.

In addition to basic film techniques, participants mentioned other qualities that they developed by making videos with more experienced creators. Sometimes benefits were more subtle, and involved developing a more comfortable, mediated presence and gaining a measure of self acceptance. Such was the case with Qwerty, who explained in an online chat interview:

> It's always strange to see yourself on camera and hear your own voice. I used to be very self-[conscious], and would almost die whenever I heard myself or saw myself. But when I realized that everyone sees me like that, and that they accept it, there's absolutely nothing wrong with it. And i've been a more mentally relaxed person ever since.

What Qwerty and others in Clubhouse Productions gained were not only technical skills, but also a sense of how to present themselves to a wider public. For Qwerty, this translated into gaining self-acceptance. Technical skills and feelings of mediated self-confidence were developed by cooperating with more expert, core members who specialized in video-making activities.

Distribution

Kids and youth whom I studied sometimes exhibited a mediated center of gravity in terms of how they distributed and framed their work. Some participants displayed intervenue distribution preferences, by strongly gravitating toward one particular online venue over another. For example, some kids preferred to post their work on YouTube while others maintained their own websites. In intravenue distribution preference, participants used multiple accounts within the same venue to showcase particular talents while experimenting with new techniques and styles. Distribution was one way that kids and youth could publicly express aspects of their technical personae.

Intervenue Distribution Preferences

Many people equate all online video with what is seen on YouTube. However, dozens of other sites exist for distributing video (Patriquin 2008). Although YouTube had caché among technologized youth who had discovered it before the general population, one group began posting videos to their websites about a year before YouTube opened. They considered themselves members of a video blogging community who eschewed YouTube, preferring instead to distribute their work on their own video blogs. I refer to this group as first-generation video bloggers, and they included video blogging evangelists such as Jay Dedman (co-author of a how-to book called *Videoblogging*, 2006) as well as Michael Verdi and Ryanne Hodson who co-authored *Secrets of Videoblogging: Videoblogging for the Masses* (2006). Other participants in this group were 20-year-old Eric Rey, who is discussed later in this chapter, and the Field family who are discussed in Chapter 4, which is on civic engagement. The two 14-year-old video bloggers named Liam and Edward mentioned previously were also part of the early video blogging community.

First-generation video bloggers did not necessarily consider video blogs or "vlogs" to be solely comprised of diary forms of direct camera address. For them, video blogging was a broad term that applied to any personally expressive video that transmitted one's point of view. Genres included comedy shows, citizen journalism, cooking programs, videos that artistically played with form, and many other genres. The point was to have one's own online space and the digital skills to express the self. Many video bloggers were current or former professional media makers including journalists, photographers, and television producers who embraced a philosophy of broadcasting one's own message without censorship or manipulation from corporate entities or site administrators.

For first-generation video bloggers, it was *de rigueur* to have one's own video blogging website. They often posted videos to video-hosting sites like blipTV and cross-linked the videos to their own websites on sites such as WordPress or similar web-hosting platforms (which of course have their own features and limitations). For example, although 14-year-old Liam and Edward posted their first videos on YouTube, they eventually stopped posting there. Instead they posted their work on blipTV and cross linked the videos to their own video blogging website. They said that blipTV offered technical advantages such as higher quality, more control over the size of the video, and ease of cross linkage. In addition, they encountered a "creepy" vibe from certain viewers on YouTube, and so they changed their video access on that site to "private." In this way, only viewers officially designated as their YouTube "friends" could see their videos. Although they retained their YouTube account, their mediated center of gravity was no longer on YouTube, but rather on their own website. YouTube studies are often synchronic, and do not attend to the many key participatory changes that occur over time on mediated sites.

Liam and Edward strongly preferred to engage socially with the community of first-generation video bloggers, rather than interact with a YouTube public. Indeed, most first-generation video bloggers (at least initially) eschewed YouTube, citing quality issues, poor compression, unruly audiences, unwanted forms of commercialization, and censorship. Maintaining creative and technical control of one's own vlog was extremely important. According to Jay Dedman:

> Having my own blog allows me to control the context of my videos. Ownership is clearly mine. I can learn to interact with my viewing community since i have full control over my site. You can't do these things on sites like Youtube (Mefeedia 2007).

One member of the first-generation video blogging social group was a white 20-year-old named Eric Rey, who requested that I used his real name. At the time of the research, Eric maintained his own video blog at: ericrey.net. He told me in a chat interview that he relocated to Los Angeles to study broadcasting, and he enrolled in a community college. However, he became impatient and wished to create web content. He was particularly interested in making cooking videos, and said that he was contemplating attending culinary school.

Like many early video bloggers outside of YouTube, he believed that participating online would bring a net positive to society. Whatever the content, from the highly personal to the more popular, personally expressive videos could promote circulation of information that was free and uncensored. He believed that such participation promoted closer forms of sociality. To him, first-generation video bloggers offered a welcoming community of similarly inspired, technically oriented participants. He did not believe YouTube was such a community, given his perception of its heterogeneous content and lack of social connections.

Eric Rey did have an account on YouTube. However, it was clear that he strongly preferred his own site. He posted his videos on YouTube to gain viewership for his main video blog. He stated in a chat interview, "what i hope for when i post to youtube is people will stumble upon my video, and then watch more and hopefully go to my website to see more." Although he had videos on both sites, his mediated center of gravity was not on YouTube. Similar to other early video bloggers, he noted that he was "not too fond of youtube [because] when you post on there you lose rights to your video and also the quality is automatically downgraded." He said that "on the upside they have millions of users searching for content."

Whereas he considered YouTube to be merely a "viral video hub," he believed that early video bloggers had formed a community, in part because they helped each other deal with questions or problems in technical areas such as editing. In describing the community of early video bloggers he stated:

> its a group of people who have the same interests and help each other out. its a very smart group of people. youve got to be a little savy to have a video blog…i like technology and things like that. so what im trying to say is the people who are in the community are internet savy, like i am

Indeed, his brother, who was also a member of the early video blogging community, had helped him with his video projects. Eric explained:

> [My brother] has always been my mentor. He has many more years experience than me in just about everything that I do. We both have the same interests, and I am doing now what he was doing years ago. So naturally if i have any questions he can answer them. Although in the past year or so I have become much less reliant on him and able to do more technical things without asking for help. Now I just look for his advice or insight on projects I work on.

As discussed in Chapter 7, kids and youth often relied on mentors to assist them at different points in their learning trajectories. Yet, when asked directly about how they learned, their tech-savvy narratives emphasized being "self-taught."

Notably, Eric stated that you have to be "a little savvy" to have your own video blog. By having one's own video blog, one could propose a more technologized identity in comparison to people who did not have their own website, but used an aggregator such as YouTube. In Eric Rey's YouTube account, out of 11 videos, 7 contain the phrase "(ericrey.net)" in parentheses in the video title. A video title is often an important indicator of a video's content and identity. By placing his external website in the *title* of his videos, Eric uses YouTube to emphasize the importance of his own website, which he considered to be superior to his YouTube channel page. The first seven videos in Eric's collection contain one sentence in the accompanying text description, which is: "Visit http://www.ericrey.net for more videos!" Here, videos function less as content and more as tactical redirects to his main site.

At the time of my study, clicking on ericrey.net redirected the viewer from YouTube to his own video blog. As of this writing, the link takes users to his Facebook page. Clearly, mediated centers of gravity change over time, and in response to changes in the mediated and technical environments within which participants operate. Although some of the early video bloggers continue to maintain their video blogs and post new material, several others have turned to social media sites such as Twitter and Facebook to post links to their work. When it was a new platform, Twitter also exhibited techno-caché. Some video bloggers told me that social media sites facilitated an immediacy of connection that they no longer received from their own websites to the same degree.

Choosing a distribution venue enabled participants to propose an identity of relative expertise. In comparison to those who did not know about YouTube or who could not make videos, posting to YouTube might characterize a participant as relatively more expert than people who did not know how to make and post videos. To those who believed in the ideology of having one's own website, posting to YouTube displayed less technical expertise than one who was "technically savvy" enough to create one's own video-oriented website. It was particularly important for some video bloggers to remain free of aggregators whose owners maintained control, commercialized videos, or otherwise interfered with individual self-expression. Intervenue specialization was one way to propose relative expertise, while also situating a participant within particular mediated social networks.

Intravenue Distribution Preferences

Intravenue distribution preference refers to how one manages or showcases content in different accounts within the same website. As content floats around increasingly amorphous online spaces, websites may become more fluid and less delineated as websites, in which case this distinction may decrease in intensity. However, it was clear in my study that some YouTube participants either crafted their account to reflect specializations or maintained multiple accounts to highlight different dimensions of their work. It was not unusual for people to have a main account that displayed more polished work, and another account for experiments, tests, and other "odds and ends" videos that they did not feel belonged in their main catalogue. For example, Therapix had two accounts on YouTube. One of them exhibited a mediated center of gravity in terms of content; he was widely known for making tutorials. He said his other account was for "scraps" and "tests."

The experiences of a video making team lead by two white teens, 17-year-old Ben (his chosen pseudonym) and 16-year-old Clyde (a researcher chosen pseudonym) highlight why it might be important for people to maintain separate accounts that enable them to challenge how social roles and interpersonal expectations impact learning opportunities. For instance, within the same site of YouTube, Clyde opened a "secret" account that was separate from the one he maintained with Ben. Through this secret account, Clyde intended to experiment outside the purview of his more knowledgeable video-making partner.

More than half of the videos that Ben and Clyde posted to their account were of the comedy, or parodic, variety. Videos included themes such as simulating passing gas, pretending to catch Clyde sucking his thumb while sleeping, parodying a public service announcement on name calling, and enacting a comedy skit in which a boy wakes up next to an unattractive, possibly androgynous person (portrayed by a male actor). Ben said that other than using email and the Internet, his parents were "clueless" about computers. Clyde said that his parents were not at all technical in terms of computers, and typically consulted him or his brother when they needed help. When asked if he was "technical" Clyde responded in his chat interview, "not [particularly], i know a little bit about computers, just enough to get by, if i ever run into trouble i talk to ben or [my other friend ned] and they help me out." This narrative indicates a relational expertise that situates Clyde as less expert than Ben or his other friend, Ned.

Both Clyde's and Ben's video origin stories include the presence of each other, rather than their parents. Clyde describes going to Ben's house one day and making videos. According to Clyde, Ben had been messing around with some "3D gaming stuff and had made a small movie." Clyde saw a camera on his dresser and said, "It'd be fun to make a movie with that green screen over there." In Clyde's narrative, Ben just happened to have a green screen "lying around." The narrative is interesting because it situates their first video recording efforts together as technologically motivated. They picked up a camera first within the context of 3D gaming activities and special effects. Using green screens typically connotes more technologized aspects of video creation. That Ben just happened to have a green screen "lying around" indexes a prior interest in visual media and in the technical aspects of manipulating images.

In terms of their individual contributions to the group's video making, Ben said that although he and Clyde initiated most efforts, about five other friends also joined in. Ben said that although everyone was an actor, typically he directed, edited, organized the group, and did "all the YouTube work," presumably referring to uploading the videos and managing the account. From time to time, he also contributed writing scripts. He characterized Clyde principally as a writer, who also directed at least one video. According to Ben, although Clyde did not edit, "he [threw] in his input when watching [Ben] do it." Although Ben and Clyde did most of the work in comparison to peripheral participants, Ben was ultimately the director and editor.

Competitive tensions, albeit joking ones, sometimes emerged between Ben and Clyde. According to Clyde, one day Ben told him that he really did not need Clyde to make videos. Clyde countered that if he had a camera he could make "just as good vids." To respond to this perceived challenge of asymmetrical techno-cultural knowledge, Clyde recruited his friend Luke, and they opened a "secret" account, separate from Clyde's account with Ben.

The plan was to launch the account with a video that seemed like the video makers had "no clue" what they were doing. Over time, Clyde would post better videos, garner widespread YouTube popularity, and unveil his true expert video-making identity to his friend. Ben would then realize that he had underestimated Clyde. In one video on the secret account, Clyde disguised himself as a mysterious vampire persona called "Vlad," who appeared in a mask and robe (Lange 2007a). He and his friend modulated the sound speed so that Clyde's voice seemed deeper. As the Vlad character, Clyde stated:

> We have a strict rule [governing] our society that there are some things that should never be seen, should never be known, [which is] more for our protection than yours. If people knew that we were doing such things, [we] would be punished, so you'll never know our real names or our real faces but you will know our entertainment.

It is difficult not to interpret "Vlad's" remarks as alluding to Clyde's and his friends' video making efforts. If his early efforts were "known," the boys might be punished, which is to say, they might be ridiculed by other YouTube viewers. They might also be criticized by Ben, who already expressed doubts about Clyde's video-making abilities. For these reasons, audiences would never know their "real names" or "real faces." However, Vlad says that YouTube would know their "entertainment."

That Clyde established a special account to develop his video making skills is not surprising in light of scholars' observations that a certain degree of anonymity or pseudonymity is often advantageous or even necessary for accomplishing self-actualization. Nissenbaum (2004:148-149) argues that having some zones of privacy is crucial for formulating "conceptions of the self" because they "provide venues in which people are free to experiment, act, and decide without giving account to others or being fearful of retribution." Clyde as Vlad enacts this concept by using a separate, specialized account that provides him a degree of insulation from his friend. He could experiment and improve his video making skills without criticism that might be creatively stifling.

Clyde made sure that his account with Ben subscribed to the Vlad account, so that Ben would see it. In a chat interview, Clyde told me that after seeing the video, Ben told Clyde that the video maker was clearly a "noob" (similar to "newbie," or person who is new at a technical activity). Clyde said he could not resist pointing out to Ben that this "noob" had at least used some cool lighting effects. Ultimately the Vlad video disappeared. Ben and Clyde continued to make videos together, and the videos they posted exhibited a feeling of sociality and interpersonal enjoyment. Although the reasons for its disappearance are unknown, the purpose of the separate account was originally to give Clyde a space to create a learning opportunity in which he could build his technical skills.

YouTube participants could express relative expertise by specializing in or at least exhibiting a mediated center of gravity in terms of how they distributed their work. In some cases, choosing or eschewing a particular online site could help the video maker propose an identity of possessing tech-savvy knowledge about what constituted an appropriate site for their videos. In other cases, what became important was to craft separate accounts that showed expert or technical competence while relegating tests or creative experimentation to a "zone of insularity" (Cohen 2000:1424) away from their main public account. Such specializations facilitated learning without risking the reputation of the video maker. The ancillary site was either shrouded in relative pseudonymity or clearly labeled as a space of experimentation.

Impact on Learning Opportunities

Kids in my study tended to specialize in terms of content, video tasks, and distribution. Whether they were novices, advanced amateurs, or pre-professionals, kids displayed preferences for certain kinds of content. They often preferred video blogging or comedy, although they experimented with many genres. For example, some participants specialized in tutorials, which helped other participants learn how to improve video-making skills. Through viewer feedback, tutorial makers in turn learned how to shape socially encoded artifacts to better assist their viewers. Bi-directional chains of learning on YouTube provided a wealth of peer-to-peer information.

In terms of video making skills and participatory roles, specialization produced both pleasures and tensions with regard to having fun and learning through a lens. On the one hand, some peripheral members never expressed the disposition or desire to gain deep technical knowledge of all aspects of video creation. They specialized in particular roles that helped them cooperate with more experienced creators to accomplish their friends' goals, but these roles did not necessarily imply access to creating or realizing peripheral members' own personally expressive visions within the group. Mentorship was not always automatic, and could be complicated when mentor and mentee were perceived as so far apart in technical acumen that they did not share even basic concepts. Sometimes peers and friends jockeyed for position within local techno-cultural hierarchies.

Nevertheless, all groups expressed a certain degree of fluidity in terms of attending to input and receiving creative suggestions from peripheral members. Being a peripheral member of a video making group that included experts helped participants gain exposure to understanding video craft. In some cases, participants gained formal technical knowledge that is taught in film schools and appears in text books on filmmaking and video blogging. In other cases, participants also developed personal confidence and mediated self-expression skills, which are important for developing a public voice.

In addition to content and skills, selecting a particular venue of distribution provided another method for proposing technical expertise. While some participants used YouTube to display techno-savvy video making abilities, other participants preferred to maintain their own website, in an attempt to remain free from the censorship policies or commercialization aspect of YouTube. Being truly technical meant having one's own website outside of YouTube. Participants also used multiple accounts on the same site to shape public interpretation of identity and facilitate learning. Some participants distinguished between their main works and other tests or experiments regulated to a special channel. Some participants attempted to create a kind of "zone of insularity" away from friends or peers who held particular techno-cultural expectations. Separate accounts enabled participants to develop skills and self-actualize without fear of unfair criticism. Selecting distribution channels became one way to negotiate technical identities while facilitating the development of digital literacies.

Having access to advanced video makers within a social group facilitated learning but also suggested that prior technical and participatory dispositions greatly influenced learning opportunities. Interpersonal dynamics, individual desire, and perceptions of technical ability influenced who might achieve access to core video-making activities, and whether peripheral activity assisted in developing digital literacies. Hanging out through a lens helped people learn and have fun, but also prompted participants to jockey for identities of relative technical expertise through video creation.

CHAPTER 3

《《◀ ■ ▶》》

Girls Geeking Out on YouTube

From technical animations to video blogs, girls are contributing an impressive kaleidoscope of videos to YouTube. This chapter describes the experiences of girls who exhibited "geeked out" or technical identities that developed from manipulating computers, cameras, and editing tools to create personally expressive videos. It focuses on girls' technological self-perceptions and techno-cultural affiliations. Those who self-identified as technically proficient often performed an affiliation not only to the act of making videos but also to particular technology-related cultural beliefs, such as learning on one's own, and supporting a historically situated Internet value of protecting free speech, even when YouTube yielded contentious and hurtful commentary on girl's videos.

Drawing from my ethnographic study, this chapter focuses on media artifacts, video-based practices, and interviews with 15 girls, aged 12 to 19. Six of the girls joined YouTube within the first six months after its launch in December 2005. Joining a site so early, before it has hit the mainstream media and garnered global attention, is a techno-cultural identity marker; displaying knowledge of eventually popular online sites demonstrates that one is technically savvy and attuned to cool online spaces. Two girls were 12 to 13 years old, three were 14 to 15, two were 16, and eight were 17 to19. Ten girls were white, three were Asian, one was African American, and one girl's ethnicity remained undetermined. Most of the girls were from the United States, although one was born in Southeast Asia and attended school in the United States, and another was Australian.

The chapter begins by describing scholarly conceptions of girls' media usage, and how technology is often ignored as an identity variable in these studies. It discusses what it means to be a "geek," and outlines this term's changing cultural connotations. It provides ethnographic examples of girls' geeking out and performing affiliations to technologies, practices, and techno-cultural values. Given that my study was weighted toward early adopters of YouTube, it was not surprising to see that most girls oriented their technical persona around making videos. Although it exhibited complications (Lange 2007c, 2007e), the participatory aspect of the site enabled girls to display relative expertise and geek out on the 'Tube.

Studying Girls' Media

Studies have moved from analyzing girls' media consumption to investigating their media production on- and offline. Early studies of girls' mass media consumption (such as teen magazines) expressed concern with how such materials promoted normative femininity, gendered consumers, and objects of male gaze (McRobbie 1981; Peirce 1990; Walkerdine 1984). More recent studies analyze girls' media production and technology use. Such studies typically focus on a specific genre such as: zines (Kearney 1998), webpages (Stern 1999), game design (Denner and Campe 2008; Pelletier 2008), lip-synching videos (Banet-Weiser 2011), websites (Mazzarella 2010), and after-school media programs (Denner and Martinez 2010; Ito et al. 2010). My study was also concerned with how girls' express identity through a medium—that of YouTube videos. It is important to note, however, that YouTube videos include many genres, such as diary videos, animation, comedy sketches, and many others.

Girls' media studies often focus on how girls produce media that negotiates non-technical aspects of the self—such as gender (Banet-Weiser 2011; Denner and Martinez 2010; Kelly et al. 2006; Pelletier 2008); age (Kearney 1998); class (Kearney 1998); ethnicity (Denner and Campe 2008); and demeanor (Stern 1999). Kearney (1998:298) asserts that media production helps girls to resist "privileged notions of gender, generation, race, class, and sexuality." Focusing on girls' media production helps scholars "more fully understand [girls'] negotiative, resistant, and perhaps even oppositional cultural practices" (Kearney 1998:289-90). Moving forward, studies need to consider girls' overt technical affiliations, not just how media helps resist notions of traditional identity variables such as gender, race, ethnicity, and class.

Most girls' media studies have excluded investigations of technical affiliations as central research loci. For example, in their study of a girl's game design program, Denner and Campe (2008:141) focused on how girls "used humor and defiance of familiar authority to play with gender stereotypes and reject the expectation that girls are always well behaved." Denner and Martinez (2010) examined how rural Latino girls in the United States negotiated identities by participating in and shaping the social network sites of Whyville and MySpace, as well as through game design. The MySpace girls engaged in "friendship-driven" (Ito et al. 2010) activities such as chatting; the Whyville girls spent their computer time learning to do new things, and exhibited an "interest-driven" (Ito et al. 2010) orientation. Denner and Martinez's (2010) study revealed a variety of girls' engagements with information technology in the same U.S. socio-cultural setting. This is a key finding because it contradicts the assumption that everyone in the same socio-economic milieu should be viewed as "one homogenous group" (Denner and Martinez 2010:217).

Yet, these researchers concluded that not all participants adequately expressed "identity" through game design. One girl who lacked an appropriate "audience" was not perceived by the researchers to be using her self-designed game as a "site for identity exploration," even though she expressed pride in her technically oriented work, was one of the first girls in the study to personalize her game with "unique features," and "her technical skills grew over time as she made increasingly complex games" (Denner and Martinez 2010:219). In their study—as in many others in girls' media—technical skills are not called out as identity variables in their own right.

Yet, many girls and women embrace technical skills and affiliations as important aspects of their identities (Bucholtz 2002; Bury 2011; Coleman 2013). Several of the girls profiled here perceived themselves as technical and used YouTube to showcase their technically driven talents and capabilities. An important goal of my study was to analyze how technical identities are created and negotiated in practice, amid changing connotations of what it means to be a "geek."

Geek Identities

Webster's Collegiate Dictionary (1979) defines a "geek" as "a carnival performer often billed as a wild man whose act usually includes biting the head off a live chicken or snake." Obviously much has changed since the word carried that particular meaning! Yet, contemporary uses of the term still connote a marginalized or socially odd male who exhibits arcane skills. A geek is typically defined as "a person who has encyclopaedic knowledge of computing and is obsessively fascinated by it but is socially inept, exhibits odd personality traits, excludes normal social and human interests, and spends free time being 'social' on a computer" (Varma 2007:360). Some researchers have characterized being a "geek" as socially undesirable (Milner 2004) or as a social stigma requiring identity "recovery" (Kinney 1993). In his studies of children transitioning to high school in the United States, Kinney (1993) argued that the social "recovery" process for geeks included joining mainstream school activities, widening one's social network, and devaluing the expectations of trendy or popular peers.

The term still holds negative connotations for many people. Bucholtz (2002:278) argues that kids are still being driven away from technology in large measure due to the "antinerd discourse of parents, teachers, and peers." For example, in a study of a high-school girls' seminar designed to attract technically savvy females to the field of computer science, researchers found that "being a geek" was an image the girls tried hard to avoid (Graham and Latulipe 2003). Rejecting the stereotype of the under-socialized, technical male, girls forcefully proclaimed, "We aren't geeks!" (Graham and Latulipe 2003:325).

In the past, geekdom was largely associated with males (Levy 1984). An influential study of undergraduates at Carnegie-Mellon University suggested that the myth of the geek male "myopically obsessed" with computers led many women who did not share such intense obsessions to question their commitment to computer science (Margolis and Fisher 2002). However, a later study conducted at the same institution by Blum and Frieze (2005) did not find such a striking gendered dichotomy. Most women whom they interviewed "seemed to be constructing a new identity that was both 'geeky' and feminine" (Blum and Frieze 2005:112-113). Both women and men were "moving toward a more well-rounded identity that embraced academic interests and a life outside of computing" (Blum and Frieze 2005:113).

Today, the term is becoming somewhat less "pejorative" because it connotes "competence in technology" (Varma 2007:360). The term's changing status is due in part to the visible, financial successes of high-technology entrepreneurs such as Microsoft's founder Bill Gates and others who exhibit lavish "geek chic" lifestyles (Margolis and Fisher 2002:67; McArthur 2009:61-62). Indeed, Moore and Love (2004) call being a technology geek a "prestigious stigma." Technology geeks often exhibit a sense of "power" and "pride" in their abilities and accomplishments (Moore and Love 2004).

Numerous studies have described technically oriented identities among women (Bury 2011) and girls (Bucholtz 1998, 1999, 2002; Currie et al. 2006). In a Canadian study of pre-teen and teenage girls, being a "geek" was "an identity that some girls embraced and actively cultivated" (Currie et al. 2006:422). Indeed girls donned buttons that proclaimed, "The geeks shall inherit the earth!", a slogan that no doubt reflects the changing shift of power of technologists in many cultures. Similarly, several girls in my study noted that they were technical and took pride in their video-making and other accomplishments.

The present chapter ethnographically explores a range of video-making and sharing practices. It takes up Bloustein's (2003) call to explore the "lived reality" of media creators that analyzes not only particular genres or single texts, but also considers girls' experiences, including social interactions that help negotiate technologized identities that emerge through sharing and producing media. Being technical is often relational; some elite hackers may see video making as a low-level form of technical competence, while members of the general population characterize audio-visual skills as "geeky." The following discussion examines artifacts, technical self-perceptions, and interactional practices to understand how girls accomplish technically oriented identity work through media.

Expressing Technical Affiliation Through Media

The girls whom I intereviewed demonstrated a wide variety of interests and abilities with regard to their YouTube participation. Two girls made no videos, and considered themselves casual users of the site; they visited only when prompted by a link sent by a friend or family member. Two girls might be considered former participants, since they eventually deleted their accounts (making it difficult to know how many videos they posted, or whether they opened other video channels). Three girls uploaded 1 video, and two of these only did so as a test or to create an image icon for their channel page (YouTube's equivalent of the personal profile page found on social network sites). Five girls posted 15 to 25 videos, and two girls posted 45 to 70 videos. One girl (who aspired to be a professional media maker) posted over 2,000 videos. One must take these numbers with caution: people on YouTube sometimes delete videos to refresh their channel page at unpredictable intervals. Thus the number of videos noted here is not necessarily the total number the girls have ever posted to YouTube. It is only the total that I observed at the time of the analysis. Such a variety of commitment to video challenges homogenizing discourses about "digital youth" that would suggest that all youth embrace the same forms of media to the same degree.

The girls' mediated centers of gravity did not always orient around making videos. Two girls, who are referred to here by the pseudonyms of Anna and Sharon, expressed no interest in making videos nor even obtained an account to comment on other people's videos, even though creating an account on YouTube was free at the time of the research and required minimal information such as a valid email. Yet, lack of interest in video making did not necessarily correspond to a self-characterization of being non-technical. For instance, Anna, a 19-year-old youth born in Southeast Asia who attended college on the west coast of the United States, considered herself "technical" and planned to develop her skills by taking computer science and programming classes. In terms of online activities, she preferred blogging and participating on Facebook. When I asked her how she used computers, she said, "mostly just email, chat, maintain a blog, school work and editing photos." Even though she was disinterested in videos as a genre, she still considered herself "technical" and oriented toward improving her skills by taking programming classes.

Similarly, Sharon, an 18-year-old white teenager, participated only casu-ally on YouTube. She mainly used computers to do Facebook, conduct re-search, and send email. Using YouTube meant visiting the site when someone sent her a link to an interesting video. When I asked her if she planned to get an account and post videos, she replied, "No. I don't think I would do that 'cause first off I don't know what I would do for a video, but also I don't really like the idea of anyone in the world being able to watch me do something." Sharon exhibits a basic but important digital literacy: posting on YouTube meant that anyone in the world with access to the Internet could watch what she did on video. Not all kids who posted videos considered the ramifications of global broadcast. In prior studies of video and text sharing (Lange 2007a; Stern 2008), many kids assumed that only people who were interested in their content would actually watch.

Ethnographic examination of the girls' video oeuvres reveals a variety of participation that may not surface when examining a single genre, such as lip-synching videos. For example, of the girls who made more than one video (eight girls), no girl made only one type of genre. The most popular genres were video blogging, sketch comedy, lip-synching, personal event videos, and hanging-out-at-home videos. Other genres included reviews of mass media works, animation, machinima, promotional videos, documentaries, how-to videos (such as painting or putting on make-up), technology experimenta-tion (such as using iLife, a suite of Mac applications for editing and publishing media), and videos for class projects. Video genres are not necessarily mutu-ally exclusive; sometimes a movie review is one of many subjects that finds its way into a video blog.

Each of the girls who made more than one video made at least one video blog of the more common diary type, in which a person faces the camera and talks about their lives. The girls covered many topics, including: feelings about school, life's challenges, love of music, information about pets, and other re-flections on life. Video blogs as a genre are often perceived by the public as narcissistic and self-centered. Such a pattern of criticism reappears with the introduction of genres that facilitate public expression of girls' voices. Yet, un-der the right circumstances, video blogs expose broadly generalizable issues that are important to young people's life worlds (Lange 2007b). For example, Crystal, a white 18-year-old teen who aspired to be a director of animation, noted in one of her video blogs that college was more difficult than she had originally supposed. In a video, she states:

> I have to tell you, life right now sucks. Going into college was a lot more dif-ferent than I thought. A lot of people said it was easy. It's not easy! I have to get money somehow you know to buy for my laptop. I'm getting a car soon

sometime so I can drive back and forth because I cannot afford a dorm at the moment and um it's driving me crazy. So what I'm thinking about doing is uh actually getting a PayPal account so I can at least like try and get some donations or um sell my art work, be selling some stuff, like I guess my PS2. I don't know I kinda don't want to give it up. I mean, PS3 is coming out but it's going to be really expensive. I might give away some of my PS2 games, but I don't think I'll be giving up my PS2, perhaps because I'm attached to it, I don't know. I guess cause I really love Guitar Hero and Kingdom Hearts and DDR. I am not selling my Play Station 2. Forget I said that!

In a genre of video that is not assumed to be particularly technical (people sit and face the camera and do not always use significant amounts of editing or special effects), a viewer nevertheless learns much about Crystal's technical affiliations as well as the challenges girls face in college. For instance, Crystal notes that college requires money to buy technical tools such as her laptop. Crystal's college learning opportunity is threatened by her lack of ability to buy appropriate technical tools. Her narrative about the difficulties of college and her proposed solutions resonate with Harris's (2004) description of the "can do" girl who is expected to continually reinvent the self in a society that does little to address the underlying causes of problems such as widespread inadequate financial support for a college education. Harris argues that societal forces impute onto girls a responsibility to exercise the right choices and internally motivated interventions to ensure success, despite the challenges presented by the infrastructure within which they operate. In her video blog, Crystal considers creative ways to raise money by selling her art or her beloved technologized possessions such as her PlayStation (PS), (a video game console made by Sony).

Crystal's personal vlog exposes deep societal problems about the practical affordability of college. This is surprising for people such as Crystal, whose father is a professor of business. In considering how she will afford laptops and cars, Crystal considers establishing a PayPal account so she can take donations for her art work or perhaps even sell her technical possessions. Crystal's proposed solution is partly a technologized one in that it involves using an online site to collect funds that would ensure successful learning opportunities through formal education. How she attempts to craft a formal learning opportunity—replete with appropriate technical tools—is recognized through her technically driven efforts to fund her college education and her performance of affiliation to devices that she is reluctant to sell.

In debating whether to sell specific possessions, Crystal's narrative reveals much about her technical affiliations. She initially considers selling her PS2 and then admits that she is "too attached" to its associated games to sell the console. She affiliates to gaming practices in general, as well as to specific games (such as *Guitar Hero* and *Dance Dance Revolution* [DDR]) and to a specific brand of video game consoles, the PS2. These technical affiliations are reinforced when she realizes it will be too difficult to sell them. She directs the viewer to "Forget I said that!" Expressing reluctance to trade away technologized devices to support her education is a performance of technical affiliation. Within a diary video blog, important clues exist as to the learning problems that girls face, the technologized methods in which they handle them, and the affiliations they perform to everyday technologies of school, work, and play.

Video blogs and accompanying feedback also enable girls to perform technical affiliations and identities. Such jockeying for technical position took a playful turn between an 18-year-old African American named Anesha, and her male friend. In his video blog, Anesha's friend says that he can attract more viewers than she can. He farcically proposes to gain attention by discussing packets of Taco Bell salsa. He says he will match her "fancy editing styles." Next, he covers the camera lens, moves to a different position, and then removes the obstruction, revealing him in a new position. Using the crudest form of "in camera" editing, he playfully demonstrates his inferior editing abilities. This friendly competition is a humorous way of performing comparatively asymmetrical technical expertise. Her friend's claim to match her "fancy editing" actually acknowledges Anesha's superior editing skills (by illustrating how poor his are in comparison), yet simultaneously enables him to perform affiliation to the idea that editing is a desirable video skill.

Anesha says that her editing style is "hardly fancy," thus downgrading his compliment. In her video, she says that she uses "Windows Movie Maker, for God's sake." This statement is an important performance of technical affiliation. Although she downgrades herself in comparison to those who use more complicated desktop editing software (such as Final Cut Pro), at the same time, she displays awareness that Windows Movie Maker is not a particularly complicated or technical editing system. Her statement shows that she is "in the know" about what really constitutes "fancy" editing skills or software packages, even if she does not use them. Performing a technical identity is relative; participants frequently situate their abilities in relation to skills that they strive to attain or to talented video makers whom they respect.

Whether underestimating one's ability is a gendered practice is an empirical question. Notably, such relative self-perceptions of ability have been observed in other technical milieu. In my ethnographic observations, male technologists who may be perceived as quite technical from certain perspectives downgrade their abilities when speaking of knowledge or skills they would like to acquire but do not yet possess. In her study of female information technology professionals, Bury (2011:44) found that one female's self-identification about being a "geek" depended upon context. If she socialized with non-technologists, she would consider herself a "geek." In the presence of more technical associates, she would feel strange trying to "compete with them technically" (Bury 2011:44). Such patterns reveal the relativity of lived technologized identities.

In her video, Anesha also performs technical affiliation by claiming to be an "editor by trade" and by planning to incorporate more editing into her video blogs. Telling her friend that she is an "editor by trade" indicates something about her perceived self-identity; she has expertise in a specific technical skill. Anesha does not simply make the claim in words. She also uses the effect of jump cuts so that each word she utters within the same sentence shows a new shot. With this technique, she metapragmatically and metaphenomenologically shows her ability and technical affiliation to editing. If pragmatics is language in use, metapragmatics includes commenting on that usage, including judging appropriateness of form. If phenomenology refers to sets of experience and their meaning, a metaphenomenological act is one that, through sharing an experience, comments on or evaluates that same experience. Here, Anesha both metapragmatically talks about the importance of editing in video-communication and shows herself engaged in it. By incorporating jump cuts in which the shot changes for each word in a sentence, Anesha metapragmatically and metaphenomenologically demonstrates her capabilities and her support of editing as an important technical skill and method of communication. In experiencing the jump cuts, viewers are invited to similarly experience editing as an important aspect of watching videos. The jump cuts enable Anesha to perform her technical affiliation to the importance of editing and they help showcase her ability to execute more advanced technical effects than speaking to a web cam.

Like most of the girls in my study, Anesha made several types of videos. For instance, in addition to video blogs, she also made machinima videos. Machinima is "a term used to describe animated films created using game engines and game play footage" (Ito and Bittani 2010:224). Anesha used the Sims2 game system to create several original animated videos. The Sims are a series of computer games that enable players to create and manipulate "sims" or "simulated people" partly by creating environments and scenarios for characters to interact. Typical activities include buying houses, partying, and falling in love (Hayes and King 2009:63).

Because their themes are often relational and domestic, and because girls reportedly constitute 60% of their player base, the Sims games are often characterized as "girls' games" (Hayes and King 2009:60). They have been criticized for "promoting consumerism and traditional female roles" (Hayes and King 2009:60). However, the Sims have also provided technical learning opportunities by assisting in improving digital literacies and broadening computer skills. Girls may engage in "modding" or making modifications to game systems or software according to specific skills and interests. In their TechSavvy Girls Project, Hayes and King (2009:61) found that:

> The Sims engages players in core computing practices, through activities ranging from creating families and neighborhoods within the game to using digital tools to produce custom content, videos, storyboards, and modding software. Just as importantly, it offers opportunities for participation in global modding communities.

Using the Sims to make a machinima video requires video and computer skills and a general understanding of how to manipulate characters, actions, and environments in the game to realize original concepts and stories.

Anesha used the Sims2 game to create original videos. She wrote screen plays, created particular characters, crafted wardrobes and sets, and then filmed the characters performing actions that she assigned to them. Creating a machinima video involves negotiation of several digital skills, including understanding Sims2 game parameters and manipulating technical aspects of video. In an online, chat interview, I asked her how this exercise compared to other forms of video making on YouTube. She replied, "There's a whole [separate] process you have to go through like creating the characters and knowing how to control them and knowing how they are going to perform an action before you even tell them to do so."

According to Anesha, the process typically takes more time than what the "common 'youtuber' does." Anesha's point that machinima is a "whole separate process" suggests that the requirements and tools used for game modding and creating game-based videos require different skill sets and forms of knowledge. Her machinima videos involve knowledge of at least three major forms of knowledge: Sims2, YouTube, and video-making in general. Not only must Anesha have knowledge of these genres individually, she must navigate between them to create videos with a compelling narrative that ideally would attract diverse viewers, including machinima fans and more general YouTube audiences.

Typically, Anesha's machinima videos (which sometimes receive more than a thousand views) revolve around themes of heterosexual romance, love, and family. In one of her machinima videos, a man picks up a baby girl from a crib and plays tenderly with her. As the girl grows up, scenes depict major life changes such as taking first steps. In one shot, her crib turns into a bed, and her shelf with toys becomes a desk with a computer. In another shot, the father bonds with his daughter by playing video games. Traditionally gendered scenes are depicted including: going to a fancy dress dance, accepting a marriage proposal, getting married, and being pregnant. During the wedding sequence, prior scenes are seen in flashback in black and white imagery. Cutting from an image of the father's face to these black and white scenes is a clever way of showing that the images are now the father's poignant memories of his maturing daughter. Anesha's father-daughter machinima video prominently displays technologies as important tropes of a girl growing up. Toys are replaced by a computer in the girl's bedroom. As she ages, she plays video games to bond with her father.

Anesha's and Crystal's stories, as well as those of many girls on YouTube, show girls' impressive variety of video genres. Contrary to homogenizing discourses that assume that all young people embrace technologies equally, not all of the girls made videos, and those who did made many different kinds. Eschewing YouTube was not necessarily a predictor of whether girls saw themselves as more or less technical, which is a relative state. Girls who did not make videos sometimes anticipated improving their technical skills through other means, such as computer programming. For the girls who did participate on the site, affiliations appeared in a range of ways—from video blog descriptions about favorite technologies to manipulation of overtly technical genres such as machinima. As with boys, interactions with other participants also helped girls' establish a relative reputation of superior technological skills. In addition to displays of skill and social negotiation of ability, another important aspect of technical performance included girls' narratives about personal technical identity characteristics. Such personal narratives offer important clues about how girls perform affiliations to particular technologies, media, and related cultural values.

Self-Perceptions of Technical Expertise

In the interviews, girls' indexes of technical ability and knowledge about computers ranged from surfing the web to learning about computer programming. Each interview typically included questions about how people got started making videos and participating on YouTube. In some cases, the interviews directly addressed whether the girls perceived themselves to be technical with regard to using computers and making videos, and what the term connoted to them. In 10 out of 15 cases, girls either adopted the label "technical" to describe their identities, or described their interests and activities in ways that indexed their facility with computers and video-making technologies.

Such findings contrast those of prior studies in which girls did not express confidence in technology or perceive themselves as having skills, but instead were reluctant to express overt interest in computers. For example, in a study of information technology use among undergraduates in the United States,

Madigan et al. (2007:410) found that although males and females perceived themselves to have similar skill levels (a perception that sometimes exceeded the researchers' judgment of their skills), female students "[did] not perceive themselves as competent users of technology."

In some studies, girls expressed technical confidence, but characterized themselves as less adept than males. In their study of Singaporean girls' uses of information technologies, girls in focus groups appeared "as confident and avid users of functional software as well as entertainment and social net-working services" (Lim and Ooi 2011:256). Further, the girls' mothers were often seen as technology adopters, thus providing them with female technol-ogy role models. Girls did not perceive technology to be an exclusively male realm (Lim and Ooi 2011). However, most participants in that study stated that men were generally more "adept" at technology then were women, prin-cipally due to their greater "exposure" to it. In their study of kids at schools in the United Kingdom, Holloway and Valentine (2003) found a number of "computer-competent" girls who could use word-processing and database programs. However, they tended to display less "overt" interest in computers than both technically savvy and less technically oriented boys. According to these researchers, although girls and boys had similar computing skills, girls were just less "interested" in talking about such subjects.

In contrast, most of the girls in my YouTube study indicated that they were technical to some degree. Girls expressed overt interest in technology by describing what they knew, how they learned to make videos and use video-making tools, and how their skills compared to other people's abilities. Interviews provide rich details about girls' past and future media making ex-periences and aspirations. Understanding these nuances is important because they prompt different interventions for how to improve girls' self-expressive, digital literacy skills, and how to encourage peer-to-peer networks of assis-tance from girls who are knowledgeable about participating online.

Knowledge and Activities

In my study, girls on YouTube indicated their level of technical ability in part by describing knowledge sets and activities that they engaged in. Two girls offer a useful comparison to understand the wide range of girls' self-perceptions of their technical ability. The first is a 17-year-old white girl who wished to be referred to by her online name of RosenbaumGrl. The second is a 15-year-old white girl who wished to be referred to in the study by the pseudonym of Allison.

RosenbaumGrl joined YouTube relatively early, in May, 2006. Her name paid homage to the actor, Michael Rosenbaum (who portrayed Lex Luther on a television show about Superman called *Smallville*). At the same time, the "Grl" portion of her name alludes to "grrrl power" movements, which emphasize female agency (Gillis et al. 2004). She believed strongly in a You-Tube community, partly because of the public support she received after discussing her health problems in her videos. She lived with her mother, who had been an assistant manager for a car rental agency. She enjoyed attending YouTube gatherings and meeting other participants with whom she had interacted over time. Her comments in interviews, videos, and on her YouTube pages suggested that her family was experiencing financial difficulties. Often mentioning struggles with her Internet connection, the single video left on her page at the time of this writing was a test video she had posted in 2009 to see if she was properly connected online. As such, the video performs a phatic function, which refers to ensuring an ongoing, open communicative channel (Malinowski 1972 [1923]).

In response to my question about whether she "knew a lot about computers," RosenbaumGrl replied that she knew "enough," but looked forward to learning more in college. In an online chat interview, I asked her what she meant by knowing "enough." She stated, "i know the basics of the computer. about how to turn it on, and how to get on the net, and how to look stuff up like using Google or AskJeeves.com or something in that matter."

RosenbaumGrl's self-characterization in some ways underestimates her abilities. She did not mention, for instance, that she uploads videos, even though it is an activity that requires more skill than simply turning on a computer and surfing the "net." Perhaps this was perceived as self-evident, since she was recruited through her video participation. RosenbaumGrl told me that some of her videos had garnered the attention of Nalts, a well-known YouTube participant who alerted others to her video-making presence and the health issues that she discussed in her videos. Her rhetorical ability to tell her story through video and inspire a successful video maker to help out also index her digital literacy skills.

Studies of video sharing practices should ideally be dynamic, and consider the ongoing flux and meaning of individual works. Her present account with one video did not index the lived experience of her past participation or future aspirations on the site. RosenbaumGrl was hampered by technical and infrastructural issues. Universal physical access to the Internet has by no means been achieved, especially with regard to creating and posting high-bandwidth media. Such "participation gaps" (Jenkins et al. 2006) in terms of class require additional study and intervention. Yet, despite her minimizations of her technical ability in her interview, RosenbaumGrl's video comments and test video reveal important information about her technical affiliations and goals, in that she coded videos as an important activity that she would like to continue and maintain after her infrastructural issues were resolved. Expressing interest in a technical activity is another way of performing technical affiliation, even if one is having technical and participatory challenges.

Allison, a 15-year-old white girl, offered a contrasting self-description in her interview. Recruited from my social network, her brother called her a "Henry Jenkins kid," meaning that she was quite knowledgeable and interested in manipulating and combining new media in creative ways (Jenkins 1992; Jenkins et al. 2006). Her participation on YouTube was relatively casual (she said she checked the site once a week) and she only posted one video.

For Allison, video was only one part of an impressively large repertoire of making media that included participating on sites such as YouTube, deviant ART (an online art-sharing site which she checked daily), MySpace (a social network site), and LiveJournal (an online journaling and media-sharing site). Allison engaged in many mediated activities such as writing creative stories, characters, and material for video games. For her, making videos was usually not a separate, planned activity. Rather, she and friends might bring cameras to a coffee shop or on a trip and post the footage, which sometimes included funny skits filled with inside jokes meant to amuse her friends and herself.

Glancing at Allison's single YouTube video does not present a complete picture with regard to her self-perceived technical ability. Her video was a comedic sketch in which she and a friend acted out a puppet-based skit with their fingers held in front of homemade sheets of white paper with drawings as backdrops. Allison said that the video was made while the girls were attending a religious convention. The girls say "random" and "spur of the moment" funny things for their amusement. Their skit is filled with secret jokes that a casual viewer would not likely be able to interpret in the same way as the girls intended. Staged more as a filmed play, the video contains no edits, and received less than 300 views, even after being posted for several years. Such a low view count seems to confirm kids' assumptions that only people who are truly interested in their more personal videos will actually watch. Of course, YouTube's view counts should not be taken too literally. It is possible for someone to download the video and repost it elsewhere, without the video creator's knowledge. As discussed in Chapter 6, family members reported feeling upset when a girl's video was reposted, without her knowledge or permission, on sexualized websites.

Despite her video's modest production values, Allison's self-description indicates a wider body of knowledge about participating in technologized, online spaces. She said she was very "knowledgeable" about computers and that she learned things "quickly." In a voice-only Skype interview, Allison portrayed herself as technically savvy by describing how she created webpages and altered HTML code. HTML stands for HyperText Markup Language, and is the basic language used to create webpages. I asked her if she did a lot of "programming," and she stated:

I do some coding, not so much programming as much as like coding. I can code Web pages and such. I do a little bit of work with FrontPage, but I don't have it on my new computer now, so I don't work with that much anymore. But I know some – I know quite a bit of HTML and a good bit of CSS. I know how CSS works, and I can always alter codes a lot. I'm really good at just taking a code and altering it to just about anything.

Allison coded webpages, and said that she knows "quite a bit of HTML" and "a good bit of CSS." FrontPage was an HTML editing tool. CSS stands for Cascading Style Sheets and is a language used to format documents by manipulating characteristics such as layouts, colors, and fonts. Her tone is confident, often using extreme terms to define her skill sets. She notes that she can "always" alter codes, and to a great degree ("a lot"). She portrays herself as not just being competent, but being "really good" at altering code "to just about anything."

Most girls in the study expressed a technologized set of skills that fell between the more extreme positions of principally using computers for basic tasks such as surfing the net and of holding complex aspirations of learning about computer programming. Narratives often situated a girl's expertise in comparative ways. For example, Anesha, an 18-year-old African American teen who was mentioned earlier and who specialized in editing, engaged in a wide range of genres including playing games, making machinima, and helping install the family's computer. She considered herself technical, although she characterized herself as being on the more "creative" side of being technical.

In their personally expressive videos and other forms of technical engagement, girls' mediated centers of gravity differed greatly with regard to how intensely they wished to participate on YouTube or to make videos. Girls' technical knowledge or aspirations could not always be "read" from the videos left on their sites. In some cases, whether or not girls considered themselves to be "technical" related to particular knowledge sets, an ability to use computing tools, and aspirations to improve their video-making craft.

Learning on One's Own

Girls in my study often expressed pride in the fact that they learned how to make videos or use computers on their own. As discussed in Chapter 7, what constituted being "self-taught" varied greatly from engaging in trial-and-error methods to using socially encoded forms of assistance such as manuals and video tutorials. In some cases, technical self-perceptions were indexed by how easily girls learned how to use cameras and editing tools. For example, a 19-year-old white teenager who requested that I use her real name of Amelia said that she was self-taught with regard to the technical side of making videos. She learned through trial-and-error, searching for information, and observation. She characterized programs such as iMovie and Quicktime as "easy" to use.

Similarly, Allison described how she learned to use computers and video tools:

> I've taught myself how to use computers, and I consider myself very knowledgeable about them, but I just – I learn everything on my own, just figure it out, and the same with cameras. It's like a cell phone. I just figure out how to do it, and it's pretty quick and easy.

Note that Allison considers herself "very knowledgeable" about computers, partly because it is "pretty quick and easy" to figure out how to use them. Unlike the respondents in Selwyn's (2007) survey, who perceived gadgets as male-oriented, Allison does not associate learning about gadgets as exclusively male territory. She says that she learned to use things like computers, cameras, and cell phones quickly and easily on her own.

RosenbaumGrl did not learn about computers from family members; she learned on her own and by "messing around." She also notes that she took a course in ninth grade about Microsoft Word and other Microsoft software. In response to my question in a chat interview about what constituted "messing around," she stated:

> just clicking differnt websites and just learning how to work the website on my own. like Myspace for example. when u set up an account on myspace it takes you through the steps on how to make your myspace better.

RosenbaumGrl's technical self-perception is a positive one, in that she felt she knew "enough" to do specific kinds of tasks, and she felt more knowledgeable in comparison to others. Notably, in her example of being "self-taught," it is clear that she is receiving assistance from the MySpace template, a socially encoded form of usage that provides suggestions on how to improve a page's look and feel. How socially encoded forms of assistance are used when one is "self-taught" is discussed in Chapter 7.

Being self-taught was important for many girls, who often associated it with being "technical" with regard to video-making tools and computers. A 16-year-old Asian teenager from the east coast of the United States referred to in my study as Wendy (a researcher-assigned pseudonym) characterized herself as a "geek" in part because of how she learned how to make videos on her own. Having posted 15 videos, Wendy was recruited for the study directly from YouTube. One of her videos, which is analyzed in Chapter 4 on civic engagement, was a documentary about a deteriorating local park. In an online chat interview, I asked Wendy how she learned to make videos. She replied, "I self taught myself basically, I'm a really fast learner and I'm a total computer geek, so eventually I learned how to do everything by myself with no manuals."

Wendy characterized herself in the strongest technical terms vis-à-vis the other girls in the study, calling herself a "total computer geek." She associates being a geek with being a "fast learner," and learning how to do things on her own, without using manuals or video tutorials. Wendy's work is eclectic and included several lip-synching videos in which she and her friends mouth the words and move their bodies to favorite songs. A textual analysis focusing solely on the lip-synching portion of her oeuvre would not likely reveal the more deeply lived technical experience and self-perception that Wendy exhibited in her interview, her other video genres, and technical practices. For example, having joined in November, 2005, before YouTube even opened its doors on a wide scale indexes inside knowledge about online media and trends. Performing technical identities includes not only posting videos, but also embracing cool techno-cultural trends, espousing methods for learning about technical tools, and aspiring to learn more about technology.

Relational Technologized Identities

I often asked interviewees to compare their video- and computer-related technical abilities to those of family members. Homogenizing discourses of digital generations would predict that kids would exhibit similar levels of ability to those of siblings, and would perceive themselves as more knowledgeable than their parents. However, kids' perceptions of their comparative abilities were more varied and did not always map to these expectations. For example, as described later in the section on geeking out on reality television, a mother Lola, and her daughter Ashley (their chosen pseudonyms) both described how quickly Ashley learned about technology and video making on her own. However, it was also clear from both of their interviews that Lola knew much about computers and was an important technology-oriented female role model for Ashley.

In prior studies of home Internet use, Bakardjieva (2005) found that learning about computers often exhibited a highly social character, in which a "warm expert," or person who was relatively more knowledgeable about computers, would alert new users to the importance of connecting and learning to communicate online. Bakardjieva (2005:99) defined a warm expert as a person who knew relatively more about "Internet/computer technology" than the "less knowledgeable other." At the same time, the "warm expert" was "immediately accessible in the user's lifeworld" and helped mediate "between the technological universal and the concrete situation, needs and background of the novice user with whom he is in a close personal relationship" (Bakardjieva 2005:99).

On YouTube, the "warm expert" might be a friend, as was the case for a 15-year-old white girl who chose the pseudonym of Melissa. In an online chat interview she stated, "I first found out about youtube, when my friend told me there was cool fights to watch on it. And as a project for school I needed to upload my video to it." Melissa was attracted not to YouTube *per se* but to specific kinds of content, which included street fights. She also used the site to upload a video for a school project. YouTube was a convenient way to participate in a class assignment.

In most cases, however, kids' interviews in my study portrayed complex descriptions of learning about technology. Instead of identifying one warm expert who was considerably more knowledgeable, perceptions of another person's expertise tended to shift according to specific tasks, knowledge sets, and personal aspirations. For example, Jordan (her requested pseudonym), a 13-year-old white girl who was home schooled in a religious family, told me in an online chat interview that she began video blogging when her "Dad and Sister told [her] about YouTube." In this respect, her dad and sister were the "warm experts" who knew about YouTube and alerted Jordan to the site. Even though she acknowledged that she learned somewhat from her dad, as the interview progressed, she later emphasized that she had learned by herself to manipulate the buttons on the camera and work the lighting. Her dad may have known about YouTube, but Jordan performs technical expertise in part by emphasizing how she learned on her own how to manipulate video tools.

Similarly, Anesha characterized herself as the family expert with regard to setting up computers. Her mother was an accountant and her father helped people find employment. She characterized her mother as more "computer literate" than her dad. She felt that neither of them were familiar with making videos. However, none of her siblings could be considered "technical" in terms of using computers or making videos. Via a chat interview she stated, "i'm usually the person who installs computers and software and things like that. but i'm more on the creative side rather than the technical side of computer use." Anesha does not portray her siblings as having similar technological abilities, thus exhibiting technical variation within the same family—an observation which challenges homogenizing discourses about digital youth.

Some girls used qualifiers when comparing their current abilities to a future self that would accumulate new knowledge, or to others whom they perceived as knowing comparatively more. For example, although Anesha unequivocally called herself "technical" in comparison to her family, she hesitated to call herself an "expert" with regard to making videos, in part because she knew other, more skilled creators. She stated, "there are people who are sooo much better than me. i wanna use [every] chance i get to practice and hone my skill untill i'm as good as them." Even though she was not as expert as others, she clearly aspired to improve her skills, which is a performance of technical affiliation to particular skills; she states that it is important to practice and hone specific video-making skills until she attains desired levels of achievement.

The girls also upgraded their ability when comparing themselves to a less technical sibling, parent, or other family member. Comparatively speaking, RosenbaumGrl characterized herself as being more knowledgeable than other family members. When I inquired whether she had help from her family in learning to use computers, she replied, "nope. did it all on my own. nobody else in my family is good on the computer, and [they're] not as [interested in learning] about the computer as much as i am."

What constituted the skills of a "warm expert" differed according to particular tasks, applications, sets of knowledge, and participatory practices. In a few cases, girls pointed to others who had helped them learn about YouTube or make videos, but in most cases, girls performed technical identities by emphasizing how they learned on their own or helped others gain technical skills. Girls also performed technical affiliation by showing alliance to certain techno-cultural values, such as ratifying the importance of knowing certain sets of information, projecting a confidence in learning on one's own, and demonstrating an ability to handle public commentary in normative ways within online techno-cultures.

Comment Control

YouTube offers a heterogeneous, interactive space in which people of varying technical abilities and communicative skills may participate. How girls handle contentious interaction and criticisms also reveals their technical affiliations. Often their treatment of comments resonated with certain cultural values upon which the Internet was founded, including forms of "horizontal, free communication" (Castells 2002:54). The telecommunications pioneer John Gilmore reportedly once argued that, "The Net interprets censorship as damage and routes round it" (Gilmore quoted in Rheingold 1993:xxii). Castells (2002:55) summarized these principles stating, "This freedom of expression from many to many was cherished by Net users from the very early stages of online-communication, and became one of the overarching values of the Internet." Strongly espousing and indeed evangelizing (English-Lueck and Saveri 2000) technical principles such as freedom of expression, even at the risk of being offended, is a way of performing affiliation to the support of core values that emerged from early, technically inflected forms of online communication. However, the Internet's openness has caused some scholars and participants concern. Studies have suggested that the agonistic or harassing tone of male-oriented, techno-centric, or academically motivated arguments in online forums have discouraged female participation through a silencing effect (Herring et al. 1995; Lange 2003; Sutton 1994).

More recent studies of females who espouse a technical identity indicate that they do not necessarily eschew such communicatively competitive environments; sometimes women embrace them. In fact, females on Slashdot espoused "geek feminism" (Bucholtz 2002). Slashdot is a web-based, computer-oriented news service targeted toward computer specialists; it offers "news for nerds." A study of Slashdot found that the site adopted the Internet value of free speech while discouraging harassment. Female hackers "[did] not seem to feel disempowered by their experience with technology, nor [did] their linguistic practices suggest that they [were] ill-equipped to participate in the sometimes combative discourse of online geek communities" (Bucholtz 2002:303). Similarly, some girls stated in my interviews that they were not discouraged by criticisms or pointlessly cruel comments posted to their videos.

Nevertheless, prior work on personal home pages and blogs shows that "social acceptance is desired as adolescents frequently view and value themselves based on how they are viewed and valued by others" (Stern 2008:108). Feedback could be very important for kids to feel a sense of accomplishment and encouragement to continue making videos. For example, a white 19-year-old teenager from Australia named Caitlin received quite a bit of success with her account. Her 68 videos each received tens of thousands to over a million views. These are impressive figures given that niche television shows see roughly one million views per episode (de Moraes 2013). Caitlin's work consists of comedy sketches, film and television parodies, and personal video blogging. She argued that receiving positive feedback was inspirational and encouraging. In an online chat interview, she stated, "One of the recent comments was: you're a really good film maker. Or [you're going to be something]. It's silly, I know. But it's one [of] my dreams, so it means a lot."

Conversely, commentary could be contentious and hurtful. People who leave mean-spirited comments are often referred to as "haters." A hater is usually defined in ethnographic interviews as someone who posts mean-spirited or stereotypically negative comments (such as "go die") without offering any useful criticisms. "Hating" in my study ranged in severity from silly criticism to *ad hominem* or even physically threatening cruelty. Of the seven girls who were asked about "hater commentary" only one admitted it was a personal problem for her. Five stated that it was a problem for other people on YouTube. Nevertheless, very few girls supported hater-reduction policies such as having to be a certain age or to have posted videos before being allowed to comment on other people's videos (Lange 2007e).

Girls generally espoused notions of free speech online and were reluctant to support policies that threatened their own ability to speak as well as curtailing the possibilities for contentious commentary. Certainly, "free speech" emerged from specific historical and political contexts, and has legal limits. How this term is generalized across different environments is important to consider. Many people interpreted this value with regards to opinions about their videos, even harsh ones. I asked Anesha how the hater problem might be addressed on YouTube. She stated, "I don't think anything should be / can be done...people have a right to state their thoughts...no matter how mean they are." Participants generally felt that haters should be ignored, although a few girls said they deleted negative comments if they crossed particular lines, such as being racist, sexist, or homophobic. In response to my question about what YouTube should do about haters, Caitlin replied:

> Nothing. Ignore them. They just want attention. I suppose the most they can do is make sure that the haters stick to the terms of agreement. Hate speech and sexual insults should all be flagged, suspended or deleted. But if we all ignored them, which sometimes feels impossible, they'd get bored and go away.

It is important to consider not only what is left on the page for researchers to see, but also the behind-the-scenes participatory choices girls make when analyzing commentary's effects. Girls' reactions are important forms of agency. Crafting reactions both internally and externally helps girls perform technical affiliation to values assumed to be associated with Internet cultures. The impact and meaning of comments are often analyzed in media studies without regard to girls' own interpretations of them. For instance, in discussing the "hypersexualized" aspect of many girls' lip-synching videos, Banet-Weiser (2011:289) expresses understandable concern that commentary left on girls' videos becomes part of a "self-branding" exercise that is not empowering. Posting comments about girls' "normative physical appearance, 'hotness,' and dancing skill" becomes a way to "control" a girl's "self-branding" in a potentially harmful way (Banet-Weiser 2011).

However, if taken to the extreme, the idea that any comment posted on a video is automatically part of a girl's "self-branding" comes perilously close to resurrecting a "magic bullet" or "hypodermic" model of communication (Davis and Baran 1981), in which any comment is assumed to be unconsciously absorbed directly into the creators' and viewers' minds as straightforwardly constructing a girl's identity. The magic bullet theory of communication assumed "that the media have direct, immediate, and powerful effects of a uniform nature on those who pay attention to their content" (Lowery and DeFleur 1995:400). Yet, not all interpretants view commentary in the same way, and many who are familiar with YouTube's contentious participatory practices understand that they include "hater" commentary that should not be taken too seriously.

Girls whom I interviewed did not usually absorb comments posted to their videos as reflecting self-truths. For example, I asked 13-year-old Jordan what she thought about a comment on her video in which someone offered tips about how to produce better images, such as by using a tripod. She responded that she hadn't thought much about the comment because her father had recorded that video. It is a common temptation to read a video maker's abilities from a single text, but video creation is often a social process to which more than one person contributes. Jordan did not internalize the comment as critical of her technical ability because it did not "apply" to her at all.

Such potentially critical comments might be better understood simply as proposed candidates of identity work and potential self-branding that may be taken up or rejected by various interpretants, including the video maker and viewers. Notably, YouTube eventually added an interactive option in which people could vote comments "up" or "down" according to readers' assessments of their usefulness or appropriateness. Researchers should consider how comments are being received by video makers, communities of interest, and general sets of viewing interpretants.

Most girls in my study attempted to minimize comments' negative effects, through interpretive or interactional choices. RosenbaumGrl and Wendy, for instance, chose to view "hater" commentary as "amusing." In a chat interview, I asked RosenbaumGrl to define the term "hater." She stated, "a hater to me is someone who just wants attention [and] who [wants] to annoy you. i usually dont respond back. or if i do i go along with them just to get on [their] nerves. its hilarious." RosenbaumGrl interactively turned the tables on her critics through aggressive forms of humor.

Similarly, Wendy found hater comments to be "funny" and never let them dissuade her from making future videos.

Patricia: Do you ever get haters?

Wendy: of course....everyone does, that's how it goes. I deal with it, and never get discourage[d] to make another video.

Patricia: Do you think that haters are a problem for YouTube?

Wendy: nah, they have their own free will to dislike things...I think it's fine. I just think it was funny that they waste their time trying to trash someone's work.

Wendy articulates the idea that participants have their own "free will" to dislike things, and that hater commentary is "fine." In addition, she downplays comments' effects by characterizing them as a waste of time. Wendy's strategies resemble those that Bucholtz found among female geeks who "responded to offensive messages by dismissing or trivializing them rather than by engaging with them seriously" (Bucholtz 2002:287-8). Rather than absorbing hurtful commentary as part of their enduring self-image, Wendy and others immediately dismissed them as irrelevant to their current or future video making.

Victimizing rhetorics about text comments do not take into account girls' participatory choices with regard to leaving or deleting the comments from their page. The phenomenology of the mediated moment of receiving a comment must be analyzed within the context of how girls externally handle commentary through hard-coded infrastructural features. At the time of the research, YouTube offered varying levels of commentary moderation. Participants had the option of allowing comments to appear on the video page "automatically" for the general public. Alternatively, participants could choose to moderate comments before being seen by the public. They could set each video's comments to be posted "with approval only," or they could disable all comments for a particular video. Whether the girls integrated the comments as part of their own self-identity is an empirical question in each case. They may have been upset by comments, but they could also ignore or dismiss them, if they seemed hurtful, trivial, or non-relevant to the content and motivations of their videos. Studies of comments as "text" rather than as part of a lived experience of interactive practices do not take into account girls' choices, which include internal, interpretive mechanisms as well as external, hard-coded options to moderate or delete comments that cross a participatory line.

Although most girls accepted commentary on their videos, a notable exception was Akmalla, who had posted only one video. She disabled all comments on her video, which she had uploaded solely to create a channel icon for her YouTube channel page. In the text accompanying the video, she said she disabled comments because people were "IDIOTS." It is important to be sensitive to each individual's lived experience with regard to Internet commentary. Not all girls are able to dismiss hurtful and vicious commentary easily. In these cases, additional interventions will likely be necessary to increase girls' participation. Girls who were able to dismiss hurtful commentary typically characterized the protection of commentary—even when pointlessly critical—in ways that resonated with those in technical cultures that have espoused historically influenced interpretations of free speech.

Girls often distinguished between garden variety haters who left stereo-typical criticisms such as "lame" and more seriously problematic behaviors from would-be stalkers or creepy participants seeking sexualized interactions. For example, 18-year-old Crystal, who was introduced earlier in this chapter, noted that she took down a lip-synching video in which she was wearing a low cut dress in order to avoid sending the wrong signals to viewers who might inappropriately seek sexualized interaction with her. In the phenom-enology of the mediated moment of experiencing the recording or viewing of this footage during editing, the outfit had initially seemed appropriate to her. Once she saw it posted within the context of YouTube, she removed it, to avoid attracting unwanted attention. Phenomenologies of viewership al-ter interpretations between the mediated moments of viewing during editing and viewing the same footage within the context of the particular culture of an online site. Crystal's choice is to be respected. However, changing one's behavior does not ensure safe and collegial commentary from heterogeneous, public viewers. For example, an innocuous video about community on my YouTube account of *AnthroVlog* received dramatically diverse commentary, including sexualized and physical threats.

Most girls in the study set their comment to "automatic," in part to sup-port free speech and to collect helpful feedback. However, if comments are set to "automatic," the site still enables account holders to delete individual comments. Many girls displayed control in terms of how they evaluated and dealt with comments on their videos. In response to my question about how she handled comments, Crystal stated:

> With me I pretty much I control the comments. I control what you say. If you say it like in a constructive criticism I'll let it slide but if you say it in a very dumb like ah, you suck. I give you a zero because I hate you. You look ugly. You know? I don't really allow those type of comments because they're really just stupid.

Similarly, 15-year-old Elizabeth stated:

> I have them as automatic because everyone has a right to an opinion of my videos. However, when I find a comment that is particularly offensive to me or might be offensive to another viewer, I delete it. I get so few comments it [is] actually easier this way.

In order to understand identity work, it is important for researchers to understand the interactive parameters of particular sites. For instance, are people able to delete comments? In many cases, girls in my study could use external, hard-coded options such as removing the commentary from their page altogether. They also could deploy internal tactics such as "ignoring" or trivializing a comment or commenter. In most instances, enabling commentary, including harsh criticism, helped the girls to display an identity of being creative and self-confident enough to leave criticism on their page.

Of course tactics such as moderating commentary may be more difficult as videos receive high numbers of comments. I noticed this through my own participation on my video blog of *AnthroVlog* on YouTube. When videos received more than a hundred comments, it could be tedious to read through all of them for public moderation. Conversely, several girls in my study noted that they get so few comments that moderating them was not problematic.

Girls exhibited interpretive and hard-coded control over the commentary that was posted to their videos, which complicates assumptions of online "victimhood" through hater comments. Not all comments were directly absorbed by girls as illustrative of their video-making personae. This lack of correspondence between comments and video makers' interpretations of them challenges the notion that comments directly illustrate a video maker's identity. Displayed comments may contain proposals of identity markers that may or may not be taken up by the video maker or other viewers. Being willing and able to handle commentary from a broad public was perceived by many participants to be an important digital literacy and practical skill. In cases where girls struggled with upsetting feedback, hard-coded or internal interventions facilitated their participation. For technically oriented participants, girls controlled comments and interacted with their publics in ways that enabled them to display alliance to techno-cultural and communicative values as well as "geeked out" forms of online participation.

Geeking Out on Reality TV

Geeks tend to argue—in sometimes excruciatingly painful detail—about minutiae or interpretations about cultural material (McArthur 2009). Valued knowledge might include information about technical systems or cultural materials such as comic books or science fiction programs that are not always respected by the general public. New literacy scholars argue that engaging in kids' organic passions may help them develop skills that are important for public self-expression. Digital cultures help kids practice dealing with feedback and "gain experience in communicating with a larger public, experiences that might once have been restricted to student journalists" (Jenkins et al. 2006:19).

A video-making team that illustrates opportunities for developing public self-expressive skills is that of a white mother and daughter from the east coast of the United States who were introduced previously in this chapter. Lola was a 42-year-old mother who helped her 16-year-old daughter Ashley by participating on YouTube. They made videos together in which they provided reviews and commentary on "reality" television shows. Parental motivations for family media making are analyzed in Chapter 5. The present discussion focuses on how Ashley drew on her home environment and benefited from parental support to help her develop technical skills, showcase her expertise, and express her opinions to viewing publics.

Lola and Ashley's work revolves around offering recaps, reviews, and spoilers for a genre of television referred to as "reality" shows. In such programs, supposedly non-professional actors are surveilled, interact, and engage in competitions. They are assumed to be interacting without relying on scripts, although even casual inspection casts doubt on the extent to which such popular reality shows are simply recorded depictions of spontaneous events. Nevertheless, these shows are popular, and by orienting their material around such shows, Lola and Ashley drew on an existing fan-base for their work. Knowing what kind of material to select to gain visibility in online spaces is an important digital literacy. Ashley and Lola have made more than 2,000 videos since opening their channel in October 2006. Their sizable oeuvre contains reviews of shows such as *Big Brother, Survivor, Beauty and the Geek, Top Chef, The Bachelor, The Bachelorette, America's Top Model, Dancing with the Stars, American Idol, Celebrity Apprentice*, and *Project Runway*, among others.

Identifying herself as a "future filmmaker" on her YouTube channel page, Ashley persuaded Lola to make video reviews together. By finding success on YouTube, they aimed to strengthen Ashley's impressive college application portfolio. Similar to other girls in my study, Ashley performed technical identity and affiliations through information and images on her channel page. A YouTube channel page is the rough equivalent of a profile page on social network sites. It enables participants to share information about themselves. The background to Ashley's channel page was customized with a repeating image in which Ashley, who is gazing back at the camera, is sitting with her left hand on her laptop computer while holding a phone to her ear with her right hand. The pose emits an impression of engaging in everyday, highly multitasked interactions with technology. The image, which repeats all over the page, saturates the viewer with the idea that Ashley is technically engaged, socially wired to others, and is unequivocally a "digital youth."

Ashley received direct participatory support from her mother, and benefited from having parents and other relatives who were deeply involved in media. Ashley's aunt and uncle had attended film school, and Lola had significant computer expertise. Lola said she joined the project to be closer to Ashley, participate in her life, and help her realize her professional goals. As Lola stated in a voice-based Skype interview:

So she asked me if I would do it and I couldn't say no because I really wanted her to get involved with this because I really feel like it's something that's gonna help her later on when she decides to go to college and go for interviews and stuff like that.

Lola characterized herself and her husband as highly "technical." Lola was an early adopter of desktop computing, and even had a computer in high-school, even though its functionality was limited. She worked on computers in fighter planes in the military in her youth, and was familiar with multiple personal computer platforms including Windows and Macintosh computers, as well as sound recording equipment. Lola noted that everyone in the family had their own computer, and there were two computers to spare. According to Ashley, their living room alone had four computers. Their home was well-outfitted for media viewing and included a digital video recorder (DVR). Lola said they would have liked another DVR but could not afford it. They had a cable television package that cost upward of $100 per month, which indicates access to many television channels.

Ashley's social-media ecology, which included access to equipment, online connections, and family support, set the stage for her successful technologized video participation. As I learned through my own participation on *AnthroVlog*, the amount of work that is required to produce weekly videos is substantial, and Lola's willingness to keep a steady flow of videos displays a strong base of social and cultural capital for Ashley to develop her technical interests. Like many middle-class interviewees in studies on U.S. family life (Lareau 2003), Ashley's mother strategically and consciously worked on "cultivating" Ashley's abilities. Middle-class parents in the United States often "engage in a pattern of concerted cultivation" in which they "deliberately try to stimulate their children's development and foster their cognitive and social skills" (Lareau 2003:5). Children growing up within a "concerted cultivation" (Lareau 2003) framework exhibit a sense of entitlement for their future. They are comfortable pursuing personal interests, as well as "sharing information and asking for attention" from institutionalized and other sources (Lareau 2003:6).

Similarly, Furger (1998) stresses the importance of female role models' influence on girls' technological self-confidence. Many girls cite their mother as one of the most influential people in their lives. A mother's recognition of the importance of technology in her daughter's life can substantially impact a girl's technological development. Furger (1998) states that this impact is felt regardless of a mother's ability. What is crucial is that a mother supports her daughter's technical development by co-learning, participating, and being inspired by participatory, online spaces. Lola supported her daughter's technical endeavors by participating as a peer and learning to navigate YouTube's technical and interactive parameters.

Lola and Ashley devoted considerable time to improving Ashley's visibility on YouTube. In an interview, Lola notes that they typically take notes on what they wish to say and then record their discussion. Ashley's schedule was usually quite full, which often meant beginning their recordings as late as 11 or 12 o'clock at night. They made videos after homework and other extracurricular activities were complete. The pace and dedication they described inculcated Ashley into a lifestyle of being "busy" (Darrah et al. 2007) as a normalized rhythm for achieving success. It was not unusual to see Ashley yawning in her videos or admitting that she was "tired." Indeed, for Lola and Ashley, the decision to make this sacrifice was a deliberate strategy to demonstrate to college admissions committees that Ashley was dedicated to a career in media.

Lola and Ashley targeted content that they enjoyed discussing but which also drew on pre-existing audiences. Fans responded enthusiastically to Lola and Ashley's commentary, opinions, and interactions with each other. Each video usually received thousands of views and several dozen comments. Their commentary typically included critiques of contestants' and producers' choices and strategies. Whether commenters agreed or disagreed with Lola and Ashley, they often shared a geeked out interest in debating the finer points of reality competitions. Viewers often attempted to perform their own identities of expertise by correcting the video makers on factual errors, and they argued about whether the "reality" show contestants were "faking" certain emotions or actions.

In terms of stylistics, Ashley and Lola tended to use minimal editing, preferring a spontaneous feeling-tone of interaction, although they sometimes edited out mistakes or spontaneous comments that ethnic or other groups might find insulting. They typically sat in front of a simple graphic of the show they were reviewing. They used modest, playful props such as coke-bottle glasses in a review of *Beauty and the Geek* to add a touch of whimsy (see Figure 1).

Lola and Ashley's banter in their videos is lively and reflects a close relationship between mother and daughter. They frequently look at each other, sometimes interrupting or overlapping each other as they animatedly exchange opinions. Such arguments illustrate how the meaning of the word "geek" has widened, to index not only ability with computer-based technologies but more generally to characterize expertise in obscure or arcane knowledge sets. McArthur (2009:62) explains:

> To be a geek is to be engaged, to be enthralled in a topic, and then to act on that engagement. Geeks come together based on common expertise on a certain topic. These groups might identify themselves as computer geeks, anime geeks, trivia geeks, gamers, hackers, and a number of other specific identifiers. Regardless of classification these geeks share the experience of being experts (Sugarbaker 1998).

Figure 1. Lola and Ashley review the show *Beauty and the Geek*. Screenshot by Patricia G. Lange, August 27, 2013

As discussed in the following paragraphs, Lola and Ashley express geekdom on YouTube partly by discussing and debating extremely detailed points in mass media works.

Lola and Ashley's style resembles that of many reality shows' judges, who may or may not have the technical training to evaluate execution of dances, singing, designing or other technically oriented competitive tasks. Enacting Andrejevic's (2004) concept of the "savvy" fan, they often position themselves as experts on the particular strategy or aspect of the competition they are reviewing. Andrejevic argues that fans of reality television must "reconcile" themselves to the fact that the reality genre is not particularly realistic. They do this by becoming a "savvy" fan who "savagely" critiques the shows in online discussion groups, but in a way that naturalizes rather than disturbs ethical acceptance of being surveilled for entertainment (Andrejevic 2004:163). As Lola and Ashley say on their YouTube page, "yes we know its not real."

An example of how they enact savvy fandom is revealed in a review of the show *Big Brother*, in which contestants, or "HouseGuests," are sequestered in a camera-laden, surveilled household. Contestants' activities are recorded for a live Internet stream, as well as a producer-edited show broadcast on television and hosted by Julie Chen. *Big Brother's* popularity has been attributed to its dual online and televised status (Andrejevic 2004). Contestants participate in contrived competitions and interpersonal drama, and one houseguest is "evicted" or voted out of the competition each week.

The following excerpt from Lola and Ashley's recap of an episode of *Big Brother 12* illustrates their format and how they geeked out on reality television. During the review, they discuss an endurance competition. The goal of the challenge was to remain on a surf board, which slanted downward as it jutted from a wall. While the contestants endeavored to keep their balance, cold water was sporadically poured on their heads. The contestants stressed how "cold" the water was, which of course the viewing audience could only appreciate through the contestants' "performances" of the cold.

In one exchange, Lola and Ashley argue about whether a contestant, Matt (who eventually won this endurance competition after some two hours on his board) appeared to receive kinder treatment from the producers, with respect to the amount of water being poured onto his head.

[1] Lola: So, Matt is 100% confident that he can go to the end.

[2] Ashley: He was up there. He was banging drums on the wall.

[3] Lola: (laughs)

[4] Ashley: He was chattin' it up.

[5] Lola: Did you notice, though, that Matt's slot was the only slot that wasn't getting like blasted on the head -

[6] Ashley: I think he was just standing behind it.

[7] Lola: - with the water.

[8] Lola: I don't think so because other people were flat up against the wall like Ragan and they were getting like blasted -

[9] Ashley: He was soaked too though.

[10] Lola: - by the water. Not on his head. It's different.

[11] Ashley: That was soaked too.

[12] Lola: Alright, well Enzo let down New Jersey because he was the next one off.

[13] Ashley: Yeah.

In line 5, Lola suggests that Matt did not appear to be having as much cold water blasted onto his head, which helped him stay on his board. Her evidence is the amount of water that appeared to be pouring out of the wall slot above him. Ashley argues in line 6 that he was "just standing behind it," where "it" is presumably the water stream. In line 8, Lola disagrees, noting that other people were also "flat up against the wall" out of the immediate stream, and yet seemed to be getting "blasted." Earlier in the competition, a contestant implied that he was "pushed" off, meaning that producers might be controlling the parameters of the game and orchestrating drama by sabotaging particular contestants. Fans of this genre seek to identify contrivances and manipulations that might change the competition's outcome. Lola suggests that such a manipulation was occurring if less water was poured on Matt. In line 9, Ashley points out that Matt's head was soaked too, and she reiterates her position in line 11.

In the videos I watched, Ashley frequently corrects her mother on points of fact. This pattern is repeated in several videos, and was noticed among commenters, one of whom told Ashley to "stop correcting [her] mom." This form of correction represents a kind of "cultural capital" which can serve as an important source of "self-esteem" among a fan's peer group (Fiske 1992:33). Correcting another person enables a performance of expertise regarding specific points. This expertise is relational because it depends upon how interlocutors respond. If the person being corrected revises his or her statement, then by so doing they are displaying a need to be corrected (whether or not they actually agree). Changing their statement in accordance with a criticism thus publicly ratifies the corrector as having the expertise to make that correction (Jacoby and Gonzales 1991).

In this exchange, Ashley performs expertise in two ways. The first is by offering a correction to a detailed fact in the show. By correcting her mother, she shows that she has the expertise to make a correction about a specific cultural artifact. The second performance of expertise occurs through the act of correction itself. When Ashley corrects her mother, she is displaying adherence to the idea that it is important to master fandom aracana as a form of cultural capital, and it is appropriate to publicly argue about small points as a way of displaying relational expertise.

Children and adults tend to argue about similar things, including: "valued resources, controlling others' behavior, rule violations, facts, and truth" (Shantz 1987:294). Members of technical and fan cultures tend to orient around precision. Ashley's attempts to keep the record precise proposes an appropriate identity both as a fan of reality television shows and as a savvy YouTube participant who sets the record straight about events in filmed entertainment. In the videos I viewed, if Lola seems to agree that Ashley is incorrect, Lola revises her statement. Lola's responses to Ashley's frequent corrections reinforce the idea of an appropriate youthful, female identity as one that asserts her opinions and makes public corrections, even to authority figures such as one's mother (See Figure 2).

Their interaction presents a publicly mediated, feminine identity that downplays or avoids the "romantic individualism" (McRobbie 2000) that has characterized media aimed at girls, as well as online media produced by girls (Scodari 2005). In the trope of "romantic individualism," girls craft their media around

Figure 2. Ashley disagrees with her mother about what happened in an episode of *Big Brother*. Screenshot by Patricia G. Lange, August 27, 2013

heterosexual romance and normatively gendered life trajectories. Girls are encouraged to exhibit a "mind of their own" that "chooses" to ratify traditional values of romance (rather than sex), passivity (rather than action), distrust of feminine company (rather than seeking supportive female friends), and seeking a boyfriend (rather than pursuing a career). Yet Lola and Ashley's choice of material and interaction through YouTube promotes a different kind of female, public persona. Ashley is encouraged to express her opinion and disagree with her mother, who acts as a supportive female friend rather than a competitor for male affection. She is also encouraged to marshal evidence to support her opinions and express them publicly, and she is supported in her choice to further her career through the technologized form of making videos.

In one video, Ashley encourages her viewers to watch because she "needs money for college." She uses her technical skills to shape her future learning opportunities by using success on YouTube to afford the right college. She communicates a career-oriented purpose for the videos, rather than focusing on romance. The videos situate mother and daughter as techno-cultural equals, who are able to evaluate the evidence and strategies of television shows they know are not "real." Through their co-participation in an area of mutual interest, learning opportunities are created for Ashley to demonstrate and improve technical expertise.

Lola supports Ashley, even when she clearly does not agree on specific arcana. Their YouTube adventures suggests that geeking out on topics of organic interest provided a meaningful way for them to explore and develop media literacies such as improving video-making skills, attracting viewers, and creating interesting content, all of which are beneficial for participating through media within a global public sphere.

Public Expression of the Self

Girls express geek identities in many ways, including making technologized forms of digital media, selecting geeked-out genres such as machinima, and conceptualizing the self in technical terms. Even in gendered machinima videos, tropes of technology are never far away. Girls perform being a geek not only through the media they create but through interactive and participatory practices such as joining a popular site early, crafting one's channel page to showcase technical ability, exercising command over interactive aspects of online spaces, espousing techno-cultural values such as being self-taught, and displaying self-perceptions of technical identities in words and images. Each performance is a proposal of identity expression that may be ratified or challenged by viewers, commenters, and other video makers.

The girls in my study exhibited varied levels of participation in making and sharing videos. They displayed different mediated centers of gravity with regard to how much they wished to make videos and how deeply they engaged in the participatory aspects of YouTube. Observing and acknowledging different levels of participation prompts commensurate interventions to improve technically oriented media skills and navigate public participation. The fact that not all kids are interested in making globally distributed videos challenges homogenizing discourses of digital youth. Further, not all young people handle commentary in the same way. Most girls in the study used internal neutralization tactics and external infrastructural features such as deletions to deal with "haters." Comments and their effects are not automatically absorbed into girls' self-perception of their identities. Yet, some girls experienced frustration with hateful forms of commentary. Asymmetrical emotional participation may encourage interventions that develop visual production and communication skills in less public ways to ensure that all kids—whatever their mediated dispositions—have an ability to create visual, personally expressive messages.

Many prior studies begin within an orientation toward investigating how boys and girls are different with regard to performing their technical identities and affiliations. Ideally, investigations should be open-ended, rather than ratifying the notion that differences must exist. Much can also be learned about technical identity construction processes by observing girls' and boys' similarities. In my study, as with boys, girls' technical identities not only included their self-perceptions, but were also negotiated in comparison to other people in their video-making milieu. Sometimes the girls' abilities were challenged, in terms of technical skills such as editing, or knowledge about technical or cultural values and artifacts. Girls took up these challenges by acknowledging their technical prowess and publicly positioning themselves in interviews, within videos, and on the site as more expert than other people in their social orbits.

Many girls saw themselves as "being technical" or being a "geek," both in terms of their knowledge base and the technical tools they used to craft mediated personae. Most genre studies orient toward analyzing media artifacts. Yet, participatory practices—such as how one learns or how one internally handles commentary—are just as important to study as the media left on one's page. Technical identities should be given more attention in future studies of girls' participation in digital cultures. Prior studies have emphasized how girls use media to express or challenge traditional identity variables, such as gender, class, and ethnicity. But participation in digital spaces also helps girls exhibit technologized aspects of identity through their choice of mediated content and displays of video-making technique. Girl geeks are successfully using the mediated nexus of YouTube to propose a technologized identity, to expand technologized learning opportunities, and to develop mediated self-expression skills targeted for global audiences.

CHAPTER 4

Mediated Civic Engagement

Frank is a 15-year-old boy from the midwestern United States who feels passionate about network neutrality. In a convincing video blog, he warns that if
corporations are allowed to discriminate and invoke unfair fees for Internet
services, opportunities for exchanging diverse information will be threatened.
Wendy, a 16-year-old girl from the east coast of the United States, creates
an informative documentary about a dilapidated park in an Asian neighborhood. She invites community dialogue about how it could be improved. Max,
a 14-year-old boy also from the east coast who dreams of being a filmmaker,
creates a powerful mashup about events that he calls the "Palestinian Holocaust." He raises awareness about the effects of war and human rights issues
in the Middle East. His video elicits hundreds of comments exhibiting diverse
opinions that often differ from his own.

Kids on YouTube are finding a voice and participating in discourses on
contemporary civic issues. Studies of civic engagement have typically emphasized the need to prepare kids for future participation in civc life. This strategy dovetails with traditional sociological models of childhood that focus on
protection and orient toward kids' future potential (Corsaro 2005). But not
all kids are growing up in a protected bubble. Kids experience disturbing issues and demonstrate a desire to weigh in. Focusing only on preparing kids
for future participation risks ignoring their current capabilities. When civic
engagement is broadly defined as forming attachments to others and helping achieve common goals, kids' ability to share information and tackle civic
problems through media becomes more visible (Golombek 2006).

Kids are also sharing information in lateral ways between peers. Notably,
studies show that websites are less successful if they orient toward hierarchical
forms of civic engagement that exhibit top-down flows of information between
organizations and publics (Bennett et al. 2011). Kids tend to share information in more networked ways, which serves as a blueprint for successful future

civic discourse. This chapter proposes a reticulated model of civic engagement, which emphasizes social connections, shared interests, and interaction around particular social and place-based attachments. These connections may blossom into mobilization around particular issues, but their roots and ongoing networked dynamic are centered around technical affiliations, technologized identities, and affective ties that diffusely propagate shared values.

Notably, how kids participate in civic issues influences the interactive constitution of their technical identities. How they engage in civic affairs is influenced by their affiliation to particular technologies (e.g., online and social networking sites) and styles of communication (e.g., documentaries, mash-ups, and video blogging). By discussing their concerns on the global video-sharing site of YouTube, kids can reach broader audiences who may not share their views. Given its agonistic environment, diverse content, and heterogeneous user base, YouTube has the potential to avoid being a stale echo chamber. YouTube's confrontational timbre exposes kids to contrasting opinions that they say are hard to find on- or offline. Sharing videos enables them to try out opinions, explore world views, and develop civic attachments and empathy.

Although civic engagement videos appeared infrequently in my YouTube study, their high quality, sincerity, and persuasiveness demonstrate kids' ability to participate in civic life and develop important digital literacies. By making ordinary video blogs or bringing a camera to a local event, kids engaged in mediated witnessing and developed their civic orientations to collective problems. The experience of learning about an issue or local place becomes intertwined with that of recording what kids observe in their communities and beyond. Phenomenologies of the mediated moment are thus inflected and intertwined with a particular kind of mediated witnessing that exhibits responsibility to spread the word about social problems. The case studies profiled in this chapter suggest that kids' style of witnessing shines light on distinctive issues of civic interest. Their experiences in creating civically oriented media enable them to develop key rhetorical and productive literacies that facilitate global participation. Discourses on kids' civic engagement should respect kids' individuality and contributions (Jans 2004), recognize their tolerance for diversity (Lange 2007e), and involve them in civically motivated media as dynamic agents of change.

Expanding Forms of Civic Engagement

The Internet is taking on a greater role in U.S. political life, as evidenced in the 2008 and 2012 presidential elections, in which influential social media practices and images were deemed crucial in securing political success (Knight 2012; Wortham 2012). Despite concerns about the Internet diverting attention away from civic affairs, recent studies suggest that time spent online does not displace civic activity (Moy et al. 2005), but rather becomes incorporated into political repertoires (Jennings and Zeitner 2003). People who are high information seekers often go online to find information that they earlier sought in newspapers and local news. One-third of Internet participants are sharing messages and videos with political content (Edwards and Tryon 2009; Smith 2008). Between 2007 and 2010, viewership for political videos rose from 15% to 30% of adult viewers (Purcell 2010).

Many kids and youth participate through technologized practices. For instance, Kohut (2008:2) found that during the 2008 presidential election campaign, 37% of youth aged 18 to 24 obtained campaign information from social networking sites. The claim that time online diminishes local social ties does not hold true across all social groups (Shah et al. 2002). As discussed elsewhere (Lange 2007d), making online media with and for friends can strengthen local friendships that prior connections (such as being in the same school or neighborhood) does not automatically promote.

Mediated spaces can increase exposure to important issues and facilitate distribution of opinions in political discourses where kids' have traditionally been excluded (Bortree 2010; de Vreese 2007). It is important to explore how each generation displays its own "civic style" (Delli Carpini 2000:345), which can manifest across different technical idioms. For example, a wide demographic of kids is playing video games, which may "expose players to a host of social issues such as global hunger, animal rights, the environment, immigration, and urban development" (Kahne et al. 2011).

Scholars of online civic engagement are attending to new forms of civic participation (Shah et al. 2002). Prior models invoked a "dutiful citizenship" rubric in which information was shared in a top-down way between authorities such as political campaigners and a populace (Bennett et al. 2011). In contrast, new forms of civic engagement exhibit an "actualizing citizenship" dynamic in which information is shared laterally between peers, and is accomplished by using social technologies and media that "maximize self-expression" (Bennett et al. 2011:839). Rather than "taking cues" from authority figures, "actualizing citizenship" involves engagement with "peer networks that pool (crowd source) information and organize civic action" through technology (Bennett et al. 2011:839).

What is needed are studies that describe and analyze opportunities for achieving actualized citizenship, particularly through video-mediated forms of witnessing, analysis, and commentary. Mediated-witnessing does not simply mean pointing a camera at something; the term is used here in Peters' (2001) sense, in that it is associated with a deep responsibility to identify and record events that shine light on social problems. The goal is to understand how phenomenologies of the mediated moment interweave civic participation and self-expression through video.

In the past, civic participation has narrowly been equated with direct political participation, or activities involving a political institution or its representatives (such as writing a letter to Congress). While these are important steps, they ignore vital forms of civic participation that enable kids and others to participate through everyday on- and offline activities. Flanagan and Faison (2001:3) call for a broader model that incorporates not only political processes involving governmental representatives but also community concerns, relevant civic skills, and "the processes whereby citizens effect change" and "become informed." Of particular interest is exploring the key skills and emotional, community attachments that scholars argue are crucial for achieving civic awareness (Flanagan and Faison 2001). Cultivated early, these skills and forms of participation exhibit outward orientations to others that extend into adulthood (Flanagan 2003).

Scholars in civic engagement recommend taking the "assets" approach, which focuses on identifying what kids already do and the unique perspectives they contribute to civic conversations based on their needs and concerns. A major way that kids can participate is through media. By making and publicly posting videos on YouTube they are developing a public voice (Levine 2008:121) that includes "any style or tone that has a chance of persuading any other people (outside of one's intimate circle) about shared matters, issues, or problems."

Civic engagement includes not only direct forms of political participation, but many activities (such as going to local festivals or library events) that help promote local place-based communities and affective attachments to them. It also includes rhetorical skills that persuade others through media about how to address collective problems. Whatever their age, people are not static in terms of skills, but rather should be viewed dynamically, as having the potential to improve and build on skills that address civic needs. Successful civic engagement is often exhibited when kids form attachments to physical places, orient outward towards a community or polity, and develop technical and self-expression skills so that civic activities feel personally meaningful.

Forming Attachments to Place

The experiences of one video blogging family in my study well illustrate how mediated family life promotes skill development and emotional attachments to place that are crucial for successful civic engagement. The Field family (Mr. Field's requested pseudonym) are Asian-Americans living on the west coast of the United States. They used video blogging to form civic attachments to their local community and to develop a mediated public voice (see Figure 3). In so doing, Mr. Field's sons learned to develop digital literacies and used video to provide information about local events and civic issues.

Figure 3. Mr. Field looks on while John searches for a video that he wished to show me. Source: Patricia G. Lange

Mr. Field's sons, who requested the pseudonyms of Bob (age 11) and John (age 9), were encouraged by their father to learn self-presentation skills by creating their own video blog. Like many of the other kids profiled in this book, Bob and John had a YouTube account. However, unlike most of the other kids, YouTube did not serve as their mediated center of gravity for video distribution, and indeed contained only a portion of their online video oeuvre. The Field family maintained their own video blog outside of YouTube, where they regularly posted videos that depicted them engaging in family activities such as going to local festivals and interviewing relatives and community members on diverse topics, such as how environmentally friendly buses work.

In addition to participating in their local community, the Field family also belonged to an online community of first-generation video bloggers. As described in Chapter 2, core members of this group began using compression techniques to post videos to their websites in 2004 and 2005, even before YouTube launched. They embraced video blogging as a lifestyle and worldview, one that recognized the potential for increasing diversity, promoting self-improvement, and facilitating social connections. Mr. Field, who had several years of experience doing business development for new media, was very active in the first-generation video blogging community. The Field family was influenced by its technical affiliations and social values. For example, Mr. Field believed in having his sons develop self-expression skills in media so that they could participate as actors on the world stage of civic life.

Many of their videos depict them engaging in fun community activities. The family's attendance at local events helped them bond with each other and promoted awareness of local happenings. For example, in one video, the family records their enjoyment of a local kite-flying festival. The video provides beautiful and dramatic visuals of kite flying, kite fights, and images of elaborate Asian-themed kites. In a voice over Bob describes long-standing traditions of kite flying in Japan. The text commentary posted to the video is particularly interesting, as it reveals learning opportunities and civic attachments that emerged from shared interest in the video. For example, one of the boys' relatives posted about another relative who also made kites. Many commenters were first-generation video bloggers who gave the boys positive encouragement about their videos, thus helping them develop confidence in making media. They posted comments such as "nice editing," and "this video makes me feel like I was there! That kite fighting looked really cool!!!"

Commenters also focused on how the video stimulated intense feelings about place. One commenter said that the video evoked nostalgic feelings for similar places he experienced in his past. Another reflected on how kite festivals encouraged togetherness in a way that gave the boys' community a distinctive flair. One commenter said, "Wonderful report! I had no idea of the history of this kind of event. People from New York City don't get many opportunities to fly kites, so it's pretty amazing to see what people do with it when they get the chance to come together." A commenter from their own local area appreciated learning about an event she had not heard of. She stated, "What a great report! Terrific job. I live near [there] and didn't know anything about this event. I learned a lot from watching your video."

Rather than "divert" attention away from local community attachments, in the phenomenology of the mediated moment, making the recording became intertwined with creating strong feelings for a local place, and provided bi-directional learning opportunities for the video makers and viewers. The online video provided information to local viewers about their shared community. The boys obtained encouragement about expressing their public voice from an online community of respected mentors, and they learned about their own family histories of kite making. The video also stimulated reflections of people's attachments to places of personal importance in their own lives, and of the importance of place generally.

Many first-generation video bloggers were former professional media makers, and they encouraged high-quality standards on video blogs. They emphasized both experimental and accepted practices of making media, such as projecting an aura of being comfortable on camera, keeping a video blog interactive, and using links to direct people to information. Although the boys were at first a bit shy and awkward on camera, their video blogs show them becoming more comfortable and sometimes joking and being playful. It is not only feedback that provides a learning opportunity, but also the experience of making videos that helps people develop skills. In an in-person interview at the Fields' home, the boys told me how they learned to correct mistakes when they did not say the right words, or when they mumbled. Their interview comments show deepening digital literacies such as an appreciation for clarity and diction in their video blogs. They recognized that the attitude that one brings to a video can affect the production and reception of its message. In an interview, John said it was better to avoid having a bad attitude. He said that when making videos, it was better to have "a calmer attitude than mad or angry."

Civic engagement requires collecting information, often through interviews with experts and stakeholders. Interviewing skills are crucial for developing a mediated public voice (Rheingold 2008), as they help people understand nuanced dimensions and perceptions of a problem. In their videos, the boys interview people about matters of civic interest. They develop their interviewing skills by asking questions about topics such as Thanksgiving memories, weather, and environmentally friendly buses.

The boys' investigative reports resemble the kind of hyperlocal journalism (Rheingold 2008; Bruns et al. 2008) that is said to be crucial for developing attachments to place and understanding specific community responses to civic issues and collective problems. For example, in one video, the boys visit their local hydrogen bus transit facility (see Figures 4 and 5). Through interviews, they learn how hydrogen buses work and how their zero emissions and lack of noise are environmentally friendly. Not only is the video blogging activity itself a technologized one, but some of the video blogs contain technical facts about fuel-efficient buses. In the video, authorities demonstrate how the buses are driven and refueled. The family's media activity worked toward constituting citizen-consumers (Banet-Weiser 2007; Scammell 2000) who understand the importance of making lifestyle purchasing and usage choices that are consistent with their techno-political values.

Although scholars often talk about "civic identity" as something to be developed as adults, in fact everyday life choices are inherently political. Whether one takes public transportation instead of driving one's car is a potentially politicized act that should be made visible as such. In the video, the boys look at prototype, fuel-efficient cars, which they may someday purchase as environmentally conscious consumers. These interactions, as motivated and emphasized through video blogging activities, display an outward focus on their community. Their video addresses concerns that begin locally but connect to larger issues of civic and political interest, such as understanding the practical steps for achieving environmental improvements through technologized purchasing choices.

Figure 4. John learns how hydrogen buses are refueled.
Screen capture by Patricia G. Lange, October 27, 2010

Figure 5. John and Bob learn about hydrogen-powered flashlights.
Screen capture by Patricia G. Lange, October 27, 2010

Mr. Field viewed his family's video blogging activity as important for helping the boys to express themselves through digital media and to form opinions in a global arena. His comments clearly resonate with Levine's (2008)
idea of developing a "public voice." Even the placement of the computers in
the Field family home symbolically reiterated Mr. Field's philosophy about
promoting video blogging as a way of orienting outward and interacting with
others. Since the garage door could easily be opened, on pleasant days, they

could open the door while they worked. In this way they could stay attuned to and potentially be drawn into what was happening physically around them. Mr. Field's home space arrangement could also serve as a blueprint for future home designs that encouraged more civic involvement and connection both locally and online. Mr. Field explained:

> A lot of our work is done in our garage, and when we remodeled the house, we have these old barnyard door style garage [doors]…and during nice days, we just open the garage door up. And, you know, they're really exposed to [the] community and the number of children here, there's children always walking by. And so it's really kind of an open invitation for conversations. It's really nice.

Although mass media tends to portray all kids on YouTube as budding movie stars who crave attention, Mr. Field's mediated participation revealed a broader civic philosophy. Media provided an opportunity to prepare his children for developing the technical and self-presentation skills to participate in civic affairs amid networked publics. He stated:

> My goal is not for my children to be actors. My goal is for my children to be aware of the world around them….[What's] our U.S. military position on the planet right now? What's it mean to the children? Right now, it really doesn't mean a lot, cause they don't get it right now. I don't think they can really comprehend the magnitude, and I don't really want to get on a political rant or a position, but as they get older, they'll start understanding governments and government influence and the power and how people use power in country objectives. What are countries' objectives? Preserve their way of life or extend their views or whatever it is. I think as they get older, they'll see that. So I just really want them to be actors in the sense of the world stage, as individuals, rather than actors, "Let's be famous in Hollywood."

Mr. Field's promotion of familial, participatory media provides a powerful illustration of how children growing up in technical environments with parents who are media savvy may internalize technically oriented ideals about how to express oneself in a networked world. Mr. Field's philosophy of using video to participate in social groups both on- and offline doubly enacts feelings of civic attachment. The media helps form affective attachments to their neighborhood. It also helps the boys learn how to participate in a process of forming attachments to future places that they experience. In addition, they form relationships with friends and mentors who share similar interests in online video. Growing up in a mediated way gives the boys tools with which to understand the events they experience and witness, and helps them process the meanings of these events for themselves and others.

Witnessing through Video

The Field family often focused on recording fun, cultural events in their neighborhood. Yet, kids also witness disturbing events that impact their lives. According to Peters (2001:709), to witness something is to observe in a way that shows a "privileged (raw, authentic) proximity to facts." But witnessing is not only an act of observation; it also involves providing a medium (such as verbal testimony in court) for others to assess what has happened. Involving both "seeing" and "saying," witnessing includes "the discursive act of stating one's experience for the benefit of an audience that was not present at the event and yet must make some kind of judgment about it" (Peters 2001:709). Ideas of universally "cherished" or "protected" children ignore the painful and dramatic events that they are forced to experience. Yet, kids may wish to explore such events to increase their own and others' understanding of them.

One way in which kids on YouTube have participated in civic and political affairs is through mediated witnessing of events in their life worlds. The first case study involves Wendy, a 16-year-old Asian girl from the east coast of the United States who used documentary-style video making to provide information and suggestions about how to improve a run-down park in her city. The second concerns Max, a 14-year-old white male, also from the east coast, who created a visual and audio mashup to comment on violence, particularly against children and families, in the Middle East. In their own ways, both Wendy and Max enact Peters' (2001:713-714) concept of witnessing, including exposing and mediating unfortunate or disturbing events. According to Peters, witnessing includes acknowledging that one is on the side of right, and one has the responsibility to bear witness so that social groups can address collective problems or traumas.

Notably, the civic style that both Wendy and Max chose is a technologized, mediated one. Their civic styles are inseparable from the act of witnessing (which includes providing information to others in a mediated form). Their media provides learning opportunities for other potential stakeholders. As kids, they also bring a unique perspective that helps adults appreciate the complexity of particular problems. By sharing their perspective, they provide input for solutions that will quite likely be mutually beneficial for key stakeholders, both adults and kids.

Improving a Neighborhood Park

Wendy's video making is diverse; her channel on YouTube includes videos of her friends creating situation comedies, as well as lip synching to favorite songs. In her online chat interview, she described having fun making YouTube videos with friends and participating in her school's audio-visual club.

She considers herself highly technical and finds it easy to learn about computers and making videos. In her spare time she volunteers for an organization that strives to improve the physical environment in underserved neighborhoods in a major metropolitan city. One of the organization's goals is to create spaces that help residents improve their social capital by addressing shared needs. Wendy's civic style (Delli Carpini 2000) included volunteering to do a documentary about improving a park. She said members of the volunteer organization were very pleased with her documentary, and she showed it to residents and others to garner input for the park's renovation.

Wendy's documentary draws on numerous skills that illustrate her mediated public voice. She visually demonstrates problems with the park and explains why it does not favorably compare with parks in other neighborhoods. In the first section of her documentary she says in a voice over that a local park—where people "sit, relax, and have fun"—was scheduled to be rebuilt. She and her crew visited different parks across the city to find, as she says, "observations and comparisons." The video documents other parks' desirable features. For example, one park is better maintained and does not contain uneven, broken ground. Further, there is a hop scotch pattern etched directly into the playground. Through these recordings she witnesses particular problems with the current park and collects ideas for desirable new features.

Wendy bridges to the second part of the documentary with a voice over in which she explains that she asked community residents how the park should be rebuilt. Having the skills to interview stakeholders is important for creating civic change. In one interview, a middle-aged white woman provides suggestions:

Wendy: Hello, so, um we're gonna ask some, a couple of questions. You're around this community or...?

Interviewee: Yes. I've lived in this community about, uh, almost thirty years.

Wendy: Thirty years, that's great. Um, you know that [this park] is getting reconstructed.

Interviewee: Yes.

Wendy: Um, what do you expect for the playground to look like?

Interviewee: I expect for it to look like and be something that the neighborhood can really use and that the neighborhood feels like it's had some impact on deciding what goes in here, what it ends up looking like. So, I'm wide open, I'd love to see a lot of things but mostly I think it has to reflect the neighborhood and what people here wanna see.

The interviewee urges that the new park reflect the "culture of the neighborhood" and later expresses concerns about safety. Wendy next interviews a middle-aged, female, Asian resident who suggests using wider spaces to give kids more "room" to run around.

The documentary includes images of an event in which kids were invited to make arts and crafts projects that illustrated their ideal vision of a rebuilt park. In a voice over Wendy asks, "Do you want changes in the park too? It's your turn to speak out." The scene cuts to a group of youth sitting in a play structure. The youth face the camera and shout out together, "What do YOU want for our park?" Wendy's documentary ends on an interactive note that mobilizes or addresses viewers directly and challenges them to reflect on their input. It encourages viewers to participate in the discussion and decision making process.

Choosing to engage in civic issues by making a documentary, Wendy displays impressive knowledge of how to tell an effective visual story that observes, analyzes, and motivates people to improve an important local center of neighborhood sociality. Her choice of civic style—volunteering to make a video—reflects and enacts her self-perception of being a technically competent teen who possesses important digital literacies. Her style of civic engagement and development of digital literacies are intimately intertwined with her technical persona.

Wendy personally witnesses how other parks around the city successfully provide safe and welcoming places for neighborhood interaction. In this sense, she is helping to reticulate others into a social network of shared values by improving a space of play and bonding. To reticulate people into a social group from a loose co-located mass means helping to create an infrastructure that will demarcate participants into a more well-recognized social network. Wendy also uses traditional mobilization techniques by inviting others to participate and provide their own input on an important neighborhood issue.

In Peters' (2001) sense, she is witnessing the problem, not only in terms of visual observation, but also in terms of creating a medium with which others can judge events and help shape their outcome. She and her crew use combinations of pans on the physical space and close-ups on happy children using equipment that one typically associates with a park, but that are missing from her local park. Wendy is an ambassador between the adults who will rebuild the park, and the adults and kids who use it to form civic attachments to the people, culture, and physical space of their neighborhood.

Wendy's documentary also includes interviewing people about their experiences and desires. She displays important rhetorical and digital literacies with regard to drawing out information from stakeholders and depicting it visually. Notably, she establishes rapport with her interviewees. By asking about their status as community participants and long-time residents, she makes the crucial move of establishing the authority of the interviewees to share their opinions. Her interviewees also confirm the importance of forming civic attachments to places by suggesting that the park reflect the local neighborhood's ethnic culture.

Wendy's documentary is powerful and exhibits crucial visual and informational literacies that display her mediated public voice. Her documentary techniques attempt to persuade others, beyond her immediate family and friends, about the importance of using residents' input to rebuild a key center of local sociality. Wendy is already civically engaged by volunteering to assist in a neighborhood improvement project with her documentary.

Within the context of acknowledging Wendy's contribution, it is also possible to explore how she might expand her repertoire of tactics to increase the efficacy of her message. For example, the video does not include interviews with children (for which there may be many reasons, including safety and privacy). Perhaps she selected interviewees that she believed would find the most purchase with adult decision makers. Wendy involves kids' input by showing images of kids using park equipment and displaying models they built of play structures they would like to see. On the other hand, it might be advantageous to recognize and integrate ideas articulated by children. Kids' input is often ignored in policy making and political affairs (Banet-Weiser 2007). Yet peer-to-peer dialogues may expand decision-making input from key stakeholders. Another step might have been for Wendy to provide a link to an online survey that the organization might use to collect feedback. Communities may implement different tactics as motivators, which may change according to individual problems, technical capabilities, and contexts.

Effective civic engagement often involves three important processes: diagnosis, prognosis, and motivators to stimulate action (Goodwin et al. 2001; Snow and Benford 1988). Diagnosis includes identifying "some event or aspect of social life as problematic and in need of alteration" (Snow and Benford 1988:199). Wendy clearly identifies a relevant problem in her video; she reports that a local park will be rebuilt because it is dilapidated and unsafe for children and families to play in and use in civically inspiring ways. Snow and Benford (1988:199) identify prognosis as an important part of the social process of effecting change. In prognosis, "a proposed solution to the diagnosed problem [specifies] what needs to be done." Wendy not only reiterates the general solution of needing to rebuild the park, she also identifies, through her own and her interviewees' authoritative witnessing, the specific things that can be done such as implementing swings, creating wider spaces, upgrading the safety and usability of the equipment, and adding local cultural elements.

At the end of her documentary, Wendy encourages viewers to share their opinions. Invitations to register an opinion enact what Snow and Benford (1988:199) call providing a "motivational impetus for participation." Motivators are "prods to action" that may involve various incentives, such as moral appeals to protect public goods or to draw people in to participate and collectively address a social problem. The kids on the play structure at the end of the documentary prod the viewer to think about what should be done to improve the park.

Wendy's subject—improving a park—is a kid-oriented topic that both reiterates and challenges notions of the protected child. On the one hand, her investigation reiterates the importance of kids having a safe space to play without risking physical harm. On the other hand, her investigative report on a dilapidated park in an underserved area demonstrates that kids do not universally experience childhood in the same ways. Many kids face real challenges such as fewer options for experiencing safe play. Wendy documents and witnesses the physical state of the park, not by passively viewing what has happened in a victimized sense, but in Peters' (2001) sense of providing a compelling and authentic mediated experience through which others can judge the circumstances and can choose to act. Her video began with a hyperlocal topic, but connects to much larger political concerns about creating safe spaces for families to bond, play, and develop crucial forms of social capital.

Raising Awareness about the Effects of War

Like Wendy, Max also chose the medium of video and the social space of YouTube to raise awareness about an issue that was emotionally important to him. He was concerned about unjust treatment of children and families in Palestine. Max enacts a form of mediated witnessing in a way that began personally, but connects to much larger political discourses. Unlike Wendy, Max was not personally at the scene of the events he depicts. He remixes others' mediated witnessing to provide information for people to reconsider the meaning of particular events. His goal was to convey moral judgments to motivate people to talk about political conflict and effect change.

Max aspires to be a professional filmmaker. He listed Steven Spielberg and George Lucas among his heroes. He performs a technologized identity by stating affiliation to filmmakers who are known not only for commercial and artistic success, but also for pushing the boundaries of technical filmmaking and impressing audiences with creative special effects. Max's identity as a technically competent teen and aspiring media maker cannot be separated from the type of media to which he aligns himself and the learning opportunities he presents for himself and others through his YouTube video.

Max created a visual and audio mashup video that juxtaposed disturbing images of people experiencing violence in Palestine with music from

Schindler's List, Steven Spielberg's Academy-Award winning film about the Jewish holocaust. A video mashup "recombines two or more pre-existing videos and/or audio sources into a new, derivative work, [which] generates new meanings through the juxtaposition of the original source materials" (Edwards and Tryon 2009). Meanings in mashups are produced via the collusion of at least two texts, "typically one text that is associated with the political realm (political speeches, Congressional testimony) and another taken from popular culture (pop songs, movies, TV shows)" (Edwards and Tryon 2009). Mashups are one example of how kids take materials from popular culture sources to create new meanings and messages (Jenkins 1992).

An audio and/or visual mashup offers a space wherein the creator becomes an online "citizen-user" (Edwards and Tryon 2009) or consumer citizen (Banet-Weiser 2007) who challenges dominant readings of information consumed in corporatized media such as news and political footage. Max's video plays a song from a popular cultural production about Jewish persecution while showing images depicting violence in the Middle East. Bringing together these ideas for two groups in historical conflict suggests that Palestinians are persecuted in lethally discriminatory ways, as were Jewish populations during the Holocaust. The potency of the mashup is dependent upon both creators' and viewers' cultural and political literacies to understand the meanings behind the media that are brought into juxtaposition to make a point.

Like Wendy, Max was motivated to produce media in order to generate action on an important issue. Although his mediated center of gravity often involved video blogs or funny videos that spoofed films rather than civic themes, he nevertheless included a video that tells an important story. Such a pattern was typical of video bloggers, who chose to video blog about highly personal subjects in ways that connected to larger publics (Lange 2007b). Max's case study serves as an example of how a hyperlocal issue (interpersonal concerns about his neighbors) connected to larger debates. During a voice-only Skype interview, Max explained why he made the video:

> That one's pretty close to me because [my] old neighbors, they used to be –
> or they still are Palestinian, but we used to live, like, right next to them and I
> would always hear, like, since I was a little kid, like, stories of [how] their family
> members that were back there, like, they would be getting, [like,] hurt or, like,
> they would just be saying that they're being treated unfairly. And then I would
> also watch, like, stuff on the news and that kinda affected me. So, I decided that
> I wanted to do something about it. I knew that I personally, like, I couldn't do
> anything about the whole situation but maybe I could, like, express my opinion
> on it and show people what I think about it.

Max explained that he and his cousin from Iran sought pictures on the web of images about violence in the Middle East and the ways in which Palestinians suffered. Although a controversial move for some viewers, Max felt that adding the song from *Schindler's List* helped him arouse empathy for people who suffer from violence and prejudice.

Max's video begins with the word "Palestine" in white letters against a black ground. The letters grow in size as the music from *Schindler's List* plays. The next title card reads, "A country which was taken over by people who know how hatred feels like," alluding to the Jewish people of Israel whose ancestors suffered during the Holocaust. The following title card reads, "But yet they commit murders everyday that go unpunished or unnoticed." Next, the video is filled with disturbing images of the bloodied bodies of adults and children, followed by images of military personnel and equipment, such as tanks and airplanes. A man carries a male child whose body is limp and whose head and neck are covered in blood.

Max's video is filled with disturbing images including a bloodied camera; a coffin being conveyed; images of families running or being beaten by soldiers; and flashing lights from bombing raids. In one image, a man huddles behind an object which looks like a barrel and a child crouches for cover just behind him. The man protectively places his arm against the child's shoulder. After several shaking camera shots, the boy is seen lying in the man's lap covering his eyes. The man's head hangs eerily to the right. His vacant eyes prompt the viewer to wonder, is he dead? Covering his own eyes, the child seems unable to bear witness.

The video is an emotional plea that uses powerful images and commentary to show Max's support for Palestinians. His video displays several important visual and rhetorical literacies. For instance, Max employs a deliberate and yet dynamic pacing that uses disquieting fade-out transitions after showing images of families facing off against soldiers. The fade outs symbolically resemble a potential moment of death and pose moral questions about the antecedents of the bloodied or fleeing individual just depicted. Set against the haunting music from *Schindler's List*, the images convey a deeply poignant tone.

Max clearly exhibits digital literacies, such as attending closely to visual structure by incorporating different kinds of shots, which include close-ups of faces in pain. He juxtaposes close-ups with footage containing longer shots of military marches as well as overhead shots, such as a man shown in a crowd of supporters. From such a high overhead perspective, the viewer is invited to become a witness, and even a god-like authority figure who is capable of overseeing human actions and having the moral authority to judge their meanings. Max's video provides stimulating visual variety that holds the viewer's attention while arousing strong judgments about war's effects, especially on families and children. Even though they are pictures of strangers in found media footage, many of his images symbolize people whom he knew personally, as he expresses his anxiety over their plight. What begins with media motivated from personal emotions ends on a highly political note. The video concludes by urging viewers to "Free Palestine."

Analyzing the technical aspects of this video can feel clinical in comparison to the dramatic, emotional text comments that Max received. Many people felt grateful to him for providing images about a situation that some people feel does not receive sufficient coverage within professional media channels (Kuttab 1993). Like many artistic mashup videos, Max's piece does not identify a solution, but rather displays a "rejection of the politics of the status quo" and attempts to identify "problems needing remedy" (Edwards and Tryon 2009). At root, Edwards and Tryon (2009) argue, mashup practices "represent a belief in the power of personal broadcasting, media creativity and remix aesthetics to contribute to a stronger and healthier participatory democracy." Indeed, the politically charged, mediated moments of making and viewing mashups are often more about "remix as a process" that "opens up a space for debate and discussion" (Edwards and Tryon 2009; Miller 2004) rather than presenting solutions.

Rather than simply preparing for future participation in civic engagement, Max's mashup shows an existing skill set and direct participation on a topic of vital political interest to many people around the world. Max becomes involved in a networked public sphere by refusing to "blindly [consume] political information" and instead uses the remix genre to "mobilize resistance against top-down, mass-media messages" (Lim and Kann 2008:99). Children are often not considered to be consumers of news stories, and are assumed to require protection from the information within them (Banet-Weiser 2007:13). Yet, Max not only shows interest in disturbing political affairs, he subverts dominant readings of corporatized media. As part of a remix genre, Max's video mobilizes others to reflect on world problems.

Contrary to prior findings that political discourse is not possible on YouTube due to its structure and culture of playfulness (Hess 2009), the comments on Max's video show that it widened "the spectrum of contestations over political meanings and practices," thus contributing "to the formation of a more open, diverse, and egalitarian political segment in the networked publics" (Lim and Kann 2008:99-100; Varnelis 2008). Max's text comments reflected a wide range of opinions on a controversial topic.

What is of value to Max, and many other kids and teens, is that YouTube offered a space in which to debate issues in a frank and passionate manner. Civic engagement scholars say that teachers are often afraid to tackle incendiary subjects (Flanagan and Faison 2001:11) for fear that they will generate uncontrollable conflict in the classroom (Lawrence and Tatum 1997) or will increase undue pedagogical burdens on teachers (Torney-Purta, Hahn, et al. 2001). Yet, democracy depends upon exchanging heterogeneous discourse, however difficult that may sometimes be (Sunstein 2006; Torney-Purta, Lehmann, et al. 2001). Studies show that "students' belief that they were encouraged to speak openly in class was a powerful predictor of their knowledge of and support for democratic values and their participation in political discussion inside and outside school" (Torney-Purta, Lehmann, et al. 2001:137). Despite the contentious tone of YouTube's interaction and discourse, kids in my study often appreciated an opportunity for self-expression.

The dialogue that Max's mashup inspired was passionate and at times hostile. Receiving both similar and divergent perspectives on his video confirms the findings of prior surveys on civic engagement that state that youth online regularly encounter and interact with people who hold views very different from their own. According to a study by Kahne et al. (2010:13), "only 5% of all youth reported high levels of exposure to views that align with their own without also reporting high exposure to views that diverge from their own." Max received hundreds of comments; his video clearly motivated people to express their beliefs. Such discourse is an extremely important aspect of civic engagement and is routinely sought in participatory media.

Max's video (which was posted in September 2006 and received 8,641 views and 399 comments as of June 8, 2012) prompted reflection and participation in at least four main areas: 1) expressing support for a particular position; 2) engaging in political debate about U.S. foreign policy; 3) expressing concern for war's impact on families and children; and 4) discussing the role of media in presenting a point of view. Although not all comments were well formed or sensitive, a number of them did use powerful rhetorical strategies such as appealing to people's humanity, citing statistics, conceding extreme positions, and reasserting free speech as a means to express opinions and engage in public discourse. Max's video was successful in that it provided a learning opportunity for himself and others to gain information about people's opinions on a highly inflammatory topic. Such factors take on greater salience in the face of information that is often ignored or minimized in professional media channels. Discussions that are polarized may also strengthen existing social ties as well as mobilize new relationships (Blitvich 2010; Freelon 2010).

Some participants agreed with Max and left supportive comments for Palestinians. One commenter said, "until Israel regonizes and gives Palestinans equality and economic hope this will never end. One race cannot dominate the world - something is [wrong]." Another commenter expressed the view that "the palestenian people are defending their land, their race, their BLOOD!.." On the other hand, some commenters strongly disagreed with

Max's position. One noted, "israel has never tried to hurt any palestinian civilian, the crimes of palestinians against israelis are 10 times worse and ALWAYS direct at civilians." Another stated:

> it does take courage to spurt senseless bullshit like "israel is the real terrorist," yes. the "real terrorist" would be the arab nations who instigated and perpetuate the palestinian refugee crisis with acts of aggression in '48 and '67 (occupation of territory captured in a defensive maneuvre is LEGAL under international law) and now refuse to help their own brothers. palestinians are a pawn in a proxy war of arab fundamentalism.

Meta-discussions about the function of media and rights of participants to express their opinions were also prompted by his video. In one instance, Max and another commenter have an exchange about the video's content. The commenter tells Max that he is concerned about aspects of what he/she calls "Muslim ideology" and its role in state affairs. At the end of one such exchange, the commenter stated:

> I have a right to my opinion, and I have the right to express that opinion on this site as I live in a free democracy. I also have the right to offend with my opinion, and in doing so I uphold the right to be offended. However, I will not go out of my way to offend, discriminate or subject abuse to anyone. I express that I'm pro Israeli, anti religon and extremely secular. Thank you.

Even though they disagree, the commenter asserts the right to express an opinion. Commenters sometimes used metapragmatic moves, or language about the use of language, to discuss what people should be allowed to say in participatory environments such as YouTube. In this case, the commenter metapragmatically reiterates the fact that he or she has a "right to offend" with a personal opinion, and upholds "the right to be offended." The commenter ends the post with a polite "thank you" for reading the comment and engaging in discourse.

Although they are in the midst of a disagreement, Max confirms his interlocutor's right to speak publicly, a right that many other kids in the study reiterated by refusing to remove comments that some might consider hurtful. Leaving such commentary on a video was a way for kids to affirm their viewers' right to free speech. Many participants whom I interviewed performed their technical affiliation to the value that online spaces should facilitate free speech, even if this meant having to tolerate "haters," or people who post hostile dissent or pointlessly cruel criticism of their work (Lange 2007e). Kids spoke about handling "haters" and their negative commentary as if it were a digital literacy that was necessary to participate fully in online spaces. Max metapragmatically reaffirms his right to free speech in his reaction to the commenter. He states:

i never said you shouldnt express yourself, if i said that then i would be a hypocrite because in making this video and my other videos i am expressing myself. you are entitled to your opinion and if i didnt want anyones opinion i would have disabled comments but i did not because i enjoy to read and hear peoples opinions on the subject matter

Max posted the video knowing that it would likely prompt strong emotions and debate, which is consistent with the goals of a political mashup video that prompts discourse. Max created a personally expressive video and displayed tolerance for personally expressive media from others in text comments. Max's mashup uses prior media in a way that stimulates additional mediated communication in a reticulated or networked ecology of viewership and discourse. It reticulates or draws a mass of others into a more delineated network or group of people who share an interest in a social problem but do not necessarily agree on a particular solution.

Media meta-commentary also included protests about the graphic nature of Max's chosen images. This discussion echoes a long-standing debate in professional journalism about the ethics of including violent images, which ostensibly offends "proprieties" and may create shock and pain in viewers (Fishman 2003). The video was "age restricted" on YouTube, due to community guidelines. Although the age restriction is not explained, a plausible interpretation from YouTube's community guideline page is that it contains graphic violence. From one point of view, such graphic images are "a means of making 'real' (or 'more real') matters that the privileged and the merely safe might prefer to ignore" (Sontag 2003:7). Therefore, some viewers might argue that authentic violent images are an important part of raising awareness and exposing problems that require solutions. This may be an especially important issue given the fact that American media rarely depict violent images that may sway political opinion, such as corpses (Fishman 2003). Sontag (2003) argues that withholding photographic images from war based on ideas about "good taste" can be repressive and a form of censorship when institutionally invoked. It can be a way to "obscure" the political problems that Max wished to reveal and provoke with his video.

Commenters also took issue with the "one-sided" perspective of Max's video. One commenter said that it was "very sympathetically produced in favour of Palestine" and urged him to look at the "whole picture." On the other hand, because news is reportedly difficult to obtain from the region (Kuttab 1993), another commenter thanked him for the video, saying that it was hard to believe "all of this is [going] on without any news coverage." Indeed Max's approach to posting controversial subject matter was applauded by one commenter who stated:

Good for you: having the courage to put out an unpopular point of view. most folks seem not to be able to tolerate things that conflict with their Walmart, McDonald's, and Pepsi culture—which inhibits and discourages difference of opinion, debate, and intellectuality. good for you

In an era of corporatized online spaces, freedom of self-expression is not taken lightly by online participants who see that structures of participation online—such as on YouTube which may flag or remove socially "inappropriate" content—can influence what is said and what is possible to say publicly. Community standards that seek to protect viewers from graphic images can become politically repressive in certain contexts. In extreme form, institutional standards can invoke the rhetoric of "protection" in ways that deny children's need for exchanging information on upsetting topics, as well as the general public's need to understand far away events with significant and far-reaching consequences. In an era of corporatized media, kids use technological means to create and share videos about frightening events that they and their peers are already personally experiencing or witnessing. In doing so, they are exercising a mediated public voice to expose and discuss controversial political policies.

Consumer Citizenship

Kids' technologized identities also influence the types of causes they support and the learning opportunities they create for their viewers. For example, Frank, a 15-year-old white boy from the Midwest is a tech-savvy teen who is concerned about what people will be able to say in an increasingly corporatized Internet environment. Frank was an early adopter of YouTube; his account was opened in December 2005, the month that YouTube officially launched. He told me in a voice-only Skype interview that he has a web design business in which he helps his clients design, make, and fix their websites. His catalogue of videos is eclectic, including topics such as soap opera parodies, hanging out with his friends, explaining YouTube's tracking statistics, and discussing ways to improve YouTube's community. Like many other kids on YouTube, Frank is concerned about being able to speak freely online, even if that means using modest production values or simply sharing an opinion. Frank is concerned that models of Internet service could be implemented in ways that complicate non-professionals' or individuals' ability to exchange opinions and information.

If discourse is a key way to influence a public of relative strangers to achieve social ends, then the battle for control over ability to exchange information through commercial services is a crucial aspect of civic engagement.

As Scammell (2000:351) argues, "The act of consumption is becoming increasingly suffused with citizenship characteristics and considerations." Consumers, Scammel asserts, are increasingly aware of their political power and can exercise it by holding corporations accountable for "acts of environmental destruction and reckless cruelty" by "naming and shaming them" (Scammell 2000:353). In this case, Frank wishes to hold media corporations and service providers accountable for how they influence everyday information exchange.

Because corporations may control media and bias opinion, Frank and others support "net neutrality," which is the idea that telecommunications carriers and Internet service providers would be legally required to offer services to anyone using nondiscriminatory rates and would provide these services without regard to particular forms of content (Montgomery 2008). In other models, carriers might choose to offer premium services to those who can pay, while providing expensive, less desirable services to users who might not otherwise be able to afford to participate online and engage in civic discourse. In addition, certain content or particular applications might be barred from circulation if network providers choose to do so.

In one video that includes multiple topics, Frank addresses his concern about net neutrality. He references a video called "Human Lobotomy," which influenced his opinions. He saw the video on a website called savetheinternet .com, which is a coalition of individuals, businesses, and non-profit organizations that work to preserve "a free and open Internet" in terms of access and content. According to the savetheinternet.com website:

> Net Neutrality is the reason the Internet has driven economic innovation, democratic participation and free speech online. It protects the consumer's right to use any equipment, content, application or service without interference from the network provider. With Net Neutrality, the network's only job is to move data – not to choose which data to privilege with higher quality service.

In his video Frank urges his viewers to view the "Human Lobotomy" video and support net neutrality. Frank addresses the camera directly to express his opinion. He passionately diagnoses the problem and motivates people to prevent the Internet from becoming another top-down medium that prevents civic interaction. Arguing that this could be the death of the Internet as we know it, he states:

> We don't want the Internet to become a one-directional media that's controlled by corporations. Because then, that means all the content we see is just what the White House wants us to see. Or only the news. We're only gonna get the news that makes the U.S. look good, more or less, where if you had like

the BBC or something you get the real truth, that's why I'm not really a fan of CNN or MSNBC or definitely not FOX or CBS News, any of the U.S. news. They just make the U.S. look good or make it come off as not as bad as it does, that's why I like the BBC and lots of other [kinds] of independent news sources because they really uh can capture how much the U.S. sucks. But you can get lots more news and learn a lot more that's going on around us so sure we've heard a little bit about Rwanda, and Darfur, and I'm sure some people have heard more than others but you don't see that much of it on the news, [although] I've seen a lot of it on other independent news sites.

Frank's message has many important attributes. First, Frank's videos provide a learning opportunity for his viewers that is motivated by his technical affiliation to the "geeky" topic of Internet communication. Second, Frank is civically engaging. He is not merely preparing to participate; he is part of a public discourse in which he urges his viewers to support an issue that is important for the future functioning of online participation, civic discourse, political involvement, and democracy itself. Finally, Frank's video is part of a reticulated discourse in which he is drawn into the conversation through media, and pulls in others through the circulation of his own video. Few viewers visit Frank's YouTube page to see net neutrality videos. They come to support a friend, who happens to believe in net neutrality. The act of reticulation means that people are exposed to issues through shared interests or friendships rather than because they seek out information on a specific issue. Viewers who support Frank are drawn into a discourse, and perhaps eventually into a social network that rallies around net neutrality. By sharing an interest in YouTube and videos, viewers eventually become exposed to an important political issue and may be reticulated into a network of net neutrality supporters.

Frank's video is also a metaphenomenological illustration of what he thinks the Internet should offer, which is a non-discriminatory space for exchanging opinion in any style a person chooses or can afford. Just as Max metapragmatically used language to comment on appropriate language use in comments, so too does Frank's experience of a video with modest production values illustrate why open Internet models are important. If the term phenomenological refers to experiences and how people derive meaning from those experiences (Schutz 1967), then the metaphenomenological may be defined as describing how people engage in particular experiences to analyze or normatively comment on the experiences themselves. Frank's way of "broadcasting himself" is a metaphenomenological act that uses the very type of mediated experience—a simple video of an opinion with simple production values—that he fears is being threatened by corporatized models of Internet service. The experience of making a video blog is a metaphenomenologically normative judgment on the importance of making just such modest media to protect information circulation outside of corporatized journalism.

Frank stresses the importance of ensuring that the Internet does not simply become another one-way medium that complicates free exchange of ideas. He "names and shames" (Klein 2000; Scammell 2000) corporatized news organizations—such as CNN, MSNBC, FOX News, and CBS News—that he feels deliver biased reports of events. Frank diagnoses a social problem, which is that exchange of opinion and information may be threatened if certain Internet service models are implemented. He offers a prognosis, which is that supporting net neutrality will prevent these threats from occurring. He also provides motivators that are both direct (to watch a video and consult the website to gain more information) and indirect (to generally be wary of news organizations that deliver a biased, inordinately pro-U.S. perspective).

Frank also uses rhetorical strategies to create the kind of public that Warner (2002) describes, namely one that is constructed through discourse. For instance, Frank says that "*we* do not want the Internet to become a one-directional media that's controlled by corporations" (emphasis added) wherein "we" would only receive certain biased forms of news. By invoking the first person plural of "we" he reticulates his viewers into a networked, social collective constructed of people and media that rally around particular values. What began as expressions of personal anxiety from a tech-savvy teen becomes sets of ideas and motivators that are articulated to wider networked publics in ways that may influence future possibilities of online interactivity and political action. By inviting a collective group of viewers, some of them strangers, into his network and engaging in consumer activism, Frank illustrates the importance of consumer critique in a globalized era. His video "brings into the daylight the dangerously hidden issue of the political power of corporations" to networked publics (Scammell 2000:354), many of whom vote or will soon be old enough to do so.

Frank performs technical affiliation to an issue coded as important in online technical cultures. By civically engaging through his video blog, he enacts technical evangelism. Technologists often evangelize practices that they believe to be important (English-Lueck and Saveri 2000) or morally necessary (Lange 2003) to improve the world and interaction within it. Frank might have evangelized his cause further by expanding his repertoire of civic engagement, for instance by adding links to petitions or websites with additional information. Expanding kids' repertoires first requires recognizing how kids are already civically engaged and analyzing the processes whereby kids are socially reticulated into networked publics, and are lending their voice to solve social problems.

Reticulated Civic Engagement

Prior models of civic engagement were often oriented around a ladder of participation that moved from the inauthentic (being excluded) to the authentic (being empowered) (Arnstein 1969). Such tiered models begin with exhibiting curiosity on an issue, proceed toward gathering information, and ultimately achieving social change through political activism. Although these models remain germane in certain contexts, the examples in this chapter suggest that kids and youth are exhibiting diffuse patterns of technologized civic interest that often begin through shared technical interests such as making media, and by developing weak but affective ties that may not be centered around issues at all. For instance, when the Field family posted a video about a kite flying event, the video provided a learning opportunity for local people to gain information about events in their community. Close ties to place are crucial for civic bonding, developing affective ties to local communities, and perhaps eventually mobilizing around shared problems, as Wendy demonstrated in her documentary. These are examples of reticulated civic engagement which extend far beyond the overtly political; they demonstrate how kids and adults engage in forms of "actualizing citizenship" (Bennett et al. 2011) by using personally expressive media to interact within and help create social networks of people who share similar values and interests.

Reticulated civic engagement is defined as the combination of knowledge, actions, media sharing, and participation that draws people into or creates a new social network of people who share particular values. The energy in this form of engagement is expended on social ties and interests rather than on particular issues, although such connections may lead to creating change or addressing social problems. Video blogging often assists this form of engagement by drawing people toward places and social networks, both local and dispersed.

Kids are part of networked public cultures, which are ecologies of people, networks, and objects that facilitate global communication and participatory connections to other people (Varnelis 2008). But how do people become networked? The examples in this chapter suggest that kids reticulate or draw other people and media into networked publics through shared interests, identities, activities, and values. Reticulated civic engagement weaves on- and offline and is centered around everyday interactions, discourse, and a shared sense of fun. It is not incompatible with traditional mobilization ladders, but it operates from a socio-emotional starting point. Consider Wendy, who overtly raised awareness and encouraged feedback on the rebuilding of a park. Her topic focused on finding ways to increase generalized social capital within a local group, by creating welcoming spaces of sociality. Her technologized form of civic engagement through documentary draws people in and helps them recognize each other as members of a group interested in interacting through shaping spaces of play.

Reticulated civic engagement can lead to or work in conjunction with mobilization on specific issues, but it often begins in a diffuse way. A potential example that appears to illustrate these dynamics is the website nerdfighters. com. The group's webpage says that its members are about "bringing nerdfighters together to increase awesome and decrease world suck." Using a particular brand of humor, they bring people together who have similar interests in things like nerdiness, gaming, and online culture. As they humorously say, "A lot of life is about doing things that don't suck with people who don't suck." World "suck" is hardly a well-defined issue to mobilize around, yet it serves to draw people in through a feeling of down-to-earth idealism and humor common in technical cultures. Funny slogans may reticulate people into a social network first, which later may yield sub-networks or shifting social configurations that support particular political positions. For instance, in the video called *Religion and Gay Marriage* posted to YouTube on May 15, 2012, a participant named John challenges so-called traditional assumptions about marriage to discuss and support marriage equality. Kids and youth are increasingly exhibiting civic engagement models in which they are connecting through media or through particular identifications such as being a "nerd."

Factors that promote reticulation processes can be social or technical, or some combination of the two. A technical feature on YouTube or other video-sharing site may facilitate particular kinds of connections. For example, on YouTube, people may subscribe to particular video makers. When Frank puts up a new video, say on net neutrality, all of his subscribers, including those who already were interested in the issue as well as those who have never heard of it, may be reticulated into a network of participants. The infrastructure of YouTube also enables people to become involved in certain discourses through the tagging system of searches of text descriptions. But such searches may lead people in directions they did not expect. For instance, searching for videos using a keyword such as *Schindler's List* might attract attention from people who like the song. They may be surprised to link to Max's video, which was about Palestine. Such viewers might enter into an unexpected discourse through a shared interest, in this case a piece of media or song. This is not yet an act of mobilization for this group, because they encountered controversial discourse through a shared cultural interest. Given its emotional content, some viewers may mobilize in quite a different direction than the video maker intended. Nevertheless, the viewers in this example are being reticulated or drawn into a networked discourse which connects people to a public discussion on an important issue.

The case studies in this chapter show that some kids are actively participating in networked public cultures to promote civic causes. Even when the process of engagement was upsetting in terms of the content or the hostile commentary that appeared in text comments, kids often reasserted the importance of being able to express one's opinion. For example, a 19-year-old white woman from the Southern United States who requested that I use her real name of Amelia, told me that social conventions in the U.S. limit certain kinds of expression. In contrast, she said that on YouTube, "people can argue with you, disagree, [and] leave nasty comments." She said that YouTube "opens doors that are usually closed" by enabling people to share their views without being subjected to silence. As she put it, "At the end of the day you can express any opinion you want and [I] think that's beautiful, it is something we need more of." Similarly, even though Max received hostile commentary on his video, he told me that he appreciated learning about other people's opinions.

Scholars of civic engagement argue that focusing only on protective concerns often neglects aspects of kids' individuality and their need to learn how to work through differences of opinion. It may be the wrong strategy to avoid any kind of contentious commentary on kids' videos. Parents and children should discuss their own personal limits, and decide how much vitriol kids should be exposed to through public media. However, washing out the visibility of emotional argumentation risks reducing kids' sense of civic obligation because the process of working through difference is marked as something to avoid, rather than deal with. Kids are often not taught in schools that achieving democratic outcomes requires dealing with diversity and working extremely hard to achieve consensus (Flanagan and Faison 2001:11). As my study and others have shown, kids often do want access to information, even if the issues are painful or produce conflict (Davies 2005:20).

Achieving tolerance amid discussion of passionate subjects is crucial for healthy democracies. Emotions, which are often framed in pejorative ways, "are related to moral intuitions, felt obligations and rights, and information about expected efforts, all of which are culturally and historically variable" (Goodwin et al. 2001:13). Although emotions are often rejected and opposed in a binary way to rational thoughts, in fact, scholars argue, "cognitions typically come bundled with emotions, and are meaningful or powerful to people for precisely this reason" (Goodwin et al. 2001:15). As Coleman (2008:201) argues, "Democracy, which has often seemed to be anesthetized by constitutionality, is rooted in expressive, cathartic, and carnivalesque practices that connect public policy to mundane culture." Rationality and emotion dovetail to help people explore and work through contentious topics through public discourse. If kids are taught that democracy is inevitable, they may be denied the tools to actually achieve it.

Models of civic engagement must investigate obstacles to the reticulation process. For instance, one of the main reasons that people do not participate in civic affairs is because "nobody asked" (Verba et al. 1995). In other cases, the problem may lie in social disconnections that result from not sharing interests or identifications. For example, I asked Frank if he discussed the issue of net neutrality with his peers. Contrary to the homogenizing discourses of "digital youth," Frank said that most of his friends and classmates were uninterested in such "geeky" topics. Frank stated:

> I don't have that many kind of geeky friends, but the ones that I do have, I've definitely told them about it, and then they've become interested in it too. But I – that's only a handful, like maybe two to five or something.

Frank's friends did not perform affiliation to the idea that net neutrality was an important issue, nor did they see it as a digital literacy about online participation. That kids have different identifications, affiliations, and commitments to technical issues shows that interventions might be needed to raise awareness about communicative technologies and policies that affect many more people than geeks. Informal learning processes broke down for Frank's social circle, given that his less "geeky" friends appeared disinterested in preserving open, networked access.

Educational interventions might include helping kids parse the comments they receive both in terms of form and content. Green (2002) discusses how "purposive" listening can help musicians improve their craft. Purposive viewing means that media makers can carefully study other videos to improve video-making techniques. Purposive commenting could also be applied to text comments that people actively read, critique, and evaluate in order to build a better understanding of what makes for interesting and fruitful online participation. Such interactive, reflective commenting—whether informal or in classrooms—might initiate a positive cycle that raised public comment quality as kids and adults developed more effective public voices. People are participating in online groups with heterogeneous skill sets with regard to public presentation. Such reflective activity could work toward developing empathy for other people, and achieve networked reflective solidarity (Senft 2008:98), which Senft defines as a political identification that sees participants as part of a collective, even though they will likely remain strangers. Posted comments, including those that are insensitive or poorly articulated could serve as learning opportunities for people to engage in meta-discourses about what makes productive civic participation.

Kids' civic styles are inflected by their technologized preferences for expressing the self through video. Some kids are already participating in civic life and can be assets for helping to solve collective problems. The kids profiled in this chapter are creating videos that detail the problems that they experienced firsthand or heard about through friends and loved ones. In some cases, it was through mediated family life that digital literacies and civic attachments were formed. The case studies suggest that kids are connecting both to local communities and to online networked publics through technologized forms of self-expression. How kids interact with their social networks and families shapes their perception about what can be accomplished by carrying around a camera in daily life.

CHAPTER 5

Video-Mediated Lifestyles

YouTube can feel like a giant, networked family album. It is filled with images of young children in daily life. No book about "kids on YouTube" would be complete without considering how families make media together, particularly in the case of parents with very young children (under 10 years old). In the United States, 30 to 49 year olds, who often have young children, are now just as likely as are 18 to 29 year olds to upload videos (Purcell 2010). To understand how kids develop media literacies through everyday video practices, it is important to consider the experiences of kids who are growing up in heavily mediated environments within the spaces of the home. Kids may not necessarily adopt their parents' media practices, but growing up in these heavily mediated environments means being exposed to their techno-savvy parents' models of living and learning in technologized ways.

This chapter focuses on parents who shared a passion for video-making. It describes how video making has changed from earlier decades of home movie making. Family videos on YouTube reflect involvement from moms, and exhibit a wide variety of content, including more mundane and technologized moments in media-makers' lives. This chapter describes displays of technical identities through depictions of technology usage, sketch comedy, and learning through pranking. The next chapter on representational ideologies deals with questions of agency, and the ramifications of kids' participation in parentally driven, online media. This chapter analyzes identities and literacies that inflect the everyday activities of families having fun with a camera.

Although most kids in my YouTube study made media with peers and siblings, some kids learned to make videos by watching their tech-savvy parents. Such an observation contradicts the popular discourse that it is only teenagers who lead the way in contemporary home video making

(Strangelove 2010:61). This chapter analyzes videos and interviews with parents who enthusiastically participated on YouTube either to express themselves in creative ways, or to socialize and communicate with other people in networked publics. Just as the kids described in the prior chapters had varying degrees of interest in media careers, so too did the parents in my study vary with respect to professional ambitions. Parents sometimes repurposed home footage for more communicative or commercial purposes, such that the ontology and meaning of the footage changed according to different phenomenological inflection points during creation and subsequent viewing.

Family videos often exhibit a quirky and playful sense of humor that is characteristic of YouTube culture, but can be found in other video making sites online and on U.S. television entertainment programs. Scholars and pundits often argue that having cheaper cameras and data storage enables a wider variety of video-making themes, but such a technologically deterministic argument has limitations (Moran 2002). For example, it does not explain why particular themes such as technologized images or pranking are chosen over others to post on YouTube, a site which displayed, at least in its early years, its own culture, norms, and social expectations. YouTube tended to have a certain "YouTube-ness" (Burgess and Green 2009a) that favored playful genres and themes. Popular genres in family media making across YouTube included conversational video blogs, informational videos, and scripted videos such as sketch comedy (Burgess and Green 2009a). An important theme also involved interactions within what some participants referred to as the YouTube community (Lange 2008a, 2008b, 2009; Rotman and Preece 2010; Strangelove 2010).

This chapter explores why parents put their young children and themselves on YouTube, and why they choose to share these moments with a wider population. Homogenizing discourses about digital generations often efface parental involvement in media making in ways that complicate understanding of how kids may be introduced to digital literacies through family media practices (Prensky 2006). Many kids are growing up amid heavily mediated lifestyles in which even the casual moments of everyday life could wind up on YouTube and be viewed by millions of people. Of course, view counts must be considered with caution; amateur and professional video makers have been known to use programs to automatically inflate view counts (Gayle 2012). Whether or not a video maker has done so must be investigated in each case. In any event, by placing their kids' human images online, creating YouTube accounts for them, moderating their received comments, and making videos together, parents contribute to early formations of how kids' interact with the wider world through media.

Mediating Everyday Life

In the past and today, family life captures the attention of the home media maker. In fact, "the most ardent makers of family pictures are parents of young children" (Holland 1991:9). One study reported that "Of amateur videos that appeared in YouTube's category of 'Most Viewed (All Time),' 67 percent featured the home or the family as the location or focus of the video" (Strangelove 2010:43). In studies of U.S. home movie making in the 1960s and 70s, Chalfen (1987) characterized non-professional work made by and for families as "home mode" media. Home movies, videos, and photographs were meant to preserve memories and to showcase life milestones and personal achievements such as birthdays and graduations. The home mode continues to be an important part of everyday video making, and connects people with absent loved ones, provides records of family histories, and creates feelings of stable family unity (Buckingham et al. 2011; Pini 2009).

However, home video making now includes a wider set of subjects and audiences (Moran 2002). For example, images from school or the workplace were generally not depicted in prior home movie making. Today, people in many other social networks including work, neighborhoods, clubs, dispersed family, and many other social groups appear in people's videos. Home mode images now include "families we choose" (Moran 2002; Weston 1992), as well as biologically connected families. Although milestone events occasionally appeared in my study, the parents profiled in this chapter did not exhibit a mediated center of gravity that was weighted toward exhibiting traditional milestones such as graduations. When they did post such content, it often aimed to communicate with or instruct others. For example, piano recital footage might serve as a tutorial to other music enthusiasts. With the availability of public video-exchange sites, home mode footage now lies on a continuum between relatively private and more public practices that are aimed at wider audiences such as dispersed relatives (Buckingham et al. 2011).

Families in my study created various forms of personally expressive media. Sometimes, YouTube videos were recorded in private contexts and targeted toward small groups; the videos might be posted on YouTube for convenience but never garnered many views. This footage most closely resembled what was previously called the "home mode." Families also created media in private or semi-private spaces that was somewhat unintentionally seen by many people outside of one's immediate family. In other cases, parents posted videos that were deliberately crafted to interest many people. These categories are not mutually exclusive; a single video might contain a number of themes (both relatively more public and private). A single video might start out as private, but it might contain amusing or disturbing content that prompted it to go viral.

One should not confuse media made at home with home mode; much of the media posted on YouTube was targeted toward audiences beyond the immediate family. Chalfen (1987) deliberately bracketed any media that was targeted to large, heterogeneous audiences from his concept of the "home mode." To address a largely ignored swath of vernacular media making, he excluded professional and advanced amateur media makers such as members of photography clubs. Although they involved family members, many videos discussed in this chapter saw widespread viewership. Even when videos depicted highly mundane footage, such as showing a child crying or someone using a computer, the intent was often social and communicative, such as in finding commiseration or empathy from other parents. Many of the families also experimented with form and created comedic videos that parodied or echoed themes from professional entertainment such as television shows devoted to pranking.

Discourses of realism have encouraged acceptance of more mundane video themes such as getting a hair cut, typing on a computer, or just running around the back yard. Some video bloggers whom I interviewed espoused support for depicting small moments of life to share everyday challenges. However, the discourses embracing the recording of "realistic" family life exhibited limits. Study participants did not post the kind of mean-spirited and brusquely candid footage—such as depictions of inebriated parents or children engaging in swearing and fighting—that has been reported elsewhere on YouTube (Strangelove 2010).

A number of striking differences appeared between themes analyzed in the past and those emerging in my study. Themes that differed dramatically included 1) videos in which moms drove video creation; 2) videos that depicted kids in technologized or mediated ways, such as using computers, playing video games, and discussing cameras; and 3) videos of families making comedy sketches and executing pranks on each other or in public. The pranks were generally benign, such as surprising people with pretend snakes, rather than the more aggressive pranks located elsewhere on YouTube, such as the brother who humiliated his sister by showing her being grounded for meeting a boy whom she met online (Strangelove 2010).

This chapter focuses on cases in which parents motivated family media creation. In each case, significant details emerged about how parents both presented themselves and their children in technologically relational ways. In some cases, the videos' overt subjects were technical, while in others, comedy and fun formed central themes. Whether or not the kids will ultimately adopt their parents' media practices, it is fair to say that early in their lives these children were exposed to models for creating media and proposing a technologized identity to the world through video.

Moms Behind the Camera

Prior studies characterized fathers as the primary drivers for home movie making (Chalfen 1987; Zimmerman 1995). They used cameras to record their patriarchal and material success, and reified capitalist ideologies of accumulation. Yet, I found that many mothers used video to have fun and convey their perspective on family life and YouTube participation. In the United States, women are just as likely as men to upload a video online (Purcell 2010). YouTube is filled with the images of mothers who include personal home mode footage as well as messages for wider numbers of viewers, such as other parents facing similar problems. Grandparents are also part of the action; I interviewed one grandmother at a YouTube meet-up who liked making video blogs and cooking videos. She wanted her YouTube account to continue after she passed away so that her granddaughter could see "grandma making a fool of herself on the Internet."

In some cases, mothers directly address the camera in video blogs and discuss what it is like to be a mom. Their feelings are highly personal. In other cases, mothers engage in a wide variety of genres that involve themes such as: playing with technology, comedy sketch, cooking, greeting or get well cards, arts and crafts tutorials, or just relaxing at home.

Four mothers profiled in this book—Cara, Jane, Trudy, and Lola—have established accounts on YouTube that are filled with images of their families engaged in everyday activities. Cara, Lola, and Jane are from the United States, and Trudy is from Canada. This section focuses on Cara and Trudy; examples from Jane's oeuvre are discussed later in the section on technologized images. Lola's YouTube participation, which was motivated by her daughter Ashley, is analyzed in Chapter 3, which is on girl geeks. Cara and Jane mostly participated to have fun with the camera and to meet other people on the site. Although Trudy also participated in the social side of YouTube, the incredible popularity of her videos—which largely depicted her daughters—enabled her to become a YouTube partner and to pursue commercialized options.

Although prior analyses of home media have identified important issues, they often lack attention to the sense of interpersonal fun and poignancy that parents in my study expressed when they recorded everyday interactions with a camera. The following discussion analyzes identity dimensions and aspects of sociality that result from making media with one's family. Moms are taking up cameras and, along with their families, are offering their perspective on what it means to express the self through video.

Commercialized Tropes of the Home Mode

Trudy (a researcher-assigned pseudonym) and her two young girls, Beth and Irene (also pseudonyms) have been making videos together for four years. At the time of the research, Beth was four years old and Irene was two. The girls are public figures with impressive viewership. They participate in an online attention economy in which viewers decide how to spend their limited attention (Goldhaber 1996). Like other YouTube participants, Trudy and her girls participated socially with other families on YouTube. They attended meet-ups offline and interacted with other video makers online through videos and comments. In one video, Beth attends a video meet-up where she reportedly met Kevin Nalty, a highly popular comedian and YouTube partner whose screen name is "Nalts." He is also a father with several children. In one video, Trudy talks about attending a New York gathering and meeting with Nalts and his family before the meet-up. Trudy and other families often connected on YouTube and pursued interaction in person, both at formal gatherings, and in smaller, informal private parties in YouTubers' homes.

On her YouTube page, Trudy describes herself as "Just a creative mom with a video camera :)." She warns viewers on her YouTube page that she checks subscribers and moderates all comments because hers is a "PG" channel, a reference to the "parental guidance suggested" film rating. Her warning implies that she will not approve comments that she does not consider appropriate for her "family friendly" channel. According to her YouTube page, Trudy joined in November 2006, which makes her a relatively early adopter, joining less than a year after YouTube officially launched.

Her videos depict her daughters doing Halloween projects, drawing pictures, singing, making and discussing art, and being interviewed by their mother. Many of their videos read as if they are more home mode, in that the girls engage in everyday activities that do not require high production values. Yet, the videos' themes captivate broad groups of viewers. For example, Trudy is a Harry Potter fan. In one video, Irene teaches viewers how to play Harry Potter chess, or "chest" as she refers to it.

Trudy likes teaching her kids about fine art and music. In one video, Beth "interviews" Vincent van Gogh. Beth asks a man dressed as van Gogh questions and he answers them. In this way, kids learn about famous artists, their work, and life histories through the videos they make. Trudy notes in her description that the information is "accurate" as it is taken from the online encyclopedia of Wikipedia. This statement is a performance of technical affiliation to the idea that Wikipedia provides accurate information and is a reasonable source for finding out about famous artists' lives. Whatever scholars' views might be about Wikipedia's accuracy, Trudy performs affiliation to the idea that drawing from this online, digital information source is an appropriate way to share information with other viewers who are interested in family-friendly ways of learning about art and artists.

The family's videos are enormously popular on YouTube. Trudy's account shows more than 118 videos posted as of December 2012, with her most-viewed video receiving more than 16 million views four years after its initial posting. Trudy posted at least four other videos that have received more than one million views. The videos in the account have a combined total of more than 51 million views and more than 75,000 subscribers. To provide perspective on viewership, niche comedy television shows such as the parody news program *The Daily Show* routinely receive in the neighborhood of one million views per episode (de Moraes 2013). Trudy's account is ranked in the top 30 list of most viewed YouTube partners in Canada. Her high viewing numbers have not gone unnoticed. Trudy announced on her YouTube page that a producer contacted her about a possible television show. She says she will keep everyone posted as she receives more information.

Trudy is a YouTube partner, which means that she receives a portion of the revenue from ads placed on her videos and on her account page. In her videos, 16-second pre-roll advertisements appear. They also appear in banner ads at the bottom of the video image, and in a square box placed to the right of the video on the viewing page. Advertised products and services include frosted cereal, light yogurt, frozen pizza, wireless telephone services, insurance, and Kmart, a discount department store. She positions herself using tropes and alliances of professional media making. For example, she copyrights her videos, with the notation "All rights reserved. Any unauthorized broadcasting, public performance, copying or re-recording will constitute an infringement of copyright." Further, she carefully points out the source of songs in her videos, thanking those who have given her permission to use them. In a video in which she uses footage from the television show *Good Morning America*, she notes that she received permission to use this footage. Trudy's careful attention to copyright situates her as different from others making casual forms of video who do not attend to legal aspects of authorship.

A friend of the girls who interviewed them noted that after years of making videos at a very young age, they have literally "grown up" on YouTube. In a rare video that includes Trudy, she and her daughter Beth are lying on the floor, with Beth's head touching Trudy's temple. Beth starts singing a song and then says good-bye and abruptly leaves the frame. Leaving when one wants to, rather than enacting a planned leave-taking is a trope of home mode video making that rejects the carefully crafted entrances and exits of professional or advanced amateur framings. Next, Trudy is lying next to Irene, who is eating a lollipop. Trudy removes a hair from the lollipop, an act that is highly mundane and is a recognizable index of a mother making her child's food safe to eat. "Mommy!" Irene yells, and Trudy responds, "Give me a kiss sweetie, I love you." Irene complies, sweetly kissing her on the cheek. Later the image cuts to

Beth, whom Trudy tickles, and then instructs to tell everyone to "watch the videos" that she made.

Trudy uses several mechanisms to promote their work and sustain viewer engagement. She uses a charming emotional plea from Beth, situated in a loving family image, to encourage viewership. In addition, she uses YouTube's navigational features to encourage viewers to move to the next or to previous videos. She also encourages people to subscribe, which at the time of the research meant being alerted at no cost when Trudy uploaded a new video. These emotional and technical features aim to prolong the mediated moment of viewership, and to keep the viewer literally tuned in. Video descriptions include exhortations to view their video playlists, which are thematic lists that YouTube participants can compile of their own videos for other people to watch. Trudy's playlists are organized around topics such as funny kid videos, parodies, art, singing, videos with Nalts, and YouTube gatherings.

Many viewers on YouTube are drawn to this channel and to the girls. I interviewed adults who think that the girls are adorable. In one case, a woman whom I interviewed at a meet-up in Philadelphia said she was inspired to participate on YouTube partly because of her enjoyment of this channel. Trudy rarely appears in the videos, which are focused on her daughters, but her love for them is depicted in the way she photographs them, asks them questions, and occasionally interacts with them on camera.

The family's channel garnered significant attention. Beth and her artwork were profiled in 2007 on *Good Morning America*, a U.S. morning news and entertainment program. In one video posted to their channel, Trudy video records Beth as she watches herself on television on the *Good Morning America* program. In the television footage, Beth is shown in one of her videos, drawing pictures of the *Good Morning America* news team. As Beth watches herself on television, Trudy records her in their home. While they watch, Trudy asks if Beth remembers drawing the pictures, and she answers, "Yeah." Beth asks, "Is that me mommy?" while pointing to her image on television. "Yeah, it's you!" Trudy answers. Beth moves toward her mother smiling in delight and hugging her; they are so close, Beth is almost off camera. The near omission of Beth's body from the frame depicts a mediated moment of physical affection that is so rapt in delight that the act of recording is almost forgotten.

The YouTube video is simultaneously a mediated moment of reception (on Beth's part as she watches her self on television) as well as production (as Trudy records Beth's viewership). Although "reception" and "production" are often seen as distinct, in this case, mediated moments of viewing and recording are collapsed. The news anchors on the show call Beth "adorable" and her artwork "advanced" and "beautiful." Diane Sawyer, a famous news personality, noted that the pictures captured "something essential" about each of the news anchors. Trudy asks if she liked being on TV and Beth answers, "I loved being on TV." Trudy tickles her and Beth laughs and says "Mommy!" as the video ends.

Trudy uses home mode imagery to promote their channel. Their fun-with-a-camera project is part of an attention economy that Trudy has been very successful at navigating by pairing home mode images with professional framings. Moran (2002)'s insightful term of "video in the text" suggests that the home mode trope can become embedded in other visual works to create a complex phenomenology of viewership. When characters see a "home video," for instance, in a narrative film, the home mode trope creates statements about the characters and plot. Home mode footage is often coded as an authentic reflection of a character's point of view. Home mode footage in narrative film is often used to index "a happy, innocent past, a time of togetherness" (Erens 1986:99). For example, a lonely, bitter character may receive complex audience sympathies if he genuinely becomes emotional when watching a home video of happier family times.

How the code of the home mode interacts within a film or video produces an emergent, or new way of interpreting a text or the events and characters depicted within it. For example, when Trudy records her daughter watching the videos that are being aired on *Good Morning America*, their video made at home is embedded within an attention economy on YouTube. It is not "home mode" in Chalfen's (1987) sense because it is intended to receive hundreds of thousands of views from unknown viewers. Yet, the charming footage of watching a very young Beth point to the odd color of her socks as they appeared when she was on television creates a feeling of home mode authenticity that contrasts to the professional television show that she is watching. The home mode status is both challenged and reiterated, given that the anchors in a widely popular television show reference Beth's publicly posted work on YouTube as they discuss her charming artwork.

The whole package of assembled footage (home videos rebroadcast on a TV show, which is being watched by Beth, whose reactions are recorded by Trudy) is embedded in a heavily promoted YouTube video. It is not a home mode video, but aspects of it visually contrast to a professional television show. The video uses home mode tropes to increase the emotional, mediated moment of viewership of a little girl who sees herself on television. In a YouTube-inflected Lacanian (1949) moment, Beth (with her mother's help) discovers her televised, mediated image as connected to her actual self.

The videos depict Trudy's love for her daughters. But she has also used YouTube's features to promote her work and gain increased visibility for their videos, thus displaying affiliation to the idea that commercialization is not incompatible with genuine family affection. Readers with media ideologies (Gershon 2010a) that differ from Trudy's may not accept this link between family emotion and commercialization. Notably, these videos are not solely motivated by the girls; Trudy is a mom who controls her daughters' YouTube images. As a mother, Trudy handled the camera in a way that showed affection for her daughters and produced (at least for Trudy) personally expressive content that garnered widespread viewership for simple and playful moments in family life. Trudy provided a media model for her daughters in which using children's footage for commercial purposes is coded as an acceptable media practice, and one that is not incompatible with genuine maternal affection.

Having Fun and Communicating

Cara, who requested I use her real name when discussing her experiences, is a mother who lives in the Southern United States. She refers to her participation on YouTube as an "obsession." She has four small children, a girl aged two, a boy aged four, and two twin daughters aged ten. Like Trudy, Cara also participates in the social side of YouTube. Cara frequently communicates with other YouTube participants, and she and her family have attended YouTube meet-ups. Whereas Trudy has more than 70,000 subscribers, Cara has about 1,000. Many of Cara's viewers and subscribers actively watch and comment on her family's adventures. Like Trudy, Cara is a relatively early adopter, having joined in October 2006, less than a year after YouTube launched. Her most viewed video, posted in April 2007, is about a hair cut she video blogged about; it received 80,000 views as of August, 2013. Her second most viewed video, also posted several years ago, shows the family doing a tie-dye project, and it received more than 43,000 views.

Many of the videos in her 90-video catalogue include family-oriented themes in which she and the kids make arts and crafts, hang out, blow bubbles with gum, dress up as pirates for a birthday party, throw pacifiers into a pool, and sing songs. Cara also likes to video blog and share her opinions about subjects such as lack of proper amounts of snow, the hair between her husband's eyebrows, getting in shape, looking for a job, favorite outfits, and leaving strawberries too long outside of the refrigerator. In a video get well card to a sick girl, Cara's family blew bubbles with chewing gum. Cara said that they ended up exchanging messages with the girl's mother and made a more personal connection with their family. She also participated in a contest for moms on YouTube and sent a video greeting card to mothers on YouTube for mother's day. Sending a mother's day greeting card is an example of a video that is not home mode, but is more accurately conceptualized as personally expressive media that is targeted toward communicating with a much wider population of known and unknown viewers.

Sometimes Cara operates the camera and sometimes her husband records her as she shares her thoughts. In one video, her husband playfully sneaks into the frame after she asks if the camera is recording. She tells him to "get out" of her movie. She is in front of the camera, yet in control of her message and image. The phrase "in front of the camera" is often used to index an experience of being recorded, but not being in control. In contrast, the phrase "behind the camera" is often used to index unseen control of media making. These phrases are strong tropes of media control, but must be empirically investigated in each case to determine actual structures of motivation and control in making personally expressive media.

Although Cara had some formal course work in web design and computer programming, she characterizes herself as being "self-taught" with regard to computers. Having grown up with a computer and a father who worked for IBM (International Business Machines, a technology firm), she has been online since she was in her early teens. On her YouTube channel page, she describes herself as a wife, mother, and "webmistress," among other roles. She lists interests such as YouTube, checking email, sewing, movies, hanging out with family and HTML (HyperText Mark-up Language, which is used to create webpages). By listing particular technical interests such as HTML, she proposes a public technologized identity insofar as using HTML or other technical activities are accepted by her viewers as "technical" acts.

Both Cara and her husband have their own YouTube accounts. However, they are cautious about releasing certain information, such as their ages. Reports show that it is possible to use birth dates to attempt fraud and identity theft (Acquisti and Gross 2009; Clayburn 2009). In withholding her age, Cara displays a digital literacy of the traceability of age to birth date, and potentially to social security numbers.

The children have their own accounts, although they are not allowed to use their real names on YouTube. Cara told me that her husband thought it important to establish their accounts early on, since the better account names are often taken quickly in new websites. Such a belief represents a digital literacy in technical and online groups. By choosing a proper name early, people can display knowledge that they were technically savvy enough to join a site that eventually became important. When the best, coolest names are taken, newcomers may resort to using less clever names, or using the same names, but attaching number strings after the name (as in John versus John457). Before any interaction takes place, identity information already yields clues about participants' technical knowledge and affiliations. These names may function as indexical links to one's arrival to a site. A savvy technologist is not so by any other name; the early birds appear more techno-savvy. Of course technologists wishing to remain anonymous might deliberately select an amorphous name. By establishing accounts for them, Cara and her husband draw on particular digital literacies to help construct their children's technical identities early in their online, participatory histories.

Cara and her husband believed that their kids should have their own online space to express themselves. According to Cara, the older girls can edit and upload video themselves. They have a better sense of the Internet, and have gained a more diverse perspective as a result of participating on YouTube. Cara said that their children should receive credit for their creative work. By establishing accounts, Cara and her husband provide a model of digital literacy in which individuals should have their own online sites and receive public credit for the work they create, even at a young age. Kids may ultimately accept or reject these parental techno-savvy philosophies, but they are nevertheless potential models of future media creation. Despite the U.S. penchant for receiving individual credit, the kid video makers whom I interviewed elected to have shared accounts in which video making activities were more fluid rather than called out as the work of single creators.

Cara's children were not permitted to send private messages to others on YouTube, and they were not allowed to comment on videos unless Cara knew the person with whom they were communicating. In addition, Cara controlled the images on her children's accounts and avoided imagery that might attract undesirable viewers. For instance, she told me that seeing unsavory comments about feet in other people's videos made her reluctant to photograph her children's feet, lest these images attract fetishists who would make disturbing requests in her kids' video comments. She displays a digital literacy gained through experience that certain sites present unwelcome participatory complications. In terms of commentary on her own channel, Cara felt that she did not want to practice censorship and would leave negative critiques on her videos. She said that YouTube should be an "open forum" where people express opinions. Nevertheless, she exhibited limits that influenced the type of family content she was willing to share on YouTube.

Even though Cara and her husband set up accounts for their children, Cara felt it was important to know their passwords. Cara moderated comments left on her children's accounts and carefully removed spam, profanity, and overly harsh comments. For example, one of her 10-year-old daughters posted a video in which she talked about having broken her wrist. Cara said the video received many responses from other people who had broken a bone and wished to talk about it. However, the commentary sometimes became excessively harsh, with one person accusing her of being "high," as in, under the influence of drugs such as pain medication. Cara, who had filmed her daughter for this video, said she deleted many of these comments and told me she would never record or share videos of her daughter in a "state" like that.

Chapter 6 explores how Cara's perspective differed greatly from that of another parent who, in the popular video known as *David After Dentist*, recorded his son acting in (sometimes discomfortingly) comical ways after being given medication for a dental procedure.

Perspectives differ with regard to advertising, and some parents may not be aware of how YouTube is using their kids' images for advertising purposes. For example, when I asked Cara how she felt about advertisements, such as the donut ad posted to one of their videos, she told me she was not aware of them and had not yet formed an opinion. At the time of the interview, Cara was not a YouTube partner, and our conversation took place before YouTube eventually announced that participants could share advertising revenue on single videos, as well as on all videos made by partners. That she did not know that advertising was placed on one of her videos is not surprising. YouTube sometimes changed policies and procedures without warning to participants. One could come back to the site after a week's absence and see significant changes. For example, even though I was not a partner, I once saw an advertisement added—without my permission or knowledge—to a video that I had uploaded on an early YouTube account I established. The reason may have been that the video contained music that had previously been approved but was later removed from YouTube's music catalogue for adding music to one's videos. Advertisements might be placed on videos even if a person was not an official YouTube partner.

In contrast to videos of past eras that displayed an ideal family aura, Cara's videos contain moments of more "realistic" and less flattering portrayals of hanging out at home. However, none of the videos challenged the family as an appropriate and loving social unit. For example, in one video, Cara provides a "shout out" or greeting card to mothers on mother's day. Cara greets mothers while being video recorded on a beach. She addresses the camera directly and says, "To all the moms. I hope you have very little of this…" The image cuts to her young daughter, who is lying on the floor crying. Next, Cara wishes that mothers will have "a whole lot of this…" and the image next cuts to Cara holding the same little girl up close, cheek to cheek. Cara smushes her lips up to her child's cheek and kisses her as both Cara and her daughter giggle in delight. Unhappiness was temporary and resolved in a close and affectionate mother-daughter bond.

Several commenters called the video "cute" and "funny." One commenter requested that she post more tantrum videos, while others wished her a happy mother's day. Although the video contains scenes of priceless mother-daughter bonding, it also shows a child crying in a way that all parents will likely recognize. Holland (1991) argues that in past media making, only smiles and not tears appeared in the family photo album of best moments. Yet here, viewers accept and encourage the posting of videos that show ordinary scenes of family life that are less than pleasant or even stressful for parents and children. In showing these videos publicly, Cara provides a model of digital literacy to her children that videos depicting private moments of unhappiness and momentary stress are acceptable forms of public, online content.

From an early age, Cara's children were exposed to several important literacies and media ideologies that included having an online space in which they could express themselves and receive public credit for their work. Their parents maintained their accounts and limited their message exchange to people whom Cara and her husband knew. Cara's kids were shown that identities are partially negotiated through the sharing of media. These included identities of motherhood, being a friend, projecting both difficult as well as fun life moments, and performing technical affiliation to certain video making practices such as joining a site early and disclosing technical interests. Like Cara, the moms in my study took up the cameras in ways that depicted their status as mothers and as media makers with their own talents, expertise, and technical affiliations. In many cases, the choice of having an account at an early age, expressing the self through video, and participating on YouTube were presented to children as models of appropriate technologically inflected forms of interaction.

Technologized Images

Many videos on YouTube depict people interacting with technological products and services (Strangelove 2010). Often these videos contain performances of technical affiliation that exhibit a person's preferences, tastes, and technological expertise. YouTube contains many technical sub-genres as well. For example, typing in the search term "playing with web cam" yielded over 5,000 results. One must always take YouTube's search numbers with a grain of salt; even casual inspection on the first couple of search result pages shows several repeated videos that YouTube administrators may have wished to promote. Nevertheless, such a high number shows that many people enjoy posting and viewing technical experimentation with devices and media.

In one video, Cara experiments with various special effects on her new web cam. Cara is seated in a head and shoulder shot, as she tries out effects such as mirror images, distorted "fun house mirror" images of her face, superimposed graphics such as stars and tigers, psychedelic colors, playful framings of her face on a playing card, and a grid of her face repeated 16 times with several different facial expressions—an effect that she says is her favorite. Throughout the video she is making silly faces, rotating her head, or waving at the camera.

As mentioned in prior chapters, identities of relational expertise are negotiated not only through actions that are displayed in a video as the person interacts with a particular technology, but also in terms of how a video maker responds to comments and questions. Several commenters ask about the kind of web cam she uses (questions about video equipment are common on YouTube) and how she created special effects. Cara posts a comment alerting one of the commenters that she posted instructions on their page. The commenter types back that they are still having problems. Cara recommends uninstalling the system, and then reinstalling it. She comments that several people have had problems with this brand of camera.

Exchanges between Cara and the commenters function as asynchronous tutorials that offer tips and suggestions about how to expand one's media creation options. Cara becomes situated as more expert than the viewers who are asking for help. Her video provides a learning opportunity for people interested in knowing more about the technology she uses. A suggestion's usefulness depends upon how it is taken up, but the comment system enables people to perform affiliations to technologies and negotiate relative forms of expertise. People can post videos or answer questions in comments in ways that demonstrate their knowledge, expertise, and critique of particular technologies. In this case, the exchange shows a mother figure (as indexed in her other familial videos) not only using technology, but providing expertise and instructing other YouTubers on manipulating special effects.

A popular question among YouTubers is "what kind of camera do you use?" It is as if the camera becomes a talisman or quick route to improvement. Questions about equipment are often asked of YouTubers whom viewers think make interesting or successful videos. Kids and youth often appear in videos explaining equipment details. For example, in another account, two girls make videos about technology with their father, who is referred to here as Nick (a researcher-assigned pseudonym). As discussed in detail below, much of their oeuvre concentrates on having family fun, often by enacting pranks on each other.

Nick runs the family account, which he describes on his channel page as a "family site that teaches family values in a funny and entertaining way and shows how a happy family functions on a day to day basis." In his ethnographic interview, he said that he had a prior account on YouTube in which he played a crime boss character. Later, he became inspired by another family on YouTube who ran a family channel, and began making videos with his girls. In stating that the account "teaches" family values, he consciously characterizes his videos as providing learning opportunities for viewers.

On their joint account, which contains over three hundred videos that were posted since joining YouTube in 2007, Nick provides information on how to get started in the entertainment industry. Providing pre-professional information attempts to position this account as relatively more professional than people who know less than Nick about the entertainment business. It is information that targets far broader audiences than their family. Nick is a YouTube partner and his family's videos receive tens of thousands of views. Their top nine videos, each of which contain material on teen singing sensation Justin Bieber, have received more than one million views each. Incorporating material on famous celebrities, as well as holding contests and encouraging viewers to comment and send in video responses, are all tactics that Nick and his family use to address a wide audience and entice viewers to interact with their site.

Nick emphasizes that although his daughters are relatively young (they appear to be under 15 during the time of his interview), they are all participating together in a fun and safe way on a public family channel with comments moderated by Nick. Having worked in areas such as law enforcement, public education, and online businesses, he lists interests such as camping, ham radio, fixing electronic devices, and video editing. By listing technically oriented interests on his page, Nick is performing technical affiliation to particular kinds of devices and communities of interest. These public statements also make a bid to craft a technologized, public identity that includes specific forms of technical knowledge. His bid is only successfully ratified insofar as individual viewers believe these interests are appropriately "technical."

Although the family focuses on having fun and pranking, in a few videos the girls describe or interact with computers, or display their musical and video equipment. In one video, the older daughter Trina (a researcher-assigned pseudonym) watches a video in which a girl performs her version of the "Numa Numa dance." This refers to a famous YouTube video called *Numa Numa* which was made by Gary Brolsma. Newsgrounds.com, a website for online video, linked to Brolsma's video in 2004 (Feuer and George 2005). In 2006, Brolsma's video was reposted to YouTube where it received millions of views (Strangelove 2010). In the original video, Brolsma wears head phones, lip synchs and moves animatedly to a Romanian pop song. The video became an Internet sensation with many parodies and references on YouTube and in mainstream, commercial media (Feuer and George 2005; Parpis 2009). Watching a video parody of this song displays Trina as a person attuned to popular Internet content.

In Nick's family's video, the camera is trained on both Trina and the computer screen, on which a video is playing of someone on YouTube dancing to the *Numa Numa* song. Trina is recorded watching this video on the computer, and singing along to it. The camera pans to her fingers at the keyboard as she begins typing. The camera then pans to the screen so that the viewer sees Trina typing and saying to the screen, "you are still good at it," perhaps referring to the person in the video. The content of Nick's video performs technical affiliation to the idea that it is fun to watch YouTube and to post comments to the site. It reinforces the idea that kids participate in online spaces not only by posting their videos but by watching, supporting, and commenting on other people's videos. It is a technologized activity in everyday life.

In prior eras of U.S. home movie making, people were generally not recorded engaging with other media such as watching television or listening to the radio (Chalfen 1987:62). It has often been argued that inexpensive cameras and digital footage now encourage the filming of far more mundane aspects of daily life (Moran 2002). Yet, as Moran explains, technologically deterministic arguments only describe possible affordances. Such abundance of footage still requires cultural and social choices about what to record and why. Simply being able to record someone typing comments on a computer does not guarantee that all families will elect to do this. In fact many do not. Performing technical affiliations to online participatory practices are being called out by Nick's family as activities that are intertwined in everyday life and are well worth the time that it takes to record them.

Aspiring to be a human surveillance camera by recording everything one sees just because footage is cheap was not observed to be a goal for any of the participants whom I interviewed. Just because one *can* record everything one sees does not guarantee that one *will*. Such a view minimizes how the mediated moment of recording personally meaningful experiences is a crucial part of the fun. In this case, showing a girl typing on a computer and participating on YouTube performs technical affiliation to the idea that going online is appropriate family fun.

Two other videos in Nick's oeuvre also perform technical affiliation to the importance of having high-quality equipment when making media. In one video, Nick's younger daughter Megan (a researcher assigned pseudonym) takes the viewer on a tour through their home music studio. Holding a microphone, she walks around the room and points out several devices, including a professional keyboard, just like the ones "they use in concerts," with "they" likely referring to professional musicians. She also points out a studio microphone, an EQ (an equalizer used for improving recorded sound quality), amplifier, green screen (for recording special effects) and computers that are networked so that they can, she explains, "transfer music and video files." The family's performance of technical affiliation to the idea that having proper equipment is important for making successful videos attempts to bolster their reputations as competent video makers and music parody producers.

The girls' performances of material largesse and attention to quality through using proper equipment was not lost on commenters, one of whom said, "6 computers awesome." Other commenters attempted (whether intentional or not) their own bid at relational expertise by making suggestions or criticisms. For instance, one commenter suggested adding padding to the room, and a microphone isolator to improve sound quality. Another commenter asked about the microphone, calling the sound "choppy." In his reply, Nick explained that the batteries were weak but they did not want to do a retake. Performances of technical identity depend in part for their success on how viewers provide uptake in the form of ratification or rejection of particular proposed identities. People making critiques or suggestions to Nick and his family position themselves as having the relative expertise to do so.

In another video, Megan discusses the cameras they use to make videos. She stands in front of a table on which there are at least 8 cameras as well as camera boxes and a computer. This image of a young girl standing in front of a bank of cameras is a performance of technical affiliation to the idea that girls can make media and be involved in the technologized aspects of media production. She mentions that they use a Canon 7D. A super title informs the viewer that the segment they were watching was filmed using an iPod Touch 4G. She also explains that they have three high-definition cameras, which video enthusiasts will understand have superior picture quality to standard definition devices.

On the one hand, this image arguably echoes Zimmerman's (1995) interpretation of past home movies' major function as displays of patriarchal success. Here the "reveal" is not that of a child opening a traditionally gendered gift such as a doll or frilly dress, but is rather a technologized display that includes females' exposure to an abundance of cameras and music equipment. The image suggests that Nick is financially secure enough to provide these cameras for his family.

However, the image differs from past eras in that a girl is depicted mentioning camera names, handling equipment, and briefly explaining their uses. Girls with cameras present an alternative gendered visual model for geeked-out identities. Family videos now casually record girls' mundane activities, which include engagement with technological devices. Recording and posting these videos to YouTube performs technical affiliation to the idea that technically oriented videos are appropriate forms of personally expressive media, and it is appropriate for girls to use these devices.

Families may engage in performances of technical affiliation not only to display knowledge of computers and video but also to exhibit affiliation to other kinds of playful technical milieu, such as gaming. I spoke to another mother, Jane (a researcher-assigned pseudonym) at a YouTube meet-up on the east coast of the United States. We discussed her interest in making videos and participating on YouTube. On her website she mentions that she is an ex-publicist and an ex-soldier. She mentioned during her interview that she was studying to be a nurse. Jane is also the mother of a small seven-year-old boy.

Like many YouTubers, she participates playfully on the site. Although they did not initially understand her interest on YouTube, Jane's husband and mother eventually supported her interest in making videos and participating online. She said she had to persuade her husband that coming to a YouTube gathering to meet "Internet people" would be a good idea. In her interview she did not express interest in professionalizing her media. Jane said that she values the relationships that come from YouTube participation and being able to communicate with people who made videos she enjoyed.

Jane posted a video with her son that is arguably a performance of technical affiliation to gaming cultures. In this three-second video, her son is seated in mostly profile view wearing headphones and looking at a computer screen. Although it is difficult to determine what he is looking at, he says, "Man, what a nub!" The tag words posted to this video—"nub," "noob," "newbie," and "wow" (presumably referencing the online game *World of Warcraft*)—situate it within gaming culture. In my previous ethnographic investigations of online gaming cultures, I observed that people who made certain basic mistakes publicly branded themselves as newcomers, and thus were often referred to as "newbies" or "noobs." According to the Urban Dictionary (2005), a "nub" may be a synonym for "newbie," or may be defined as "One who sucks at a particular video game, they are not new to the game, but possess some [detriment] that prevents them from playing well, no matter how long they practice playing the game." Unlike the new initiate who makes initial mistakes but eventually learns and outgrows this unfortunate status, a "nub" has had plenty of time to learn but persistently makes poor decisions.

This brief video shows a boy criticizing someone he "sees" online for being a "nub." The video depicts a young boy displaying a relational technical identity in which he is more knowledgeable than the irritating "nub" whom he performatively criticizes. Analogous to the technical equivalent of "baby's first steps," which illustrate a child's milestone of learning to walk, the video comically shows a child's early performance of relational technical expertise within a gaming milieu. Whether staged or not, the image visually displays a young child not only interacting with a technological device, but also performing affiliation to the idea that it is appropriate to participate in gaming, to relationally evaluate others, and to participate in ways that do not reveal one to be a "nub" who makes basic mistakes.

Families and children perform technical affiliation in their videos on several levels. They are depicted interacting with specific types and brands of technical devices such as cameras and computers. Videos also depict YouTubers playing with form or creating special effects with new technical tools. The performances help posit a public identity of a competent video maker and online participant who is knowledgeable about the right technologies. In addition, the idea of posting such a video, in which one interacts with technology, is a performance of technical affiliation to the idea that such videos constitute appropriate material for YouTube. Putting up a video displays a digital literacy that they are appropriate content for the site even when the performance is one of a highly mundane, technological intervention such as entering a comment on a computer. Not everyone would agree that such content is worthy of posting or would ratify this as a "digital literacy." Literacies are contextual and negotiated; those who do put up these videos code them as legitimate for display.

Videos with technologized themes often incite viewers to engage in their own performances of technical affiliation through compliments, questions, or technical criticisms. It is often through interactions with commenters that relational bids at expertise are offered, contested, and negotiated. Whether or not a particular performance is successful depends upon how interactants ratify or challenge a performer's bid at demonstrating expertise. Family video making offers one model for how one performs technical affiliations and identities of relational expertise. Technical affiliation can be performed in many ways, but it is often executed in humorous ways that reflect not only aspects of YouTube culture, but also share a joyful spirit of video-mediated play that moves on- and offline.

Comedy Sketches

The comedy sketch videos encountered in my study were very popular on YouTube. They often included funny characters, brief narratives with a comedic punchline, or videos that played with form to create humorous effects. In some cases, the humor of the video relies on understanding prior professional media forms that use specific tropes and communicative strategies. For example, in one comedic video, William (a researcher-assigned pseudonym) uses a "bleep" sound effect when reading a bed time story to his son. It appears as though he is reading him a "naughty" story. William is a father and enthusiastic participant who met other YouTubers in part because he posted videos about losing a younger son to sudden infant death syndrome. His videos about his coping process received an outpouring of support and social connection. William is working on a script for a film and has achieved a certain niche audience with thousands of views for each of his videos.

In the bedtime-story video, William reads his son a story by Dr. Seuss. In editing, William "bleeps out" certain words using the same tonal sound effect that is often used on television to prevent audiences from hearing censored material, such as profanity. Reading a seemingly profanity-laced story to a very young child creates, for some viewers, a comedic effect. Bleeping out innocent words is not novel; it has been done countless times elsewhere on YouTube and in television comedy programs. But executed in the right way, it can strike viewers as amusing. Some called the video "awesome," "cute," "funny," and stated "LMAO" (laughing my ass off). Later, William posted another video which depicts the same scene without the bleeping effect; it is a tender moment between father and son.

The video's text description reveals that he posted the un-manipulated video because his wife was concerned that not everyone would understand the "joke," and might assume that her husband was reading inappropriate material to their son. The description of the non-bleeped version states, "My wife is very nervous that people won't get the joke. The joke, by the way, is that adding a 'beep' can make even Dr. Seuss look naughty. Anyway, here's the beepless one. Still worth watching, because my son's adorable." One can understand why his wife might have been nervous; Chapter 6 illustrates how viewers may respond passionately and critically to material that they feel is not appropriate for children's media making in the home.

Using such humorously juxtaposed images of children and profanity is not limited to YouTube. Just as advanced amateurs include their children in media, so too do professional media makers often involve their children in projects to achieve comedic effects. An example is found in the popular video called *The Landlord*. Although it was reposted to YouTube, it was originally posted on April 17, 2007, to a professionally managed website called funnyordie.com. The website contains short, comedic videos that were created by or feature famous professional actors and comedians. The website was launched by well-known actor Will Ferrell and his frequent collaborator Adam McKay, who is a professional screenwriter, director, and actor.

The Landlord, which stars Ferrell and was co-directed by and featured McKay, received more than 80 million views on funnyordie.com as of July 2013. The video depicts a landlord, played by a two-year-old child, who demands rent money using profanity. She threatens a financially struggling tenant, portrayed by actor Will Ferrell. The child in the video is reportedly Pearl McKay, who is Adam McKay's daughter (Borrelli 2012). She demands her rent, calls Ferrell's character a "bitch" and an "asshole," and threatens to evict him. When he asks her why she needs the money so quickly, she says she needs to get her "drink on" and that she wants "four beers." Little Pearl is barely able to say the lines; her dialogue is displayed in subtitles, most likely to facilitate viewer comprehension. Part of the comedy lies in the fact that as a two-year old, she does not understand her lines' profane content. The film also enacts the classic comedic power inversion in which a father figure in the form of tall actor Will Ferrell expresses vulnerability and cries as he is harassed, ridiculed, and threatened by an adorable, small child in a blue dress with frilly, yellow sleeves.

To see William's bleeped-out bedtime story as a genre particular to You-Tube or to aspiring amateurs ignores a long-standing trend in entertainment genres that involves children in images crafted for comedic effect. Examples have included professionals who have involved their children in their professional media, such as in the situation comedy *The Adventures of Ozzie and Harriet*, which ostensibly depicted aspects of Ozzie and Harriet Nelson's family life. Other examples include television shows that broadcast home made, non-professional videos such as *America's Funniest Home Videos*, or comedy programs such as *Kids Say the Darndest Things*, in which kids were asked questions and provided unintentionally humorous responses.

Involving children in media is not limited to YouTubers but is part of a comedic tradition. Anticipating the kind of content that will be popular in online, attention economies is a form of digital literacy. Striving to be popular in digital media does not necessarily mean inventing approaches novel to the digital or online realms; in fact many successful online works echo or integrate elements from traditional media such as television. Parents on YouTube in my study used their children's images in their personally expressive videos to participate in the public space of YouTube and to have fun; how they chose to participate provided a model to children that their images might be used not only for parental self-expression but also to showcase their parents' ability to manipulate form in technical ways. Some families expressed a sense of humor and bonding by making comedic videos, which helped certain family members display affiliation to technical values, video-mediated forms of learning, and popular online content. Humorous, parentally driven videos also provided models of appropriate digital and participatory literacies to their children as they grew up on camera.

Pranking

Pranking videos are popular on YouTube, and was a preferred genre for several families in my study. Pranking has a long tradition in numerous cultural contexts in the United States. Pranking serves many social and cultural purposes including relieving boredom (Gmelch 2000). Overcoming boredom is also a reason some people cite for watching YouTube videos or playing online in general. Other reasons include: experimenting with temporary inversions of normal power relations (Bakhtin 1994 [1965]; Jorgensen 1984); raising one's social status in the eyes of one's peer group (Jorgensen 1984); exercising creativity and mastery of physical circumstances among people in technical cultures (Peterson 2003); and bonding with others in a cultural or peer group (Peterson 2003).

Pranks on YouTube vary from benign jokes to physically dangerous stunts. Some videos show kids engaging in unflattering behavior. For example, Nalts, who is a very popular YouTuber, enjoys putting kids (and adults) up to pranks in public while he films people's reactions. Nalts is a father with several kids. He is a YouTube partner and talks in his videos about how he enjoys being paid to make videos. As a partner, he receives revenue from advertisements placed on his videos. He also sells related merchandise, such as t-shirts and hats. He is a very early adopter of YouTube, having joined less than two months after the site officially launched.

Nalts's videos receive hundreds of thousands of views, and he has twenty videos that have received tens of millions of views. I observed him at several YouTube meet-ups and in other people's "collab" or collaboration videos in which footage is made by several participants and compiled to transmit personal messages. Clearly, he enjoys participating in the social side of YouTube and has interacted with many of the families discussed in this chapter. For instance, interviewees told me he hosted private get-togethers with families who met and played together just before public YouTube meet-ups. For example, Cara visited Nalts, and told me that as a gag, her family arrived to his house wearing Nalts t-shirts.

Many of Nalts's videos revolve around pranks. One video, which was posted in March 2007, had received a cumulative total of more than 13 million views as of July 2013. In the video, a teenager enters a library with a device that emulates the sound of a person passing gas. People either ignore him, shake their head, or look surprised. In one shot, kids "wave away" (or perhaps try to ward off) a bad "smell." In another shot, the teenager is shown seated, reading *Outlook 2007 for Dummies* (see Figure 6). The teen's "character" in the video is depicted as interested in a Microsoft application called Outlook, which is most often used as an email application and is on the lowest end of the technical spectrum of online interaction. He is learning about it not through hands on-experience (which is a method that is coded as a superior way of learning by many tech-savvy kids) but rather by reading a book from a well-known series targeted to rank novices or "dummies." This character is so dull that he even needs to read a book for dummies about how to use a simple email program. Combined with his socially inappropriate act, this image is a performance of technical affiliation to the idea that this person would rank low on any technical hierarchy. The act of reading such a book adds to the humorous effect of a not-so-bright person who is rude in a library.

The teen moves through the library activating the device while Nalts, who refers to himself as "youtube's oldest 14 year old" films reactions. Unable to control his glee, he giggles while operating the camera. He is not merely filming events as a co-producer of the video, he is experiencing the mediated moment of recording and viewing the action. Recording an action is said to preclude meaningful participation because recording requires detachment and results in inauthentic forms of experience. Sontag (1977) made this argument

Figure 6. A teen pretends to read a book called *Outlook 2007 for Dummies* in one of Nalts's prank videos. Source: Kevin H. Nalty. Screenshot by Patricia G. Lange, February 15, 2011

when referring to tourists who mindlessly take snaps of famous locations without looking at or emotionally experiencing them. But filming something does not always presume detachment. The phenomenology of the mediated moment must be investigated in every case. Nalts' participation represents a deep level of engagement in that he is filming the action, and simultaneously creating and viewing a mediated moment of mirth. Mediated moments of participation, recording, and viewership become collapsed in ways that heighten Nalts's enjoyment of the prank.

In another video, Nalts puts another child (whom he says is a relative) up to picking his nose in public while he films people's reactions. This video, posted on January 2, 2009, had received over 700,000 views as of July 2013. In order to record reactions before people recognize the prank, Nalts positions himself some distance away from the action. This presents a problem for recording sound. For adequate comedic effect, the video requires the sounds of discomforted by-standers. To deal with this, Nalts's video description explains "I had a second camera in [the nose picker's] jacket to pick up his sound. I took the main camera outside or far away, and laughed like a school child." The pranking video thus includes information about how to video record something from far away while capturing adequate sound to be edited in later. The prank video offers a sound tutorial that can be used in far wider applications than pranks. Viewers of the pranking video thus receive tips on how to execute technical effects. Part of the fun results from bonding together with friends and family to execute the pranks on other people. They are all (to different degrees) metaphorically "behind" the camera, in terms of their role in producing the action. Their level of participation differs from that of the people who are unwittingly captured on video as part of the prank.

Among the families discussed in this chapter, Nick and his girls also enjoyed pranking each other and video recording the results. Sometimes Nick pranks the girls. In one video, he throws an object that looks like a spider at them. He has also pretended to be hurt, or to seem to be choking on something. In the choking video, he tells his daughter to get to the phone. However, he quickly revealed that he was just joking, not choking, before she dialed emergency services. In one video, he made a garden hose move like a snake. He wiggled the hose in their path as they were supposedly coming home from school, causing the girls to scream.

The girls also prank each other or their father. In one video, older sister Trina pranks Megan by putting flour in a hair dryer. As the air blows out, so does the flour into Megan's face and hair. Pranks on Nick include putting water in his shoes, removing a ladder while he was on the roof, and pouring water on him from behind. Sometimes the videos feel staged; someone else is obviously in prime position to film the three of them, with the action well-positioned and in frame before the prank occurs. Having suspicions that Nick is "in on" the pranks against him does not necessarily derail the fun, nor does it negate the visual effect of seeing a prank enacted on a father figure by two girls. The visual image transmits a trope of classical power inversion in which a father and authority figure is depicted in a vulnerable state, such as when Nick's face is comically covered in white flour. Conducting pranks is arguably a way of showing affection (Thomas 2002:206) or challenging authority (Thomas 2002:48). Both girls display a performative challenge of authority to Nick, who acts in youthful, playful ways.

The ephemeral visual inversions of power do not appear to challenge the relational, familial hierarchy. Nick is the father and he remains in charge of many aspects of their life, such as managing their YouTube page. As Nick explains, "I promised my kids I would never get angry or yell at them when they prank me unless it is something that is far too wrong but they know better than taking things too far. Once I realize something is most likely a prank I just laugh it off." To say that they know better than to take things "too far" is to underscore the fact that the girls know their boundaries and how much they can push the temporary inversion of power in a brief prank video. Pranking videos are a far cry from the idea of family media in past eras that focused on recording life milestones in ways that emphasize patriarchal emblems of material success (Zimmerman 1995). Comedic pranking videos may invoke authority-figure power inversions, however temporary, that tie into popular online content and attract viewers.

The family pranks led by Nalts and Nick resemble those found in videos seen in other contexts, such as in technical cultures and in popular television shows. For example, in technical groups, such as students at the Massachusetts Institute of Technology (MIT) and other universities, technically oriented students often pranked administration officials in ways that demonstrated imagination and originality (Peterson 2003). When quoting "his" work on the history of pranking, I use the listed author's name of "Peterson." However, astute readers from the MIT community might recognize that the initials of the author (listed as Institute Historian T. F. Peterson), involve the same letters as a famous MIT acronym, which is "I hate this fucking place." It is perhaps not surprising that a book on pranking would include a bibliographic joke.

Long before "hacking" became associated with acts of technical manipulation and prowess on computers and software, it was applied to creative pranks executed in physical spaces (Levy 1984:23). MIT pranks include things like painting the Great Dome building at MIT to look like R2-D2, a robot in the film *Star Wars*, or parking a police car atop the dome. "Peterson" (2003:x) argues that students valued hacks as part of their education, as they taught them "to work productively in teams, to solve engineering problems, and to communicate to the wider world."

At MIT, pranking ethics include injunctions to be "safe," "leave no damage," "do not hack alone (just like swimming)" and "exercise common sense" (Peterson 2003:10). Similarly, Nick and his family provide warnings to be safe. Their videos often contain disclaimers to ward off potential harm resulting from mimicking their pranks. For example, the flour from the hair dryer prank includes a warning to avoid implementing it on someone with wheat allergies. Nick's family's videos share with the hacker spirit an expression of power inversion, as hacks in technical groups can be used on people in authority. The videos also share a sense of whimsy, creativity, and performative play within social limits.

Pranking behavior can also yield learning opportunities and reveal asymmetrical digital literacies between YouTube participants. In one video, a YouTuber whom I will refer to as Ted records what he jokingly calls a "stalking" trip to another YouTuber's house. I will refer to Ted's target using the researcher-assigned pseudonym of Malcolm. Ted and Malcolm had interacted briefly online prior to Ted's "stalking" trip. Ted's wife, Lynn (a researcher-assigned pseudonym), told me that it was quite easy for her husband to find information about Malcolm, although Malcolm's YouTube account does not disclose his full name. By tracing links that Malcolm placed on his YouTube account to his other website, Ted was able to find his real name. He then entered his name into Yahoo! People Search, an online directory (one of many available choices), and located his address. Next he used a mapping website to find directions to his house.

Both in our interview and in the prank video, Lynn expressed reservations about meeting another YouTuber in this way. Although I have observed many YouTubers meet in small, private gatherings, or through organized, public meet-ups, interviewees say that typically messages are exchanged and people agree to meet after interacting online. This pattern of getting to know others online and then meeting offline is a long-standing trajectory of Internet sociality (Kendall 2002; Rheingold 1993). By jokingly referring to his behavior as "stalking," Ted enacts a prank in which the family surprises a YouTuber, and illustrates how he has left quite a bit of information about himself online that is traceable through commonly available online directories and websites.

As Ted's video opens, the family is seated in the car and the camera is trained on them as they drive. Ted says, "Welcome to the first episode of the YouTube stalkers." Lynn laughs, and her husband explains that they are going to Malcolm's house. Later in the video Ted says, "The wife thinks this is a little bit of an inappropriate activity." Lynn goes on to say in the video that if he thinks Malcolm is cool, why not send him a message and ask to "get together and hang out"? In the video on their way to Malcolm's house, Lynn smiles nervously and says she hopes they do not get "arrested." As they park the car, their children are overheard in the back seat asking, "Is this his address?" The kids are participating in an observational way in their dad's techno-driven, pranking behavior.

Near the end of the video, Ted knocks on the door of a house in a wooded area. A woman opens the door and Ted (perhaps nervously) says, "Hi I'm looking for Malcolm." She asks who he is, and he introduces himself. Malcolm eventually comes to the door, and Ted says happily, "Hi we're taking YouTube to a whole new level of inappropriateness." Stepping outside and carefully closing the door behind him, Malcolm seems surprised and cautious, but does not appear to be angry or frightened. He smilingly responds, "Oh my God."

Lynn, who holds the camera, moves to get closer to the door to focus on Malcolm. However, Ted and Lynn never force their way into the private spaces of Malcolm's home; they remain outside his door. Ted explains that, since Malcolm put him in one of his videos, he thought he would do the same. They talk about the video until Malcolm recognizes him from their exchange on YouTube. Malcolm jokes that he looks like "a normal human being" in person, and then asks "How did you ever find this place?" Malcolm's responses influence viewers' interpretations of the video-mediated experience. Perhaps considering where his fellow YouTuber's footage will probably wind up, he never covers the camera lens, retreats into the house, or angrily tells his "visitors" to leave. Malcolm's smiling and joking responses add to the feeling-tone of the mediated moment of the prank; they shape potential future moments of viewership. Had his reaction been angry or upset, the pranked moment might yield altogether different future viewing responses.

Most of the commenters found the video very funny, calling it "cool," "great," and "awesome." Although some viewers questioned the authenticity of Malcolm's surprised reaction, one commenter noted that either way, it was "funny." A few used words like "creepy" and "scary." Perhaps the most extreme negative reaction came from someone who questioned the wisdom of stalking someone that way, recording it for "fun," and bringing their children along to the prank. This viewer mentioned blocking Ted's account and requested that he not watch their videos.

Some viewers who do not participate on YouTube socially, who are not part of technical cultures, or who do not enjoy pranking might view this act quite negatively. Critics quite likely question the appropriateness of bringing children to a prank in which a fellow YouTuber is paid a surprise visit from someone whom they do not know well. In a sense, Ted both enacts and interrupts common stalking fears that many people attribute to the Internet, but which require no high-tech solutions for people with sufficient interest. For example, one high-profile stalking case resulting in the death of a celebrity was facilitated from information that was originally publicly available in local Department of Motor Vehicles offices (Johnson 1995). Ted enacts aspects of a common Internet stalking fear by surprising Malcolm using publicly available information, but interrupts it by having fun rather than causing harm.

Through the prank, Ted shows Malcolm the ease with which it is possible to locate someone on the basis of information they share online. He reveals a crucial digital literacy that involves understanding the ramifications of leaving intentional or inadvertent digital traces. However, even the most cautious online participants are finding it increasingly difficult to maintain privacy as social network and other sites freely circulate personal information—with or without participants' knowledge—for profit to third parties (Leavitt 2011).

In technical cultures, pranking is often about control over a technology, and pranks often demonstrate "an ability to play with the ways in which that technology mediates human relationships" (Thomas 2002:48). Ted demonstrated to Malcolm that he had the technical skills to control technologies of information and track someone down on the Internet in ways that many people are still not aware of. His prank was a performance of relative technical ability; he showed that he knew more about how information is disseminated online than did Malcolm.

During her interview, Lynn said that the video was genuine and that Malcolm was kind of "freaked out" because he and his wife believed that it would be difficult for people to discover where they lived. Lynn said that many YouTube participants do not really understand how much information is now available online that links people back to personal information such as their home address. Lynn explained that afterwards, her husband told Malcolm how he uncovered his personal information and discussed ways to remove sensitive information. Ted interacted with Malcolm in a technologically inflected way. Ted's actions were consistent with those of hacker cultures that espouse the notion that if information is available, it should be used. If someone exposes themselves to vulnerability, that person should be made to understand the consequences of their choices. Like the pranksters at MIT who leave detailed instructions for the maintenance crew to dismantle their pranks, so too did Ted reportedly work with Malcolm to understand his online identity-sharing practices. Lynn says that they became friends, which is not necessarily surprising. "Affection through mayhem" is often one way that males signal affection for one another (Rotundo 1998; Thomas 2002:206).

From a certain perspective, the video can be read as a clever hack. A technical vulnerability is exposed by a person who performs technical affiliation to the idea that such a technically inflected act is funny, and that one should expose vulnerabilities and educate others to avoid more serious problems resulting from one's indiscriminate digital footprint. In the phenomenology of the mediated moment of having fun through a video-mediated prank, a (perhaps discomforting) learning opportunity is born. It is not only Malcolm, or YouTube viewers, but Ted's kids along for the ride who receive this education. Learning opportunities emerge from the technical affiliations and identity proposals that are crafted by participants in an imagined community (Anderson 1985) of YouTubers who often share a similar sense of transgressive humor.

Growing up on Video

Although kids and teens in my study generally reported making media with friends or on their own, families with young children connected with other video-making families in technologically inflected ways. Many parents on YouTube were media enthusiasts who enjoyed recording everyday events tinged with comedy and whimsy. Finding a sense of acceptance, fun, and creativity on YouTube, families created learning opportunities when they dealt with the technical aspects of making videos, crafting appropriate online content, and discussing crucial digital literacies, such as how personal information is shared online.

Past studies that have been critical of patriarchally driven home media often miss the warmth and sense of fun that some families experience when they involve their kids in their personally expressive media. Not only fathers, but mothers are taking up the camera. Moms are sharing their perspective not only on what it means to be a mother, but also to display technical identities and to explore commercialization opportunities on YouTube. People may play with technology for fun while simultaneously showcasing affiliations to technologies and techno-cultural values and practices.

Many of the kids mentioned in this chapter are growing up in families that highly value video-mediated lifestyles and frequently record small moments in everyday life. Family members learn about making media together, and kids receive models for making appropriate media and achieving digital literacies. The case studies demonstrate parents' willingness to record mundane, technologized interactions such as entering comments on a computer, playing games, and manipulating cameras and special effects. Cameras and footage may be cheap to obtain, but parents are choosing to record specific kinds of technically inflected practices that reveal significant identity work. Kids may ultimately accept or reject their parents' models for making videos and crafting technologized identities; either way they are introduced to technical identity practices and digital literacies. The next chapter analyzes how recording personally expressive media in the home triggered passionate debates about appropriate mediated interaction and public video sharing.

Many subsequent generations of "digital youth" will grow up with parents who themselves grew up with technology and who impart particular cultural values and technical affiliations. Researchers should consider to what extent families, like individuals, have mediated centers of gravity, and how these dispositions influence informal learning. Families oriented toward gaming, for example, may have different learning styles and technical identity inflection points in comparison to the YouTube families profiled here. Researchers should devote energy to cross-cultural family comparisons in which different parents exhibit asymmetrical abilities with regards to technology and media.

This book argues that technical affiliations and identities should be considered as variables in their own right. They cannot be read from any other traditional variable, including gender or class. For example, even though technology has long been coded as a male activity, many moms whom I spoke with were highly influential and technically competent media makers. Further, as noted in Chapter 2, not all males automatically achieve the same level of technical expertise. Certainly, any unfortunate interactions between variables (such as whether or not low-income families struggle to gain technological advantages) should be rigorously studied. But technical identifications are not isomorphic to any identity variable, including income. Many girls in the study talked about financial difficulties, as discussed in Chapter 3, and yet they displayed strong affiliations to specific techno-values and practices. As digital youth grow up, many will have children and impart their own techno-cultural values and practices to future generations. Family media making will thus always provide a fascinating and worthy locus of study for understanding informal learning about media and technology, including (and perhaps especially) for those kids who fiercely espouse an ideology of being "self-taught."

CHAPTER 6

‹‹‹◄ ■ ►›››

Representational Ideologies

Try the following thought experiment. Describe your life without mentioning anyone you know. Now imagine making a video that illustrates who you are but never depicts family, friends, neighbors, coworkers, teachers, schoolmates, fellow commuters, or anyone else with whom you come in contact. Personally expressive media involves using words or images to share the self. But it is hardly possible to accomplish autobiography without involving biographies of other people (Henwood et al. 2001). Media makers commonly incorporate the stories of people whom they know and love in order to work through problems, express the self creatively, and experience and enjoy a shared life cycle. Once a person begins to depict or even describe other people, they have entered a zone of representation.

For many years, professional image makers, anthropologists, journalists, and others have struggled with how to represent people in media, and what role subjects should have in a representation's creation (Gross et al. 1988, 2003; Gubrium and Harper 2013). It has been an especially important question for anthropologists (Lutkehaus and Cool 1999; Ruby 1991), whose goal is to represent other people in words and images to provide insight about the human condition. Given that video is easy to distribute globally, image makers of many different varieties, experiences, and abilities are dealing with these thorny questions, sometimes in full view of other people who have their own contested, tacit, and shifting ideas about representational media.

This chapter explores learning opportunities on YouTube that appeared within the context of negotiating representational ideologies, or ideas about what constitutes appropriate ways to record and share human images. It describes how both kids and adults negotiated digital literacies regarding human representation. In some cases, adults felt very comfortable distributing an array of highly personal images, whereas several kids were more circumspect about how their images should be shared online.

On YouTube and other video sharing sites, video makers are faced with many choices along the representational chain of mediation. They must choose whether and how to record, edit, distribute, or delete particular images, in consideration of their own or others' wishes. Sometimes, people new to making media have not yet established practical rules. Writing about the challenges of representation in visual anthropology and documentary, Ruby (2000:138) argued that if people had ready-made and glib answers to the question of how people should represent others, they were probably not to be "trusted." In other words, these issues require ongoing negotiation and sensitivities to particular circumstances and individual needs.

In a world where images proliferate, the stakes of making personal media are high. That images remain online with the potential to circulate indefinitely presents problems. People often fear the "nightmare reader" (Marwick and boyd 2011:125-126) or unintended viewer such as a relative, teacher, or employer who exercises judgments that may negatively impact one's future. Images may be downloaded and shared in ways that damage personal reputations, as several amateur and professional celebrities have discovered (Associated Press 2007; Feuer and George 2005).

This chapter discusses tensions that arose when kids whom I interviewed represented themselves online or participated in other people's media. The discussion is intended to be a co-productive exercise between the author, readers, video-makers, and viewers in ways that invite personal reflexivity and critical attitudes about video-making practices, especially in terms of interpersonal mediated boundaries and acceptable uses of human images. The goal is not to adjudicate between participants but rather to "conscientise" (Kuhn 1995:9) or make visible certain representational ideologies and their moral underpinnings. The vignettes in this chapter may function as "triggers" that arouse emotional feelings about media, and invite readers and media makers to collaborate and discuss appropriate forms of media in their own image-creation and representational contexts (Fisch 1972; Gubrium and Harper 2013). Underlying beliefs may tacitly inform interactions during a mediated moment, but may not be well understood as representational ideologies by media makers, image subjects, and viewers. This chapter aims to facilitate direct and ongoing discussion about how human images are created and distributed in emotionally charged, public contexts.

The Phenomenological Roots of Representational Ideologies

The concept of representational ideologies emerges from a tradition of scholarly reflection on how beliefs about communication and media intertwine with behavioral norms and values in a social group. In this context, ideologies are sets of beliefs that motivate action and promote particular socio-cultural hierarchies. Representational ideologies draw from the concept of media ideologies (Gershon 2010a), a term that owes its legacy to scholarship on linguistic and semiotic ideologies. Language ideologies "envision and enact ties of language to identity, to aesthetics, to morality, and to epistemology" (Woolard 1998:3). Irvine (1989:255) characterized language ideology as, "the cultural system of ideas about social and linguistic relationships, together with their loading of moral and political interests." In other words, ways of speaking have deeply normative, moral associations about what is considered right or wrong for members of particular cultural groups.

Keane (2003:419) introduced the concept of "semiotic ideologies," which involve "basic assumptions about what signs are and how they function in the world." Keane (2003:419) argued that different "ontologies (what is 'natural'?) underwrite different sets of possible signs." Semiotic ideologies inform the possible kinds of "agentive subjects and acted-upon objects" that are observed in the world. Drawing on these traditions, Gershon (2010b:283) argued that it is important to understand the underlying sets of ideas that people use, both overtly and tacitly, to communicate through a range of media. According to Gershon (2010a:3), "media ideologies are a set of beliefs about communicative technologies with which users and designers explain perceived media structure and meaning." Gershon investigated how people accomplished publicly mediated forms of ending a romantic relationship. She explored how particular choices (such as breaking up in person or changing one's relationship status on the social network site of Facebook) affected the feelings and dignity of the person who did not wish to end the relationship. Focusing on media ideologies reveals particular concerns that shape perceptions about socially appropriate uses of media, as well as who has the agency to communicate across them.

Extending this line of thinking, this chapter investigates tacit representational ideologies, which may be defined as sets of beliefs that creators, participants, and viewers use to interpret the ontology, structure, and meaning of human images, including their normative uses, appropriateness, moral basis, and consequences. Whether articulated or not, representational ideologies underlie appropriate interpersonal interactions through media. They contain moral assumptions about media agency, in terms of who has the right to record and share an image.

Producing media is loaded with moral assumptions about what it means to be a mediated person. Adults and kids hold a wide variety of views about appropriate image creation and use. In describing linguistic ideologies, Silverstein (1979:193) argued that they were sets of beliefs that users *articulated* to rationalize or justify certain linguistic usages. This characterization assumes an ability to communicate ideologies. My study found that people were not always able to articulate or even know what their representational ideologies might be, especially since many media makers were experimenting with video or had not yet encountered certain problems prior to participating on YouTube or their own websites. It was when human images transgressed moral boundaries that ideological parameters were often revealed and contested.

Speaking with regard to professional image-making, Ruby (2000:141) once noted that morality underpins the production and distribution of any human image. He argued that different phenomenological positions of mediated processes demanded particular moral obligations that should be respected. First, creators have a moral obligation to themselves, to make the personally self-actualizing and authentic media they wish to make. Second, a media creator has a moral obligation to respect the dignity and rights of the people who are represented, described, or analyzed in media. Third, human image representation should also have some benefit to viewers, such as providing education or entertainment. Other obligations might be targeted toward media sponsors or entities that paid for or otherwise facilitated media creation or distribution.

This chapter is concerned with exploring interpersonal obligations and how people respond when they perceive that media makers have failed to honor them. Key questions include: What are people's ideologies with regard to representing human beings in personally expressive media? How do interactive experiences of making media reveal appropriate representational ideologies? How are representational ideologies contested and resolved? What happens when honoring the moral obligations to one person or entity means ignoring the needs of another? How do mediated interactions teach others about such ideologies? Making media can be challenging, especially when honoring one's intentions may result in moral conflicts at different points along the experiential chain of mediated moments.

Caught on Video: Having Fun and Playing on YouTube

Scholarly conceptions of play have characterized it as a voluntary activity that is "fun," and occurs within its own limits in time and space. It happens in certain spaces, and time has a different kind of duration. People become "absorbed" in a kind of "magic circle" of activity that "is never imposed by physical necessity or moral duty" (Huizinga 1949:8). Play can be "enchanting" and "captivating" in ways that lie outside the normal moral duties, tasks, and chores of everyday life. In this sense, having fun and playing with a camera can present special challenges in that it is difficult for some people to take into account all the ramifications of particular media, when one is absorbed in the activity of creating the media, including attending to its technical parameters and interpersonal focus. Considering an image's potential future impact is not impossible but often becomes difficult as one engages in fun and play.

Sometimes the experiential moment of fun for one party is not fun for someone else. Videos on YouTube sometimes depict unflattering behavior. For instance, some parents found it amusing to record a child crying or throwing a tantrum. Not all adult media makers agree that this is appropriate public media content. One participant in a study in the United Kingdom (Buckingham et al. 2011:79) said it was improper to video record a child crying, as the image might harm their future reputation. In a number of YouTube videos posted by adults, children are depicted engaging in behavior such as passing gas or picking their noses. Sometimes a mother can be heard saying or placing text on a video in which a child's nose picking is light-heartedly referred to as "digging for gold." Those who believe these images are amusing for viewers hold a different representational ideology than those who believe they are visually unpleasant or may harm a video subject's future reputation. In the eyes of those who see them as disadvantageous, the video maker has violated the ethical obligations to respect video subjects and to please viewers.

Discourses of "realism" in video laud the recording of everyday activities in spontaneous ways. Such discourses have resulted in a far wider depiction of home life than has been reported in prior eras of home movie making in the United States (Chalfen 1987). Scholars have criticized processes of "patterned elimination" (Chalfen 1987) in which unrealistic idealizations of home and family are created by eliminating unpleasant images and focusing instead on "compulsive smiles," that can yield repressive mediated life histories (Citron 1999; Holland 1991; Kuhn 1995; Zimmerman 1995). Holland (1991:2) states that "the children's party may bring tantrums, but the pictures will show laughter." Holland (1991:2) argues that, in many home movies of past decades, "however untidy or unsatisfactory the experience," the picture will show "appropriate emotions." These criticisms have been especially strong from feminist and Marxist scholars who were concerned with the oppressiveness that patriarchal, family media making could inflict upon mediated subjects, such as kids. In contrast, the videos of many parents with small children on YouTube show a much wider range of family images that are far from ideal and include depictions of highly mundane or even distasteful behavior.

People in my study sometimes became caught up in video play, and did not realize how their video might be interpreted. Later, the video maker might recognize how their recorded behaviors might lead to negative consequences. In interviews, I asked participants if they had ever taken down a video from YouTube. Interviewees such as 18-year-old Crystal (her requested pseudonym) often cited issues of quality and safety as primary reasons for video removals. Crystal, who was introduced in Chapter 3, is a fine arts major in college who enjoys making video blogs and lip synching videos. Having joined YouTube in December 2005, she was an extremely early adapter of the site. She told me that she typically watched her videos as she edited them, and again after she posted them on YouTube. She explained her decision to take down a few videos:

> It's mostly because I feel like it might like um endanger me to like the public like if somebody looked at it and realized I lived on this address or um if I post my video of myself like dancing a little bit like too provocatively, a pervert might like, you know. And I'm worried about stuff like that so I would take those things down. Like this one time I posted a video of myself in a dress and I noticed that it was a little bit too low cut and I had to take it down. It was like in two days I noticed it and I took it down right away.

In this example, Crystal had fun making a dance video. In the phenomenology of the mediated moment of recording, she did not recognize any potential problems. Nor did she see problems when she watched the video during editing and uploading. Upon viewing herself in the video two days later, she removed it, lest it prompt unwanted attention from a "pervert" or someone with inappropriate sexual interest in her. The video took on different meaning during the mediated moments of viewership when it appeared online. In Crystal's representational ideology of herself, it was inappropriate to appear in public dancing in a revealing outfit. The mediated feelings of fun and play that occurred during recording, initial viewing, editing, and distribution were reconsidered during a later moment of viewing, once the video had been posted online within the cultural context of YouTube.

Viewership is a crude category that should be reconceptualized more finely across different moments of experience. The phenomenology of viewing can be divided into the experiences of self-viewing and public viewing. Self-viewing maybe further divided into multiple moments, including initial manipulation of the video (one usually has to watch one's footage during editing) as well as self-viewing after the video is posted within a particular context of viewership. After two days, Crystal decided that the activities she engaged in while having video fun might prompt unwanted viewership from other people. Crystal displayed a representational ideology in which her intention to express herself and have fun did not outweigh her moral obligation to keep herself safe. Different obligations to the mediated self initially conflicted. One obligation was to express a moment of mediated fun; the other goal involved protecting her safety.

Decisions to remove videos were not straightforward for all participants. As discussed in Chapter 3, Lola and her 16-year-old daughter Ashley strengthened their mother-daughter bond by making videos and learning how to participate on YouTube together. Prior to their interviews, I noticed a video in which Ashley "danced for subscribers." Lola explained that she helped with the music in the video, which she felt was appropriate. Lola said that it helped Ashley express her interest and talent in dancing and that her viewers might enjoy it. Lola's representational ideology attended to their project's obligation to honor Ashley's self-expression and facilitate viewers' enjoyment of her talents.

However, the video's unauthorized reposting on a pornographic website prompted Lola to reconsider the video's distribution status.

> *Patricia:*   So that one you felt was safe for content on YouTube?
>
> *Lola:*   Well, I didn't – she was fully clothed and she wasn't doing – I don't think any really suggestive moves and she does love to dance. She studies dance. And, yeah, so I thought um it would be good to get subscribers.
>
>   But when we first had posted that video up, somehow it got linked to a like a porn site so then I was upset about that. My [other] daughter was really upset. My older daughter. And she's like, "Mom, you gotta take that down. You gotta take the video down."
>
>   And I didn't want to take the video down but I did. And then I reposted it a second time but then I disabled the embedding quality so that they couldn't um have it link to any outside web site. Just on that one. The other ones can be embedded.

In considering ethical obligations, Lola struggled with the decision to remove the video. She displays the digital literacy that one can choose to disable embedding functions for future videos. But an additional digital literacy would acknowledge awareness that a video can be re-appropriated even if YouTube's embedding feature is disabled. Many websites enable users to download YouTube videos, allowing the downloader to re-edit and re-post videos without the original video maker's knowledge.

In this case, the rights of the video makers outweighed the obligation to produce media that diverse viewers might enjoy. Lola said that Ashley's sister felt the video should be removed. In an interview, Ashley expressed no particular concern about the video. She said she hoped it would bring additional subscribers. At the time of the research, YouTube subscribers were people who chose to be alerted at no cost when a video maker posted a new video. The idea of "dancing for subscribers," Ashley said, began as a joke. Lola, Ashley, and Ashley's sister expressed different representational ideologies about appropriate YouTube participation for a 16-year-old female. Their attitudes also reflected an ideological hierarchy in which the video makers' rights outweighed that of the corporate entity of YouTube, which would likely benefit from having videos with attractive girls dancing.

The examples of Crystal, Lola, and Ashley all involve a teenager's or adult's conscious use of female representations in an online context. Notably, their opinions and behavior changed during different mediated moments. In the initial playful moments of mediated recording, certain behavior was coded as acceptable. In contrast, during specific mediated moments of viewership and image-appropriation, media makers reconsidered their behavior. But not all participants have the knowledge, world experience, or agency to reflect on how their image is being used online. Reputations are partially forged not only from one's own personally expressive media, but also from the ways in which one is represented in other people's videos.

When people in my study made media for fun, they did not always consider the ramifications of the media's content, and how a child's images may circulate in ways that kids would not understand. For example, in one video, I noticed a mother recording a scene in her living room. As the camera quickly pans across the room, the viewer also happens to see a boy in his underwear watching television. The boy's behavior is most likely a fairly typical one that plays out in homes across the United States. The video's content is not a carefully crafted image of repressive smiles, but reflects a discourse of realism in which the casual moments of life are coded as acceptable to capture on camera and to distribute publicly. I queried the mother about this image choice. Even though the camera does not linger on the boy (whom I surmise to be somewhere between 3 and 5 years old), I was concerned about seeing his public depiction in a state of partial undress. She explained her point of view about this topic in an interview with me:

> When you first start out, I didn't really think that much of it, you know because they were little. It was kind of like okay; babies walk around naked on the beach. You know, stuff like that. It's not that big of a deal, or in diapers, you know?

> Now, I wouldn't do it, um but no one's ever commented on that, really. Well, they might [have], but nothing that's really like come up as a negative thing. I'd have to go back and look at the comments and see if there's actually any specific comments about it. Um, so there's nothing really that's flagged me to be like oh, I should take this down.

> And he's in there so briefly, and there's nothing tagged about it, like there's no tags like "little boy in underwear" or anything that would cause creepy people to search for that and find it in that way.

In this example, the mother explained that when she first started out, she did not think about such images' interpretations or impact. Indeed, the children's very young age at the time of recording situated them in a cultural context that accepts a different standard of public presentation and dress than those of older children or teenagers. In many cultural groups in U.S. culture, very young children routinely appear in public in diapers. Part of the explanation also involves being caught up in a mediated moment of fun in which the mother did not necessarily consider the future impact of a fleeting moment in her video.

This mother believed that the representation of her son had not violated her moral obligation to him, or to her viewers. No viewer called out the video as problematic. She noted that the image went by quickly, and she had not provided tags or keywords that would attract unwanted attention to the image through search techniques. Of course, it is a type of digital literacy to understand that people can access the video in other ways, as happened to Lola and Ashley. If someone downloads the video on an external website, the downloader could then add tags that attracted unwanted attention. Since such a procedure might happen off of YouTube, the video makers may never learn about these undesirable uses of their children's image. Not all "participants" in media understand the ramifications of their involvement. In this case, a very young boy was focused attentionally elsewhere and may not have realized he was being recorded. Even if he knew he was being recorded, at such a young age, he would not likely understand the ramifications of his image circulating online, potentially in perpetuity.

On the one hand, it might be argued that as generations of children grow up "online," in publicly mediated ways, the benchmark of what is considered a normal mediated representation may change for some cultural groups. In the past, teenagers might have had to suffer while a romantic date viewed the baby pictures that a parent proudly trotted out in family photo albums. In the future, a teen's boyfriend or girlfriend may have seen these images online long before prom night. If most people in a particular cohort experience these practices, then people in that cultural group may have similar "embarrassing" baby pictures on the web.

On the other hand, not all socio-cultural groups may embrace these practices as appropriate norms. Children growing up in more publicly mediated or unfortunate ways could be coded by future employers as not fit for particular occupations and activities that would require stricter representational ideologies and standards. Kids who grow up in families that are more protective of their children's images may have socio-economic advantages in comparison to parents who display their children in their underwear, picking their nose, or exhibiting unflattering behavior.

Contemporary discourses about media realism argue that the repressive smiles of past home image making should be replaced by depictions that show life in its untidy and imperfect reality. But these discourses vary with regard to appropriate parameters of realism. It is important to consider the potential consequences for broadcasting casual moments of everyday life. In some cases kids and teens can reflect on their own behavior and decide how their image may be used. Yet, younger kids may not understand these ramifications. Notably, much of the media discussed above were adult-motivated. The tensions between viewers, and within media makers themselves at different points of experience, demonstrate that advanced age does not guarantee that everyone will agree on standards of image appropriateness. Nor do all adults carefully consider the consequences of how their children's video-mediated representations will be used or interpreted.

Altered States

Kids on YouTube were sometimes depicted in altered physical states, such as on pain medication or using drugs such as alcohol. In some cases, these depictions were meant to reflect reality; the child really was on medication. In other cases, the depictions were pretend, and were used to comedic effect. Parents in my study disagreed about the appropriateness of publicly depicting kids in altered states for entertainment or commercial benefit.

Cara, a mother of four, maintained a representational ideology in which it was unacceptable to record her child on pain medication. In a video in which her daughter discussed breaking her wrist, some commenters accused her of being "high" on drugs. She had not taken drugs, and Cara said she would never film her children in a "state" like that. Cara's perspective clearly differed from those of other parents on YouTube. In a well-known and widely circulated YouTube video called *David After Dentist*, a young boy is filmed by his father while on pain medication. In this video, seven-year-old David is filmed while in the back seat of a car in the parking lot of a dentist's office, where he had just had a tooth removed.

In the video description, David's father, David DeVore (hereafter referred to as DeVore), explained that he took the video to show his wife (who could not accompany them) that their son was fine. He also wanted to reassure David about his recovery. At first DeVore circulated the video to only family and friends. Later, the video was posted publicly on YouTube for convenient sharing, and thus is an example of how a home mode video might eventually be seen by millions of people. On his website, DeVore stated, "I chose to make it public thinking no one would think it would be as funny as we did. Shows you what I know!" The practical reality is that sending video files in private ways is still difficult, and YouTube became popular because it facilitated the sharing of higher bandwidth media such as videos. Of course, people might deliberately post funny home footage in the hopes of attracting commercialized attention. According to the family's *David After Dentist* website, David's family first wondered if David was being mocked, but elected to leave the video up when they decided that viewers seemed to feel it was "cute" and "funny."

The choice to show David on medication after a medical procedure represents a dramatic departure from Chalfen's (1987) description of home mode media in the United States. David is depicted on medication at a moment in life that is not coded as an important milestone or a source of personal progress. David's speech is slow and his head moves around as if he is dizzy. He asks his father, "Is this real life?" This is a humorous quote given that he was on pain medication and the video is posted to YouTube. This quote has added to the video's enormous popularity. At one point David begins to lift himself up from his car seat and screams in a rather primal way. He asks about his stitches, states that he feels "funny," and asks why this is happening to him. His father explains that it is the "medication" (that is affecting him this way). In terms of consent, some viewers may see the video as problematic in that it not only publicly distributes a video containing the image of a child who most likely does not understand the ramifications of this choice, but he is also on medication, an altered state of consciousness that shows him in a vulnerable state.

Posted on January 30, 2009, the video had received more than 120 million views, 21 video responses, and more than 120,000 text comments as of July 2013. It has been parodied in numerous ways. For example, it was spoofed on a popular YouTube channel called *The Annoying Orange* and by Chad Vader (a YouTube character dressed in a Darth Vader costume resembling the evil overlord in the film *Star Wars*). It has also been parodied by the teen-aged pop singer Justin Bieber (who himself was reportedly discovered on YouTube). On September 28, 2010, it was referenced by a character on *Glee*, a U.S. television show about high school show choirs. Upon awakening from a dream sequence in the dentist's chair, the character of Rachel asks, "Is this real life?" in a widely recognized quotation of the *David After Dentist* video (Donnelly 2010).

The text comments posted to the video include indexes of laughter at how funny his behavior is, expressions of empathy as people recalled their own dental experiences, comparisons to its parodies, and remarks about the irony of David asking confusedly "Is this going to be forever?" in a video on YouTube. Although the anesthesia's effects will wear away, his representation is in a video that is online, and could be circulated indefinitely. On the day that I watched it, the video had a pre-roll advertisement before the video began and an advertisement on the right side of the video from an insurance company.

Over the top of the video was a personalized banner, which indicated the account's partnership status (meaning that the owner of the account was sharing advertising revenues with YouTube). The video also included information about where to buy t-shirts and stickers related to the video.

The family, who received criticism for this video, has reportedly earned "in the low six figures" from both the video and related merchandising (Horowitz 2010). DeVore is quoted in the press as saying, "We said we will make a family adventure out of this and see what happens. Nothing has happened that we felt uncomfortable doing" (Horowitz 2010). Although using kids' images for profit has been a regular pattern in entertainment industries, platforms such as YouTube enable a wider array of media makers to amass such kid-driven revenue. For a select few, earning six figures on a grass roots video is significant income and may be deeply valuable for a family with children in an uncertain economy. Discourses of realism might argue that such moments are a part of everyday life and are to be acknowledged rather than hidden.

In some cases, kids' or teens' images are used to depict them in mock states of altered consciousness, as a kind of joke. But the question becomes, at what age or within what cultural contexts do comedy videos by amateurs or professionals make it difficult to know if a behavior is just a gag or real? What consequences might those videos have, either way? Teenagers are told that pretending to be drunk on one's social network page, or being "tagged" or identified in pictures in real or faked scenarios of inebriation or other undesirable states could have serious consequences for them. In a real-world example, a student named Stacy Snyder was reportedly denied a teaching certificate in part because of social media imagery she posted (Mayer-Schönberger 2009). Wearing a pirate hat and holding a cup, she appeared in a photograph with the caption, "drunken pirate." Such images reach an unacceptable limit of playfulness when "nightmare viewers" such as school admissions committees or potential future employers find them and make negative judgments (Marwick and boyd 2011).

Viewers encountering a video for the first time may interpret it in numerous ways, as reality or fiction depending upon the viewers' social distance to the video's subject and creators. Drawing on Meunier's phenomenology of cinematic identification, Sobchack (1999) argues that works can be interpreted as different genres depending upon a viewer's prior experience and relationship to the video subject. For example, a potential employer who sees a work of fiction (say, teenagers pretending to be drunk), and who has no knowledge of the video's context or personal character of those involved, may believe that they are seeing personal documentary. Whether or not the behavior actually happened, they may read into the video a "truth" of the teenager's situation, which includes a willingness to post real or fictional drunken images of themselves. The same fictional video can be consumed as a funny home movie parody by friends and as a documentary by others.

Popular discourses often stress the fact that kids are not always aware of the ramifications of circulating their images. In fact, not all adults are aware of what will happen when they post a video. In some cases, it is a particular event that brings into awareness unforeseen consequences that occurred when media left the "magic circles" (Huizinga 1949) of recording and initial manipulation. People whom I interviewed found that publicly posting videos could lead to misappropriations, critiques, and judgments about one's moral decisions in making and distributing media that contained kids' images. Parents did not always agree that states such as being on medication exhibited appropriate representational ideologies for children. Posting such videos often resulted in comments and debates through which standards, norms, and contingent representational ideologies were explored, sometimes in strongly emotional terms.

Everyday Media Skirmishes

People often record videos as a way of interacting with the video's subjects. The intention is not only to record something for the future; it is about experiencing the present through a camera. In many cases the fact that a moment is being mediated often codes the people or activity as having the status of being worth recording (Holland 1991). Individual mediated moments take on heightened emotion and may become more fun—or more stressful—because someone is recording it.

Videos depict only a small moment in time, and reflect only a part of what it means to record someone's image. What happens behind the scenes in terms of how participants negotiate a video into being does not always appear in a final video. Viewers are not necessarily made privy to the moments in which people resist or reluctantly participate in the active shaping of media. Sometimes people engage in everyday media skirmishes in which friends or loved ones disagree about the appropriateness of recording or distributing media. One person might wish to record someone, and the subject might express reluctance or outright opposition. Many of us have been annoyed when a cranky relative staunchly refuses to be photographed at a wedding or birthday celebration. Conversely, we may have felt irritated when a predatory family photographer or friend insists on taking our picture even when we do not wish to be photographed.

When image creators and subjects are not in alignment, an argument or media skirmish may ensue in pursuit of a mediated image. How these everyday conflicts are negotiated and resolved often reveals tacit representational ideologies about who has the right to make and distribute human images, and for what purpose. Disclosing these negotiations on camera becomes one way to enact discourses of realism which acknowledge that making media is not always smooth. However, displaying these negotiations and resistances directly in a video opens media makers up to public judgment and critique when representational ideologies collide.

Feminist studies that critiqued the oppressiveness of patriarchal media making to document material success often ignored a mediated subjects' participatory role (Sontag 1977; Zimmerman 1995). In critiquing the oppressiveness of male authorities in home media, such scholarship risks reifying a one-way trajectory of empowerment that does not reflect all media subjects' participatory experiences. Yet, participants' responses, protestations, or even challenging looks to the camera are important forms of agency during these mediated moments.

Sometimes people are coaxed into creating an image that is intended to give people joy and contribute to a family's shared legacy. As a child, I can remember scowling at many a picture reluctantly taken of me. Later, I began helping to shape my mediated image by smiling for pictures that I knew were destined for the family album. People's response to their own image may change during different mediated moments of recording and viewing, and they may regret not having media that documents their childhood histories.

On the other hand, some people may smile for the camera and participate even though they are inwardly reluctant to be recorded. The video may appear to be fun for all, but actually contain disturbing oppressions and silencing that will not encounter criticism when posted online. For all of our claims to postmodern sophistication at knowing that images are not always what they seem, people often tend to believe what they "see" in home videos and photographs.

When media skirmishes occur, they present learning opportunities for participants to work through representational ideologies during various mediated moments. Many of these issues were thrown into dramatic relief after a video was posted by Michael Verdi, a well-respected and important figure in the first-generation video blogging community. First generation video bloggers were often technically savvy and began working out ways to compress videos and post them to their own websites before YouTube opened to the public. They often embraced discourses of realism and fiercely advocated a democratization of the lens, to encourage personally expressive media that is not controlled by corporate or government entities.

Verdi posted a video entitled *Because Why Not?* to his personal video blog (michaelverdi.com) on November 25, 2007. The 1 minute and 53 second video depicts Verdi video recording his seemingly reluctant daughters at home.

The video was also posted to YouTube, but received very few views and no contentious feedback on that site. In contrast, the video spurred an argument within his own community of video-blogging peers. His daughter Dylan was 14-years old at the time of the research; her sister Lauren was about 10 years old. To appreciate the video and the commentary that ensued, it is useful to know a bit about the family's background, including his daughters' experiments with video blogging and Verdi's passionate support of media creation as an important form of contemporary literacy.

Verdi requested that I use his real name when discussing his contribution to the research project. He, like many video bloggers on and off of YouTube, believed that media makers should receive proper credit and attribution for interview comments and works that are referenced and discussed in public contexts. Verdi co-authored a book with Ryanne Hodson, called *Secrets of Videoblogging: Videoblogging for the Masses* (2006). The book is a how-to manual that assists video blogging newcomers. When I interviewed Verdi, he was a creative director for a company that assisted with marketing for companies involved in virtual worlds and social networks. He was also a performance artist and a co-producer of a machinima web series. Machinima is a genre of media in which participants can record actions from 3-D (three-dimensional) computer animations, such as recording characters' actions in a computer game to create new original stories.

Verdi strongly believed in promoting video blogging so that individuals could have a public voice and develop the skills they needed to distribute their message. Verdi received The Vloggervangelist Award at a special ceremony honoring video bloggers called The Vloggies, which was held in San Francisco in November 2006. A conflation of the words "vlogger" and "evangelist," the award was bestowed by PodTech, a company that creates branding and social media strategies. The goal of the award was to recognize and honor "a vlogosphere activist who [had] done an extraordinary job promoting the vlogging medium" (N.A. 2006). Verdi was recognized for his "tireless work in helping people build and establish their vlogs" and for establishing NODE101, a network of people who provide informal tutorials at gatherings so that people could learn to video blog and create personally expressive media.

During his interview, Verdi said that everything that comes from Hollywood now looks "gorgeous," "sounds fantastic" and has "great special effects." But the really important part of making media came from telling one's own story and having creative ideas. Many first-generation video bloggers believed that everyone should have the digital literacy skills to make their own media. They believed that human connection and social change were made possible through more personal mediated communication (Lange 2007b). Although Verdi and his daughter Dylan have accounts on YouTube, their mediated center of gravity was not on that site, but rather on their own video blogs. Many people in the first-generation video blogging community believed that one should have one's own site, and not be subject to a video hosting site's social dictates, censorship, or technical limitations, or any commercial influences that might compromise self-expression. In this sense, not having obligations to particular sponsors or patrons is a type of media ideology that privileges media-makers' intentions over those of third-parties that facilitate media distribution.

After experimenting with her own video blog, Verdi's daughter Dylan was named the "world's youngest video blogger" by ABC News in a piece profiling people of the year in 2004 (Vargas 2004). An ABC News crew came to the Verdi home to interview her about her online activities. An 11-year old at that time, Dylan was quoted as saying that she blogged about things she'd seen or heard of, or "just anything that happened to [her] that day that [she was] thinking." Getting comments, she said, made her feel "good," because "somebody else cares what [she had] to say." Michael posted a video telling the story, which included footage of Dylan watching herself on the ABC News program and seeming excited and pleased to have been profiled so prominently on the leading edge of new media.

Michael told me that shortly after he started video blogging in earnest in 2004, Dylan became curious about his cameras and activities. He suggested that she make a video blog. She had already maintained a text blog for several months. Working in the editing program of iMovie, Michael says he helped Dylan learn how videos were made from clips, and how clips could be rearranged to tell certain stories. In this mentorship narrative, Michael, like other technically oriented parents in the study, helped co-create learning opportunities for his daughter to improve her technical and self-expressive skills.

Michael's decision to assist his daughters displays a representational ideology in which it is acceptable for girls under the age of 15 to have the ability to create and transmit their own message and human images in a public way. When I interviewed Michael, he stressed that when he was their age, it would have been deeply meaningful to have these technologies and platforms to express himself creatively to a global forum. In contrast to critiques of patriarchal home movie making, Verdi espoused the idea that his daughters and indeed everyone should have the skills and tools to make their own media. He taught his daughters to video blog because he wanted them to have their own mediated space in which to express their point of view.

In the first video that Dylan posted to her blog, called *Record Player*, she discusses receiving an analog record player for Christmas, which is an unusual gift given the availability of other formats and services such as iTunes that distribute music online. Anticipating viewers' puzzlement, she explains in the video that she had been curious about her father's record albums and wanted to hear them, so she was happy to have received this gift. In her video, which functions as a tutorial, she listens to punk rock music and teaches the uninitiated how to use a record player by gently placing the needle on the record. Dylan is an archaeological media ambassador bridging old and new media.

Dylan went on to video blog for about two years. Typical topics included discussing her activities on Neopets, an online site in which people can adopt pretend pets and play games to enhance the pet's attributes. She also video blogged about clothes, her cello, wearing braces, hanging out with her grandmother and her father, and ear hole plugs. Dylan displays a talent for video blogging; she speaks to the camera in a comfortable, natural style. The camera work in her second video feels dynamic, as she holds it close to her face, uses animated expressions, and carries it around the room as she provides commentary about the items within it. By the time of his interview in 2007, Michael told me that she had largely dropped video blogging; her archives on that particular site show her last video posted in July 2006. Even kids growing up in highly mediated environments do not always display an ongoing disposition toward particular media.

Michael said that Dylan principally video blogged for social reasons, and most of the people watching and commenting on her video blog were adults in the video blogging community rather than peers of her own age. Although this was "cool" for her, Michael said, "it wasn't where her friends [were]." Such an observation contradicts the fact that teen cohorts in all social groups are always on the leading edge of technologized activity, with adults lagging behind. Among first-generation video bloggers, parents and adults typically led the way in supporting heavily mediated, everyday lifestyles. Dylan Verdi was evidently not typical of her teen-aged peers; she was Internet-savvy and engaged in video blogging. When Michael started in earnest, he said, many people in the United States still had to dial up to go online, and many people did not know how to retrieve videos online, much less know how to make and upload them.

Verdi's younger daughter Lauren also launched her own video blog a few months after Dylan. She posted far fewer videos, and her last video was posted about a year after she began. Again, such a pattern disrupts the discourse that all kids' mediated centers of gravity reveal equal ability and interest in all forms of technology and online participation. Within the same household, Dylan video blogged more than Lauren did. Lauren's first video, posted on February 6, 2005 primarily concerned discussing and displaying her Brownie vest and badges. The Brownies are part of the Girl Scout organization in the United States, and they accomplish activities such as improving sports and craft skills and fundraising through cookie sales.

Other topics in her video blog include riding horses and sending mother's day greetings. Michael told me that in general she did not spend much time at the computer.

Michael Verdi's own video oeuvre contains an eclectic mix of styles and media. He sometimes blogs about his thoughts and feelings, as well as covering events such as the media conferences he attends. In one video, he directly addresses the camera (and his audience) and talks about his sadness at losing family members to cancer. In a civically oriented message, he encourages viewers to contribute to the Leukemia and Lymphoma Society. He also documents his participation in a triathlon to raise money for the organization.

One category of videos on his site is "family." On his blog he notes that he is the "proud father" of two "amazing" girls whom he enjoys photographing. In the video *Because Why Not?* Verdi approaches his daughters and video records them as they go about their everyday life. As the video opens, Lauren is searching for something in a drawer and the camera is trained on her in profile. She is not smiling. On the screen, the text reads, "She is not amused."

Michael's voice is heard saying, "Lauren, what's up baby? Why are you in that outfit?" She looks at the camera with a wary expression and responds, "'Cause I just came back from dance." Michael pans the camera down to her feet so the viewer can see her outfit. He asks what they were dancing about, and she responds, "The Nutcracker." Michael asks if she will perform a little of her dance for him. Lauren looks at the camera/Michael with a hesitant look and he laughingly says, "What?" Their conversation continues:

Lauren: (smiles) If you're going to put it on the Internet, then, no.

Michael: (laughs) Who says I'm gonna put it on the Internet?

Lauren: (in a sing song tone) Yes, you are daddy.

Michael: Why, why would I put it on the Internet?

Lauren: Cause you put everything you tape on the Internet.

Michael: Not *everything*.

Lauren: Yes.

Michael: No, really, not everything. I leave some stuff off.

Lauren rolls her eyes and a subtitle reads, "I don't think she's buying that."

The video transitions next to Dylan, who is seated at her laptop computer. She looks over her computer at the camera and says, "Dad, please stop." The camera lingers, and she says in an irritated tone, "Dad." Michael responds, "What?" She says softly, "I said, please stop." He responds, "I'm not doing anything Dylan." She rolls her eyes and looks at the camera. The subtitle reads, "She is not amused either." Michael lingers facing her, and she says in an exasperated tone, "What?!" They continue:

Michael:	Nothing. I'm not doing anything
Dylan:	You're being weird and annoying.
Michael:	No.
Dylan:	Yes. Why are you doing that?
Michael:	Why not, Dylan? Look at me! Blow me a kiss! (an audible kiss is heard). Love you Dylan! (Dylan looks back at her father and then back down) Love you Dylan! (She once again glances back at her father.)
Dylan:	I mean, is this - does this have some sort of purpose to it?
Michael:	No purpose at all.
Dylan:	Why then, why?
Michael:	Because.
Dylan:	Because why?
Michael:	Because why not? (remaining audio trails off)

One of the final shots depicts Dylan looking at her father in a different light, perhaps almost smiling behind her computer screen.

The video spurred a vigorous discussion, receiving 32 comments (although Verdi eventually closed the comment forum) that represented diverse reactions. Many of the comments were supportive of Verdi and his family and interpreted the video as an instance in which one party wanted to make media of loved ones, and the photographic subject expressed reluctance. Most commenters interpreted these media skirmishes as a part of everyday life between parents and kids. They index one way in which kids start exerting their independence by taking control of their image creation in the home. A few comments were quite negative and felt that recording the girls after he had been asked to stop (in Dylan's case) was not appropriate and potentially violative of their expectations of privacy within the home.

What is extremely interesting about the video and the responses it garnered is that it showed that even in a community of people who were interested in the liberating and democratic possibilities of heavily mediated lifestyles, people did not always hold the same representational ideologies about what it meant to record human images, especially loved ones. Even after Verdi and his family responded to the negative commentary and explained that the girls were not as upset as some of the commentators had assumed, the explanations and contextualizations did not dissuade all viewers from having strong reservations about the video. Verdi expressed exasperation in his interview with me that the topic had been discussed at length by many video bloggers on the Yahoo! Videoblogging discussion list, an online forum for exchanging ideas about video blogging. He told me that the highly critical commenters knew him and were aware of his consideration of media ethics in his video blog. Verdi's case study provides an important learning opportunity, especially for new media makers. One cannot always predict how one's media will be received. The responses reveal several tacit representational ideologies that conflict and are sometimes contingent as they are based on specific assumptions and contextualized interpretations.

Working through this case study reveals the concerns that opened this chapter. For instance, what is a media maker's moral obligation to him- or herself to make the most authentic media that they deem is most personally expressive? What are one's obligations to one's children, whose human images are represented in media that may exist in perpetuity online? What are media makers' obligations to viewers? What happens when these obligations cannot all be honored simultaneously? By examining this case study, readers are invited to reflect on their own practices and perhaps discover their own shifting and conflicting representational ideologies.

A few commenters expressed concerns. For instance, one comment (#21) noted that children should not have their own video blog until they understand the "ramifications" of having one. This commenter stated that he "doubted" that girls as young as Lauren "understood the pros and cons of self-publicizing your life to thousands of strangers." Some of the reactions were quite strongly worded. One such comment came from a female video blogger:

COMMENT #8

Why not? Wow indeed. Because growing up as a young woman is already hard enough. Because they're kids and deal with enough social pressure as it is. Because documenting your own past online is your choice – and you take away their agency by letting your parental whims follow them into their virtual (and tangible) futures. Because you don't use a pseudonym. Because you don't obtain consent – in fact, you seem to get the opposite. Because you're supposed to set an example: when someone you love and respect says stop, in any situation, for any reason, you do.

My dad is a slumlord. When I was a kid, we'd go to collect money and he'd have me sit in the car and lock the doors while we went to "talk to clients". If they saw that there was a kid in the car, there was less chance they'd kill him. I'd never trade that for this.

Verdi reacted very negatively to being compared to a "slumlord" and to her suggestion that she would rather have a slumlord for a father rather than someone who recorded her image against her will. This commenter points out that documenting one's experiences online should involve choice. In her view, Verdi took away the girls' "agency" by letting his desires or "whims" overshadow consideration of the potential consequences of having this media forever online.

Another commenter, who was a close friend of commenter #8 above, said that the video made him "uneasy" and "sad." He says that he "can only judge based on what you let me see." Such a comment contains a representational ideology that as a viewer, he has a *right* to judge the representations of others he sees online, and he has the right to determine whether they contain problems such as failure to respect a mediated subject's wishes, especially in the assumed private spaces of the home. Many readers may feel a right or obligation to speak up about images that seem to violate a person's rights.

On the other hand, many comments were supportive of Verdi and recognized the girls' reluctance as typical for kids who do not wish to be filmed at particular moments. For parents, even small moments of a child's life can take on heartfelt poignancy, and recording a child sends a message that the person and the moment are worth recording and preserving for other people (and themselves) to see. Discourses of so-called realism contradict earlier ideas that it is only more dramatic and progressive moments of the life cycle that are worth recording. Notably, whether or not media appear online, even the most personal recordings are often targeted at wider audiences, such as future unknown generations of family members (Holland 1991). In many U.S. cultural groups, media is not necessarily for the mediated, but for other people who have deep feelings or connections to the people depicted.

Media skirmishes occur in text as well. Some commenters read the posted *criticisms* as violative and defended Verdi. They argued that what happens on camera is not the "whole story" with regard to a single piece of media's ontology, or story of how it came to be. One commenter characterized the video as important because it realistically captured people's media experiences. Here discourses of realism situate the video as revealing some of the more messy or non-ideal moments that past eras of video making were accused of excising from the frame. In response to commenters who expressed concerns about the girls having online video blogs at a young age one commenter stated:

COMMENT #22

...I totally understand what you're saying and you make some good points about kids needing a maturity level to make decisions about this kind of thing – and how it can be traumatic for a parent to keep a camera trained on them all the time (I have friends who underwent that kind of treatment with Super 8 home movies!). What I'm responding to here, I think, is what likely happened off-camera – a kind of understanding and permission on the part of the kids to post videos of themselves online, even if on-camera they were resistant. And the resistance I see in the video is more of a grouchy, "aw dad, not now!" kind of annoyed attitude, not a retreat or fleeing from the view of the camera. In other words, it does seem to me that this video is a collaboration between father and daughters that captures their relationship (both the creation of the video and the posting of it online), rather than a father exerting power or control over his children's images and privacy.

This commenter astutely observes that resistances are of different types and degrees. In other words, a person who secretly takes pictures shapes a different level of subject agency than a person who pursues someone during a media skirmish at a party. The commenter also offers a phenomenological perspective by stating that mediated moments have different inflection points both on and off camera. It is possible for people to express reluctance during the mediated moment of recording, but later give permission during the mediated moments of editing and distribution. According to this representational ideology, it is possible to separate different moments in the media-making chain of experience, and to recognize that different moments may produce contingent feelings that change one's relationship to the original footage. One may be annoyed during filming, but the event may become funny during editing.

Verdi's immediate family such as his brother, wife, and mother also lent supportive commentary and sometimes expressed shock at the more negative criticisms. Verdi's brother noted that "resistances" or media skirmishes are typical in everyday family media making, and refraining from taking kids' pictures can also have ramifications when kids grow up without having adequate media from their past to index parental attention and affection. He stated:

COMMENT #18

...to all those that have an issue...If your parents had put the camera away every time you showed any resistance at all, how many fewer memories would their be of your childhood? What teenager/young adult doesn't try to hide [from] the camera from time to time? I for one have never met anyone who was scarred for life or had to go therapy, or had issues to deal with because their parents showed them love and attention and made attempts to capture their existence on film. On the contrary, people have issues when they don't get attention, when they don't know they are the center for their parents' world and when they go into the family albums and as they are thumbing through the pages have to sit there and wonder…"why in the hell are their no pictures of me."

Being a person in the United States today means having a mediated presence. According to commenter #18, a failure to record family images suggests parental neglect.

Similarly, Verdi's mother (comment #29) noted that she had received similar looks from Michael and his brother when they were growing up. Her comment is interesting because Michael himself went on to enjoy making his own media and living a heavily mediated life style (at least during the time of my research). It is not only the camera shy, then, who sometimes avoid having their picture taken. Even people who have an interest in media at times engage in media skirmishes. In some cases, these skirmishes may have less to do with media *per se*, and may be more reflective of kids asserting their individuality to their parents as they are growing up. Media skirmishes simply become one way to express this independence.

Michael Verdi's wife Rebecca argued that the negative comments did not consider the context of the family's media making choices and interpersonal relationships. She especially took issue with commenters who had imputed problems from their own mediated pasts onto their interpretation of the Verdi exchange. This comment is interesting because it asserts that one's own phenomenological experience cannot be mapped onto and equated with another person's subjective experience of a particular event. She stated:

COMMENT #13

…Some of your comments eluded to the relationship between Dylan,
Lauren and their dad. Unfortunately you don't have a clue. The video is not a
reflection of a thoughtless, self centered father; its a reflection of father who
could choose to post a video about anything else but he chose to post about
his daughters. Daughters he has the utmost respect, pride and love for.
Michael knows what his [boundaries] are when it comes to videoblogging in our household, please don't assume you know what they are. Please
don't transfer your own childhood issues or sensationalize our teenager's
responses. This video is does not rob anyone of their privacy, its simply two
girls who love their dad.

Moving beyond the particulars of the Verdi video, the debate opens up a broader issue about representational judgments. Is it part of one's civic duty to identify and protect people who appear to be "wronged" by particular mediated practices? Does the video touch a nerve that had actually been long debated within a community of media makers who had grappled with contradictory emotions about video blogging? On the one hand, video bloggers often passionately believed that media could have personal and civic value. On the other hand, they often struggled with how to honor their own personal expressivity as well as the needs and integrity of the people whom they recorded.

In the last comment he posted before closing the comment forum, Verdi addresses his criticizers (some of whom, he points out, do not allow comments on their blogs). Although he admits to sometimes putting up provocative videos, Verdi claims that he had not intended to stir controversy with the video. It was simply a moment in time that he thought "[captured]" something recognizable and "true" about "a father-daughter relationship." To use Ede and Lunsford's (1984) term, he had "invoked" or imagined an audience of like-minded viewers who would appreciate its truthfulness and authenticity. Nevertheless, his "addressed" audience or those who actually watched the video included both sympathetic and critical viewers, a common risk of public media sharing. Verdi stated (#32b) that he was not trying to be provocative but rather sought "moments that capture something we'd like to remember and, I hope, contain a little bit of truth that others will recognize in their own lives. I think I got a tiny, true piece of a father-daughter relationship here. That's all I was trying to do. I didn't make this to start a 'debate about online identity of minors and the role of parents.'"

In addition, Verdi posted a video in which he and his daughters responded to the critical commentary. In the video, Michael, Lauren, and Dylan sit side-by-side facing the camera and react to the debate. Lauren protectively and supportively touches her father's left shoulder. They stay close partly to remain in frame. Such bodily positioning also projects an aura of emotional closeness and support.

The video opens with Michael asking the girls what they wish to say. They respond:

Dylan: I think all the comments left are really, really stupid (laughs). You, you guys are seriously digging way way way too into this and you're act - like you're treating my dad as if he's some like creepo pedophile person. As if like, like I had to like beg and plead and he like, he like shackled me, and it's like "No! You're going on the Internet!" I mean, hello, I had a website, I had a video blog at some point. Obviously, it doesn't bother me to be on video. I mean I was only like that because I had woken up like 20 minutes earlier and I'm not a morning person.

Lauren: And I just didn't want to perform my ballet. I didn't say I didn't want this on the Internet.

Dylan: This is ridiculous.

Michael: [He explains he will restore the comments he had removed.]
Really, you guys. I'll say this. None of you have children. And
so, you're speaking about a bunch of shit that you don't know
anything about. Okay? You don't know anything about it. And,
you're also making a lot of assumptions about my family, and
about our relationship, and about what happened all in and
around and outside of that video. You don't know shit! So
please stop making shit up about shit you don't know about.
Okay? Thank you.

One of the most interesting aspects of this response video is Verdi's
suggestion that the viewers who criticized him did not know what had
happened "all in and around and outside of that video." This is a phenomenological assessment that creates a learning opportunity for viewers to
understand that their interpretations in their own mediated moment of
viewing may not be the same as those of the video's creators. Speaking
within the context of youths' personal websites and blogs, Stern (2008:111-
112) noted that text bloggers were often disappointed that people over-
generalized who they were as people on the basis of a mere "snapshot" of
themselves provided online. Understanding the moral obligations and ontology of a media's creation, in Verdi's view, depended upon knowing what
his relationship to his girls was, and what happened in the moments and
negotiations that surrounded the video but were not necessarily depicted
directly within it.

Dylan also calls up important context in which she argues that she had
her own video blog and was not necessarily opposed to appearing online.
Dylan grew up in a home in which video blogging was coded as an important
digital literacy skill. The idea of teaching girls how to video blog reflects a very
different philosophy in comparison to the way scholarship in past media eras
portray fathers as wielding cameras, while girls were encouraged to remain
media subjects (Zimmerman 1995).

In his interview for my study, which took place just days after the video's
posting, Verdi explained his frustration with some of the commentary, which
had principally come from people with whom he had interacted in video
blogging circles. Contrary to many first-generation video bloggers' and the
general population's fears that participating on You Tube would attract aggressive criticism from unknown persons, the harshest comments appeared
on his own website and came from people whom Verdi knew, at least as acquaintances. The criticism appeared because different parties interpreted the
moral undertones of the mediated act in very different ways. Such a variety

of interpretations and critical commentary complicates the meaning of terms such as "haters," given that at least some commenters are passionate because they are reacting to a moral issue.

During the interview Verdi said that the girls had seen him working on the video and they had "cracked up" when watching it. His frustration was with the commentary that suggested that he would ignore his children's wishes with regard to putting video up online. Verdi stated:

> But there was this underlying assumption that I would - that I would be the person who would put something inappropriate of my kids up on the web, like something that my kids explicitly told me, "Dad, please don't put that on the Internet" and I said, "Ah, screw you. I'm putting it on the Internet." (Patricia chuckles.) Right? What kind of an asshole father would I be if I was doing that? And so the thing that was *insulting* to me was that these people who, again, I know they haven't watched every single video that I've made or anything but you know, they've known me at least peripherally for like three years now, and they've heard this whole story about Dylan and the whole thing. Uh, uh, two of them were like part of the video blogging list when you know, there was like two dozen active people posting and this was *the* story that we were talking about, so they've heard this all before. [Again], I've met them all in person, and that they would come to my blog and, and assume that I did this horrible thing against my children's will is just infuriating and insulting to me.

Media subjects/participants have a range of options with regard to accepting or resisting being recorded. They may run from the camera, put their hand over the lens, verbalize resistance, or ignore the media maker. In one video on YouTube, I observed a very young child, perhaps not yet 5-years-old, tell her mother to put down her camera. To say that the media maker "[takes] away their agency" risks washing out the range of available choices and reifying an assumption of unidirectional control. On the other hand, children may not realize the range of available choices, or may feel reluctant to exercise them when directed at a parent, with whom they have a particular relationship. Many parents post media without their children's knowledge or understanding. Moving away from the particulars of the Verdi example, kids in other situations may be scolded or punished for not participating in media (say, on the day that expensive family portraiture is scheduled and children decide to "opt out" behaviorally by playing in mud).

It is interesting to observe how Lauren and Dylan reacted to being recorded and to explore potentially different levels of agency with regard to mediated moments of recording. Looks can yield interpretive messages. In several instances, Michael made requests or issued directives for the girls to execute certain behavior. For instance, he requested that Lauren perform some of her dance for the camera. Lauren declined this request and explained that it was because she did not want the dance to go online. She exercised a particular level of agency in refusing to dance. One could easily imagine a scenario in which she smiled pleasantly and danced even though inwardly she did not wish to dance. Since these images would simply look like kids dancing for dad, they would not likely receive any criticism. They would emit no external indicators of a child's discomfort. People would likely believe what they saw, and would accept the video as appropriate, even though it would arguably be more offensive than a video in which someone is depicted as exercising their right to refrain from performing such a dance.

Lauren exhibited an important digital literacy by establishing the parameters of what she considered to be an appropriate level of the video's distribution. She would not perform the dance if the video was to go on the Internet, a statement that implies that she was aware that the video did have the potential to go online and thus could be seen by many people. She modeled a kind of digital literacy to other children that it is possible to resist media that is being made in a number of ways, through looks (such as eye rolls), verbalizations (saying "no" to dancing), and a refusal to honor a request even if made by a loved one.

Media skirmishes bring up a host of interesting questions. For example, while viewers might use Verdi's video to recall their own troubled media histories, is it right to assume that his video enacts the same social circumstances? What are the responsibilities of viewers to point out problems when they see them? How severe does a video transgression have to be before people feel the moral obligation to intervene, whether or not their own experiences are similar to those observed in the media? What level of context is necessary to judge any mediated act? Is receiving background on the Verdi family helpful for judging the status of the mediated act? What level of relevance should this background information be accorded when adjudicating media's appropriateness?

Some commenters might argue that no matter what happens during editing, a person's declining to be photographed should always be respected. But what happens if people laugh about it later? Can the mediated moment of recording (when a person requests someone to stop filming) be ethically separated from the mediated moments of editing and distribution? Can a video's moral-ontological status change according to different interpretations along the phenomenological chain of mediation?

Also, what does it mean to leave some of life's messiness in play, rather than only depicting cheerful smiles? Does a rejection of realist discourses of media making necessitate a return to rarified patterned eliminations and forced smiles that would be undetectable as problematic by viewers? Moving forward, it seems clear that video makers, subjects, and viewers should frankly discuss these issues with their own families, friends, and fellow video makers, to understand people's interpersonal boundaries, ethical obligations, and representational ideologies.

The Moral Contradiction to the Contextual Lament

Once something is recorded, subsequent readers or viewers do not have access to the original circumstances of the media's creation for interpretation. Lacking the context of an artifact's ethical-ontological foundation may complicate future interpretations. Complications spawned by media's interpretive distance from its creators has long been debated by philosophers from Plato to Derrida. Arguably, writing has an iterable quality that is intelligible at some level even if "the moment of its production is irrevocably lost and even if [one does] not know what its alleged author-scriptor consciously intended to say at the moment he wrote it" (Derrida 1972:9). Plato argued that if writing "is ill-treated or unfairly abused it always needs its parent to come to its rescue; it is quite incapable of defending or helping itself" (Plato 1973:97). People interpret media even when they are not privy to the author's intention, but the media itself cannot provide a defense against interpretations that do not align with those of its creators.

Many people will not understand or will simply disagree with a media maker's original intent. Media viewers become an "imagined audience" (Brake 2009; Marwick and boyd 2011) whom a media maker may not know. "Context collapse" (Marwick and boyd 2011; Wesch 2009) occurs when multiple audiences interpretively convene in one artifact. In other words, many possible audiences may view and react to the same mediated artifact in vastly different ways. Tensions may arise when interpretations of media creators and viewers are not symmetrical. Viewers may interpret a media maker's recording as morally flawed. As Strangelove (2010:58) points out with regard to YouTube videos, "The lack of context can make it difficult to understand the action in a home video. Innocent behavior can be seen as deviant." Of course, the opposite argument can also be made. Things that look innocent, such as a smiling daughter dancing for daddy (though she really did not want to), may be problematic.

A common complaint about online interaction is the lack of so-called context. Many scholars have offered their version of what is termed here the "contextual lament," which generally assumes that if adequate context could be revealed, then misunderstandings between a media maker and a viewer would inevitably be resolved. The contextual lament is predicated on the idea that computer-mediated communication lacks many subtle cues such as winks and nods, and that it is the lack of these and other contextualizing cues that creates misunderstanding. The contextual lament asserts that if people who are interacting online could simply get to know each other, misunderstandings about people's actions would be minimized (Tannen 1998).

Perhaps it can empirically be shown in certain cases that getting to know others, and most especially developing empathy for someone's seemingly exotic mediated philosophies, may truly settle misunderstandings. The problem is that social interaction alone does not guarantee that tensions with moral underpinnings will be easily resolved in all cases. Imagine getting to know someone who is deeply racist about hiring practices. Will any amount of understanding the context of the ontology of their beliefs change one's own stance with regard to the appropriateness of such unfortunate behaviors? Getting to know a person who is racist will never prompt acceptance of their morally bereft beliefs and practices.

When people hold deeply different positions on behavioral morality, much more interactive work is needed to achieve agreement or even respectful understanding. Note that comment #31, cited previously in this chapter, suggests that strongly worded criticisms had less to do with the video itself and more to do with being on different sides of an intensely moral debate that revolved around whether children should participate online. Harsh criticisms are often motivated by deeply felt, morally driven emotions and desires to protect parties who may not have full consent as to how media is created and distributed. When morality is at stake, passion and critique often follow—even if the interactants know each other to varying degrees.

The contextual lament exhibits several theoretical conundrums. The first is, what is meant by "context"? The word is often used in a singular form, as in desiring to know "the context of the situation." Yet, the concept involves multiple layers that may interact or conflict. What counts as appropriate context may change over the course of an interaction as prior moves influence responses.

In addition, people may "see" or draw on levels of context that prove their original, moral assumptions, rather than admitting as evidence levels of context that contradict these assumptions (Gellner 1970 [1962]). Within the context of analyzing anthropological studies of human behavior, Gellner (1970 [1962]:130) stated that, "the amount and kind of context and the way the context itself is interpreted, depends on prior tacit determination concerning the kind of interpretation one wishes to find." This contextual pre-disposition is not limited to anthropologists, but to anyone trying to answer the contextual question, "What is going on here?" Gellner's argument can be productively applied to mediated interaction. People who believe that a behavior is legitimate will recognize those contextual factors that validate their original judgment of the act. Aspects of context that contradict the act's validity may be innocently overlooked or willfully ignored.

Finally, even when people do have access to contexts, they may not attend to them. Verdi complained during his interview that his whole video blog provided relevant context to interpret the *Because Why Not?* video. First-generation video bloggers tend to see the video blog, rather than any single video, as what constitutes one's "work," but Verdi understood that most viewers would not likely have watched all of his videos. Yet, even if people actively attend to available context, they may continue to hold asymmetrical moral judgments about behavior and values. What some people read in Dylan's media skirmish with her dad was a violation of a right to privacy during the moment of recording. For these interpretants, the phenomenologies of Verdi's or Dylan's actions before or after the mediated moment of recording did not count as legitimate interpretive evidence. To interpretants who choose to focus on the mediated moment of recording to judge the video, it did not matter that Dylan had a video blog prior to the skirmish or that during editing the family deemed the video acceptable for posting.

Verdi draws on different levels of context to defend his video choices. He introduces the idea that being a parent and understanding how parents in the United States typically interact with their kids through media will be, for some readers, a crucial aspect of context. In his response video, he argues that people who do not have kids do not understand what it means for a parent to make media in the home in general, and in his home in particular. Verdi also mentions that those who criticized him were not privy to what happened "all in and through the video." He suggests that judgment is not possible even within a particular mediated moment without understanding the many feelings and experiences that surrounded the decision of recording.

Representational ideologies have temporicities that influence how people interpret media. It is not the availability of context that is at issue in this case study, but rather, how and whether people admit as evidence particular levels of context to validate or challenge prior beliefs. What counted as relevant context was often influenced by representational ideologies that people previously held. Posting media online in this way presented a number of learning opportunities. Through these experiences, people might see models for how to handle being mediated. Girls see other girls making requests about video recording in the home. Video makers learn that despite their intentions, posting one's media online invites an array of interpretive views that may not always map to one's own. People wishing to protect others may find themselves in text-based media skirmishes with media creators or subjects. The moral contradiction to the contextual lament means that fundamental differences in interpretive morality often drive media interpretations, and no amount of adequate "context" will easily resolve certain passionate, morally laden media skirmishes between video makers, subjects, and viewers.

Playing by the Rules

What can media makers and participants do to handle representational discrepancies? Why do people seem to hold such different representational ideologies? Giddens (1991) argues that people's risk calculations are elided because of the vast distance between a decision and its impact in time and space. Risks that are remote from daily life, such as how an image might impact a toddler's college acceptance, may be "too far removed from a person's own practical involvement for that individual seriously to contemplate them as possibilities" (Giddens 1991:130). Part of the goal of this chapter was to "conscientise" (Kuhn 1995) how present media choices might affect people in the future. Stacy Snyder's "drunken pirate" incident, described earlier in this chapter, demonstrates how seemingly playful imagery from people's pasts has reportedly complicated their future job opportunities (Mayer-Schönberger 2009).

Decisions about understanding which media may have negative ramifications become more complicated as more video is taken in the casual spaces of the home. Is the implication of these findings that we will all be reduced to what Marwick and boyd (2011:125-126) call the "lowest-common-denominator" philosophy of online participation? Will we all resort to making media that is so bland that it will not offend the sensibilities of anyone, anywhere, at any time? Are discourses of so-called realism and the quest to avoid stilted family perfection compatible with representational ideologies that express concern over the ramifications of interpersonal media skirmishes? What do the learning opportunities of the case studies in this book yield for future generations of video and media makers?

The ease of recording and distribution engenders serious responsibility on the part of media makers to maintain sensitivity to the people with whom they interact on video. One might wonder where the boundaries lie for media makers who advocate heavily mediated lifestyles as a way to secure important digital literacies for themselves and future generations. I raised this question in an interview with Ryanne Hodson and her partner Jay Dedman. They are first-generation bloggers who strongly support the use of video to create personally expressive media. They mentioned that they had very few interpersonal boundaries for making media that contained the other's image. The only incident that potentially crossed a line was when Jay took a 30-second close up of Ryanne sleeping and posted it online. He called this video "beautiful," "cool," and "something you rarely see." Ryanne said he had not told her he would put it up. Had she been asked in advance, she said, it would not have been a problem.

Interactions like these become learning opportunities in which participants recognize potential asymmetrical boundaries with regard to acceptable media-making practices. These and other incidents prompted Ryanne and

Jay to discuss, in an open and sincere way, what was okay to film and what was not. Was it acceptable, for instance, to film Ryanne when she was upset and crying? While some people may feel sensitive about being filmed in this state, Ryanne and others embrace it as part of real life that is worthy of recording. Establishing parameters ahead of time as Ryanne and Jay did helps negotiate ethical obligations between media participants. These types of interactions indicate that it is possible to play by the rules and have fun. Indeed, Huizinga (1949:11) argues that "all play has its rules."

But what should a media maker do when they do not know people's interpersonal boundaries? For some video bloggers, it is deemed better to film first and ask questions about distribution later. However, whenever media is taken, there is always a risk that it might find its way to a much wider audience than was intended (Kitzmann 2004). Such an observation would suggest that people should think carefully and slow down the mediated moment of recording to consider future ramifications of taking a particular image. One can think of the process as slowing down (Eriksen 2001) the mediated dimension of interpersonal experience as mediated by a camera.

To use another metaphor, one might think of the vast proliferation of images as a "loud" experience; thus "controlling the volume" (Baron 2008:32) is beneficial in order to consider who is being recorded and why. People might consider how their comfortable media "volume" levels may be different from those of other people. Participants on YouTube may aspire to achieve what James (2009:80) calls "good play" or forms of activity that are "meaningful and socially responsible." This chapter aims to be co-productive in involving readers to reflect on their own mediated, ethical parameters. The goal is also to encourage media makers and participants to be co-productive about establishing acceptable interpersonal video-making practices, and to acknowledge that their own representational ideologies may differ from those of other people.

Many kids are growing up in heavily mediated spaces within the home, and these images are often circulated online. In these mediated moments, kids are offered various models of appropriate digital literacies, including image ethics. In some cases, these lifestyles and representational ideologies may be so naturalized that they are not even recognized as things that kids are "learning." They simply become aspects of one's embodied, digitized, mediated worldviews and habitus (Bourdieu 1977). For many kids, it is through experiencing interpersonal mediated moments that they form tacit representational ideologies while growing up on the 'Tube.

CHAPTER 7

<<< ◀ ■ ▶ >>>

On Being Self-Taught

Vignettes and cases studies detailed in the prior chapters demonstrate that kids learn many things by making videos with friends and family. Yet, a funny thing happened on the way to the ethnographic interview. When I asked kids directly about how they learned to make videos, they often portrayed themselves as nearly autochthonous learners. Many kids espoused an ideal of being self-taught as part of a performance of technical identity. Such a value is common in technical cultures and among "nerds" and "geeks" who believe strongly in the importance of learning outside of school or formal institutions (Bucholtz 1998). Kids performed technical affiliation to the importance of being self-taught by de-emphasizing the contributions and impact of the media ecologies in which they grew up, as well as the social sources of support and direct assistance they received. Many kids' definition of "learning" was relegated to highly traditional and formal versions of knowledge acquisition based on sit-down classroom models. Notably, the definition of the term self-taught varied; kids labeled many different methods as appropriate ways of teaching themselves about technology, computers, and video.

Discourses on "digital youth" and "net generations" often emphasize kids' independent, informal learning as they master tasks and tools in online environments (Prensky 2001, 2006; Tapscott 2009). Homogenizing discourses based on age tend to characterize children as highly technical and parents as indifferent or unknowing. Yet the meaning of being self-taught is rarely interrogated in prior research. It is often a taken for granted term that elides the variety of meanings and identity implications that it connotes to kids.

The present chapter analyzes kids' learning narratives, or reflections on how they acquired particular forms of knowledge. Learning narratives are personal stories that describe how people learn to use a device, accomplish a task, or adopt particular attitudes and literacies that code sets of knowledge as important or worth knowing. On YouTube, learning narratives are part of

Patricia G. Lange, "On Being Self-Taught" in *Kids on YouTube: Technical Identities and Digital Literacies*, pp. 189-215. © 2014 Left Coast Press, Inc. All rights reserved.

participants' "technobiographies" (Henwood et al. 2001) of how they learned particular skills and cultural worldviews with respect to making media, using technology, and participating online. In learning narratives about YouTube interviewees describe, account for, interpret, or organize prior experiences in using videos and computers.

Despite this outward stance, kids' learning narratives often contained clues that their learning processes were varied and social. Learning narratives that emphasize being self-taught despite internal contradictions in interview statements ultimately reveal idealizations of the self (Portelli 1991). Kids often performed technical affiliation to the normative ideology that technically competent youth *should* be "self-taught" rather than receiving formal instruction. Yet this ideology may not work for kids of all dispositions who encounter widely varying learning contexts, and who may not be conducive to being self-taught. Yet, to be considered a "geek," in this milieu, one is ideally self-taught, rather than "copying" from others.

This chapter discusses interviewees' varied connotations of being self-taught and the term's conceptual relationship to informal and trial and error forms of learning. It analyzes different aspects of learning narratives and explores kids' stances toward the use of socially encoded forms of information. The chapter discusses how kids and youth use discourse strategies—including disassociation and minimization—in their learning narratives to handle dissonances between perceptions of solely self-motivated knowledge acquisition and lived forms of socially-influenced learning. These dissonances and subsequent reparative strategies reveal how kids' learning narratives intertwine with their performance of affiliation to normative ways of learning, and thus help them perform their identities as technically competent kids.

Polysemic Connotations of Being Self-Taught

Although routinely claimed as the only, main, or best way for kids to learn, the notion of being self-taught is rarely theoretically explored across technical and non-technical activities and social groups (Prensky 2001, 2006; Tapscott 2009). Being "self-taught" is often equated to concepts such as "self-directed learning," "informal learning," "hands-on learning," "trial and error," and "tinkering," to name just a few. For example, in her study of musicians playing popular music, Green (2002:5) stated that one type of informal learning includes being "self-taught," which she defines as drawing on the assistance or even "encouragement" of family and peers, as well as by "watching and imitating musicians around them." For Green, being self-taught is consistent with very social forms of learning that occur outside of formal institutions.

According to some definitions, being self-taught includes watching or being mentored by a peer, or receiving assistance through socially encoded forms of knowledge. A socially encoded form of knowledge is one in which someone has prepared media with the goal of providing information, instruction, or assistance to other people, who may be known or unknown to the encoder. Artifacts such as tutorials and manuals are socially encoded in that someone has flagged the information within them as important for someone else to know. The artifact mediates an asynchronous social encounter between people who are typically unknown to teach other. Such artifacts are hardly neutral cultural objects that simply exist in the world; they were made by someone with the intent of influencing or helping someone else. Socially encoded forms of knowledge include artifacts such as text-based, frequently asked question (FAQ) files; manuals; text comments posted to a video; and step-by-step, video tutorials. Sometimes people create such artifacts to perform their technical identity more than to provide assistance; the artifacts showcase the abilities and reputation of the FAQ file author, text commenter, or tutorial maker, rather than provide sincere instruction (Lange 2003; Perkel and Herr-Stephenson 2008). For example, a terse manual may be written not with the goal of democratizing access but rather of addressing fellow technologists who have substantial familiarity with the technical information being codified. In other cases, such artifacts are helpful to novices. People often produce them with the goal of helping people acquire new skills, concepts, or participatory competencies.

In contrast to the social connotations of being "self-taught" in fields such as music, some studies on computer and Internet learning in the United States suggested that participants distinguished between being taught by friends and family and being "self-taught" (Hoffman and Novak 2000; Katz and Aspden 1997). Being self-taught was seen as distinct from learning from friends or through work, but these latter categories were also distinguished from learning from "formal coursework" (Katz and Aspden 1997). Similarly, in a study by Wheelock (1992) on information and communication technologies in homes in northeastern England, learning from others was contrasted to learning on one's own. According to Wheelock (1992:108) more men tended to identify themselves as being self-taught. In contrast, wives tended to learn from other people, such as their husbands, sons, and daughters. She noted that children often learned through "networks of friends and relatives, especially the sons" and in several families, "children taught each other" (Wheelock 1992:108). My data suggest that it is not gender, but rather perceptions of technical identity, that correlate with whether or not someone feels that being "self-taught" is important.

Using socially encoded forms of knowledge such as tutorials is not a naturally better way to learn; it is a cultural choice, as indicated by the fact that it is not always regarded as a legitimate way of being "self-taught." A study of tutorials in the online participatory art-exchange site of deviantART revealed tensions with regard to stances toward "tutorials" (Perkel and Herr-Stephenson 2008). Researchers identified three connotations for the term "tutorial": guides, walk-throughs, and tutorials. They defined the last of these as "step-by-step sets of instructions on how to achieve a certain outcome" (and is the meaning of the word "tutorial" invoked in this book) (Perkel and Herr-Stephenson 2008:7).

Notably, tutorial makers on deviantART display reluctance to use *other people's* tutorials. They preferred doing things "themselves," and chided tutorial users for "cheating" and "copying" other people. One tutorial maker suggested that tutorials "actually stunted learning, by keeping people from learning on their own and continuing a reliance on copying the approach of others" (Perkel and Herr-Stephenson 2008:17). Even though participants requested tutorial makers to create tutorials, many tutorial makers eschewed them for their own learning experience. Given that tutorial makers are perceived as more technically "advanced" than their viewers (at least in the subject of the tutorial), their rejection becomes part of a performance of their technical affiliation to particular ideologies of learning and participation in online sites of creative production.

For some video makers and technologists, it may seem "obvious" that being self-taught is the best way of learning. However, not all creative communities ratify the value of being self-taught. Scholarship on so-called "self-taught art," reveals that being self-taught is not as well respected as having formal, institutional training. Self-taught art tends to exist outside of what Becker (1982) called "art worlds," or those interconnected social and material networks of artists, critics, distributors, and buyers who collaborate to produce and qualify only selected works as "art" (Fine 2004; Jones 2001). Fine (2004:4) states that, "as far as the art market is concerned, [self-taught artists] lack social capital, ties to the larger community, aesthetic theory, and are not fully integrated professionals in the mainstream art world." A similar argument has been made with respect to YouTube video makers. According to Sherman (2008:164), "deprofessionalized artists working in video, many sporting M.F.A. degrees, will be joined by music-video-crazed digital cooperatives and by hordes of Sunday video artists." In the United States, the Master of Fine Arts degree (M.F.A.) typically requires 2-3 years of formal study. Informal video makers are often negatively judged against those with formal training. Despite the fact that some technical discourses portray it as a universally accepted method, being self-taught is a cultural construct that requires empirical investigation to determine its efficacy in particular contexts and for specific individuals.

Many YouTube participants whom I interviewed rejected both in-person social interactions such as informal mentoring and use of socially encoded materials. These were seen as inadequate paths to achieving technical ability. For many participants, "trial and error" forms of learning helped to construct a technical and competent participatory persona. However, inconsistent statements in learning narratives revealed an inability for some interviewees to retain a "pure" portrayal of being self-taught through trial and error methods alone.

Trial and Error

Normative claims of being self-taught resonate strongly with prior research on technical communities in which those who learned on their own appeared to receive more respect than those who learned in formal or explicitly social ways (Lange 2003, 2006). Learning on one's own becomes a kind of tacit cultural knowledge or "hidden curriculum" (Portelli 1993; Snyder 1970) in technical groups. A technical person may or may not be explicitly told that learning must occur on one's own to receive social acceptance, but participants in computer and network oriented environments tacitly infer through feedback and social criticism that members who have been "self-taught" develop more respected social reputations.

For many scholars and participants, being self-taught is equivalent to or at least includes trial and error methods of learning. In technical environments, other names for trial and error include being "hands on" (Levy 1984; Thomas 2002) and "tinkering" (Levy 1984; Thomas 2002). In his history of computer hackers at the Massachusetts Institute of Technology (MIT), Levy (1984) noted that early computer users espoused the importance of trial and error methods. "Hackers" are computer users who control computers and software in expert ways. According to Levy (1984:40) an important part of the hacker ethic is that "essential lessons can be learned about the systems—about the world—from taking things apart, seeing how they work, and using this knowledge to create new and even more interesting things." Being "hands-on" is a cultural "imperative" for these elite technical groups (Levy 1984:40).

In addition to having access to devices and programs, obtaining freely available information on technical systems was also crucial for early computer cultures. To avoid having several technologists create the same new computer program, hackers circulated information and programs already in existence. The idea was to distribute information so that others could benefit from encoded, collective wisdom and build on this knowledge to find new ways to work on systems and creatively improve them (Levy 1984:40-1). This cultural legacy of sharing information is seen in commonly available networked resources that facilitate on-demand teamwork, projects, and collective forms of intelligence (Benkler 2006; Gee 2000). Video tutorials on YouTube, in which people provide tips and tricks on using digital editing software or manipulating features of the site itself, echo the practice of freely sharing on-demand information.

On the other hand, Thomas (2002:42-46) also argues that technologists in elite computer cultures generally disrespect people who draw on prior resources without really understanding a system's technical underpinnings. In some technical groups, people who use scripts or programs that have been pre-written for a particular task become labeled as "uncreative," or "derivative." Because they draw on prior forms of knowledge, they are often perceived as far lower on techno-cultural hierarchies.

Trial and error is not a guaranteed method of success for all individuals with different learning dispositions and self-perceived social identifications (Becker 1997; Holloway and Valentine 2003; Livingstone 2009). For example, in Bakardjieva's (2005) study of the introduction of the Internet into homes in Canada in the late 1990s, a key figure in many of the study participants' Internet introduction was the "warm expert" who was more knowledgeable than Internet newcomers. Warm experts were not only helpful but socially available to the participant whenever needed. In her study, Livingstone (2009:52) observed people struggle using trial and error methods for even simple information-finding tasks, especially on websites that provided little or no feedback for "mistakes." Trial and error may have more salience at different times in a user's or task's life cycle, and may vary according to task type, desired outcomes, time constraints, and individual learning dispositions.

Holloway and Valentine (2003) argued that high levels of autonomy and lack of didactic instruction that kids encountered in school-based computer sessions impaired rather than facilitated learning. Afraid of displaying incompetence, and receiving apparently little formal instruction, girls in these technology classes were "concerned about the ways in which their identities might be read by their peers if they [showed] an interest in technology" (Holloway and Valentine 2003:67). Such observations reiterate others' findings about the entangled way that perceptions of identity influence uptake of worldviews about literacies and learning opportunities in specific social contexts (Buckingham 2008; Hull and Schultz 2002; Street 1993; Szwed 1981).

In my interviewees' learning narratives, YouTubers' discourses of being self-taught, including trial and error methods, were often an important part of performing technical identity. But as discussed below, the meanings and symbolic loadings of being self-taught varied widely not only across interviewees but within an interviewee's self-portrait of the resources that they used to improve. Explicitly prompting interviewees to provide a learning narrative often proved to be beneficial for discovering more nuanced ethnographic understanding of the implications of being "self-taught" on YouTube.

Learning Narratives

An important part of understanding kids' experiences on YouTube included investigating how they learned about computers, videos, and online participation. Interviewees were typically asked about how they "learned," or "got started" making videos and participating on YouTube. Of particular interest was probing autobiographical descriptions that often contained both positive and negative identity associations with respect to ideas and practices in video making and technical cultures (Bucholtz 1999). In her study of nerd girls, Bucholtz (1999:211-212) defined negative identity practices as "those that individuals employ to distance themselves from a rejected identity, while positive identity practices are those in which individuals engage in order actively to construct a chosen identity." According to Bucholtz (1999:211-212), "positive identity practices define what their users are, and thus emphasize the intragroup aspects of social identity," while negative practices emphasize difference and therefore highlight and reify "intergroup" identities.

A common theme in learning narratives that I recorded included discourses of being self-taught, especially through trial and error methods. Such discourses initially seem to bolster arguments about kids independent, technological learning. Consider the remarks of a 15-year-old white female from the Southern United States (who requested the pseudonym of Allison and who was introduced in Chapter 3). A colleague who suggested her for the study referred to her as a "Henry Jenkins' kid" because of her impressive participation in many creative online genres (Jenkins 1992). Upon further investigation, her mediated center of gravity was not on YouTube; her participation on YouTube was casual and less intense than other mediated activities.

Allison described herself as very technical. For instance, she was familiar with HTML (HyperText Mark-up Language) and CSS (Cascading Style Sheets), both of which are used for creating and designing webpages. For Allison, learning about video tools came easily.

Patricia: So how did you learn do use the video tools?

Allison: Um, trial and error I guess (laughs). It's like any – whenever I learn anything with computers, I've taught myself how to use computers, and I consider myself very knowledgeable about them, but I just – I learn everything on my own, just figure it out, and the same with cameras. It's like a cell phone. I just figure out how to do it, and it's pretty quick and easy.

Patricia: Do you find yourself reading a lot of manuals to do the computer stuff?

Allison: No. (laughs) I must say I've never read a single manual for anything, even for like a computer program, like even Photoshop. I've never read a manual, unless we're in like graphic arts class where he's like we're required to read the manual, but I already know just about everything from figuring it out. It's not – I don't know – it's just, it's all easy.

For Allison, being self-taught and using trial and error forms of learning were positive identity markers. She considered herself "very knowledgeable," using the adverb "very" to emphasize her expertise. Further, she used the generalizing word "everything" (rather than a more modest phrasing such as "some things") to characterize what she has learned "on her own." Figuring out using devices, she said, was "pretty quick and easy." When I queried her about using "manuals," she eschewed them, even for learning about computer programs. Reading a manual was a negative identity marker from which she distanced herself. She associated them only with the most formal kind of learning, that which is "required" in a "class."

Such an assessment of manuals contrasts with other technical norms where reading the manual prior to engaging in manipulation of technical programs and systems is *de rigueur*. For example, the well-known acronyms "RTM" for "read the manual," or the less polite form of "RTFM" for "read the fucking manual," can be invoked by technical experts "to brush off questions they consider trivial or annoying" (Raymond 1996:389). Raymond notes that showing that one has read a manual is often seen as a necessary preface for asking questions that may seem obvious to more knowledgeable technologists (Raymond 1996:389).

As discussed below, however, not all learning narratives are as polarized as was Allison's. People whom I interviewed displayed varied stances with regard to socially encoded forms of information and instruction. In addition, many of the narratives contained contradictions about what it meant to be self-taught. Once the discussion moved away from the initial and perhaps symbolically loaded interview prompt containing the word "learning," other forms of instruction and knowledge acquisition surfaced in kids' recollections about technical learning opportunities.

Social and Socially Encoded Forms of Knowledge

As stated above, a socially encoded, mediated form of knowledge is created by someone (or multiple people) with the purpose of providing information or instruction to other people, often unknown to the encoder. For many interviewees, being self-taught was compatible with using socially encoded forms of instruction such as books, manuals, and tutorials. One example is found in the responses of a 23-year-old white male from the Southern United States who asked that I use his real name of Charles Trippy when discussing his remarks. Charles was a very popular member of YouTube. He successfully used the social network features of YouTube and Twitter to promote his work. On YouTube, he routinely received hundreds of thousands of views for his videos. He joined in May 2006, which makes him an early adopter of the site. As of November 30, 2012, he had more than 700,000 subscribers and at one time was ranked as the twenty-second most subscribed participant of all time in the category of "comedians." His videos focus on comedy themes, or humorous depictions of everyday events such as bathing his dog, dealing with the micro-blogging site of Twitter, or sneezing while driving.

During his interview, he noted that creating videos was at first an "outlet" or even a kind of "joke" that eventually took off. He routinely works with three other people, primarily male friends who are writers for the material in his videos. Charles said that his girlfriend "sometimes" contributes by being a "critic" or acting, when he can persuade her. But he says he does all of the "editing." His friends specialized in tasks such as writing, acting, and editing. He characterized himself as technical in terms of using computers and making videos.

> Patricia: Would you say that you're particularly technical when it comes to like using computers and making videos and things like that?
>
> Charles: Oh, yeah.
>
> Patricia: Where did you learn all that from?
>
> Charles: Self-taught. Just kind of read books, looked on tutorials online, watched videos. Like tutorial videos.

When I asked Charles about how he learned, he immediately mentions being "self-taught." Although he earlier noted that his video work is often very social and involves his friends, being self-taught is at the center of his recalled narrative. He says that he considers himself "technical" when it comes to using computers and making videos. Being self-taught is closely associated with a technical identity. When providing examples of what it means to be self-taught, he includes a range of socially encoded forms of information, including books, tutorials, and videos. Charles's learning narrative displays an acceptance of several types of socially encoded forms as legitimate methods for learning on his own.

Similarly, a 20-year-old Filipino-American male college student from the Southern United States stated that he did not have anyone to "teach" him how to work with computers. He requested being referred to by his real name of Brian. For Brian and his friends, making YouTube videos stemmed from recording everyday, ordinary activities that they thought would be fun to post on the site. The videos are often amusing. For example, in one video, two youth battle each other (one in medieval armor) in an impromptu scuffle in their college dorm's corridor. The comments they received were often personal from friends or people in their dorms who were interested in the events depicted, but were unable to witness them first-hand.

Early in the interview, we discussed Brian's background and family life with regard to learning about computers. Interestingly, he noted that he had a 15-year-old brother whom he described as a technology "user" but far less technical than himself. Although he described his brother as competent in terms of searching for things on the Internet, watching videos, and playing games, Brian said that his younger brother was unable to format hard drives or do "anything" that involved "fixing" a computer. This pattern contradicts the prediction in popular discourses that all youth under the age of 18 outperform their elders with regard to using technology. His characterization illustrates how young people *in the same household* exhibit a variety of technical abilities. Brian's and other participants' stories invite further ethnographic investigation of people's varying dispositions with regard to the types of technology they wish to become experts in, or try to learn at all.

Brian considered himself quite technical, as he often fixed or even built household computers. Although he said he was not a computer programmer in any "way, shape, or form," he noted that he was the one who repaired problems with the family's wireless Internet connections and he formatted hard drives. His self-portrayal resembles that of the "warm expert" as described by Bakardjieva (2005).

Patricia: How would you say you learned to work with computers?

Brian: By my own time. I didn't really have anyone to teach me.

Patricia: So how – how did you learn on your own?

Brian: Just tinkering around, reading manuals, testing stuff myself. Not electrocuting myself or anything, but I guess – I guess I just taught myself how to do computers all around.

Brian's narrative is interesting because he equates learning on his own with "tinkering around" and "reading" sources of information. In my ethnographic observation, understatement was often a way that technologists expressed a sense of humor. Here Brian uses dramatic understatement, saying that he successfully avoided "electrocuting" himself, and thus was able to teach himself general computer skills. Avoiding self-electrocution is a baseline (but an important one!) for achieving computer proficiency. His humorous understatement symbolizes his perceived technical prowess. It is not likely that anyone will really electrocute themselves using a home computer. Note that for Brian, learning on his own was compatible not only with "tinkering" and "testing" but also with "reading manuals." Brian uses the expansive phrase of "all around" to characterize what he has taught himself with regard to computers. Brian coded things like being able to "tinker" and "test" systems as positive indexes of having a technically competent identity.

For Charles Trippy and Brian, being self-taught was unambiguously coded as a positive identity trait that was clearly associated with acceptance of socially encoded forms of information. However, in some cases, the meaning of being self-taught needed to be probed and investigated in more detail. In her interview, an 18-year-old Asian female college student who requested that I refer to her by her screen name of mirugaiSC used linguistic phrasing that placed the acceptability of socially encoded forms of information in a more ambiguous position. Her initial remarks could be read in different ways; they may be interpreted as describing socially encoded forms of information as part of, or as distinct from, being self-taught.

MirugaiSC had a single sibling, an older brother (separated by 15 years) from whom she learned to play video games. Early on, she watched him and observed what he did onscreen. Yet she says he did not deliberately "teach" her any gaming tips or tricks. In her technobiography, gaming was very important; her mediated center of gravity was not posting videos to YouTube, although she had posted a few videos and she enjoyed watching videos through links sent to her. She especially enjoyed watching game videos and Japanese animé music videos. Her parents were not particularly "technical"; email was the extent of her mother's main computer usage.

In her interview, mirugaiSC mentions that she was taking a "multimedia literacy" class in college. The class was basically an introductory video making course. She stated that learning editing, although "tricky," was important because "everyone's making videos now," and therefore "it feels good if you know how to do it." Here, she alludes to a social standard for understanding what is an important skill to learn, namely making videos, even though she said she did not make many "home videos." Although she posts very little to YouTube, she sees video making as a worthy skill to develop to keep pace with her peers and to feel a sense of personal accomplishment. Her class editing team used the desktop editing software, Final Cut Pro, which she describes as "difficult," and "complicated" to use. Even though she appeared quite technical, video software required additional mastery through formal coursework.

MirugaiSC said that she originally became interested in video through the purchase of family video-making equipment. I observed that getting started through receipt of a material object often launched a learning trajectory. She and her father "learned together" to work cameras and make videos, although he did not video blog. In her learning narrative, she describes how her parents initially purchased equipment, but it was she who became an expert in using it.

> *Patricia:*   You seem very, very technically savvy 'cause you've got all these games and, you know, camera phones, and digital cameras and production tools. So, who's teaching you all this stuff? Like, how did you learn, say, how to use a digital camera at 14 or how to connect to the Internet and stuff like that?
>
> *mirugaiSC:*   A lot of stuff – well, I think – well, my dad and, like, my parents would buy some piece of equipment, but I would basically have to be the one to learn how to master it and, like, learn how to use it properly, so I could help them out. They – like, if my dad has computer problems or the camera isn't working, I can usually fix it. And a lot of it, I guess, is, like, just reading the manual or being self-taught. Like, PhotoShop and that kind of thing, I kind of learned myself and through online tutorials 'cause I was just curious about it.

This learning narrative portrays being self-taught as a positive identity trait and is consistent with a technical persona. MirugaiSC describes herself in ways similar to that of the "warm expert" (Bakardjieva 2005) who "fixes" computer problems at home. She says that much of her expertise comes from "just reading the manual or being self-taught." Further she says she learned by herself "and through online tutorials." Her phraseology is a bit ambiguous. On the one hand, her distinction between using a manual "or" being self-taught, would seem to indicate that these types belong to two separate categories; she is using "or" in the sense of either/or but not both. In this sense, using a manual is not equivalent to being self taught. The same is true of learning by herself "and" through tutorials. It may be argued that "and" is being used to distinguish between two separate categories. On the other hand, invoking these terms so closely together in the same phrasing could connote an inclusive sense of both terms as part of teaching the self.

In a follow-up clarification exchange over email, mirugaiSC's offered further explanation of her views. For instance, she said that tutorials go "hand in hand" with being self-taught, indicating that tutorials were a legitimate form of learning on one's own. Whereas manuals do not provide the specific information you may need to learn a technique, a "step by step" tutorial provides this assistance. According to mirugaiSC, "I would have to say that tutorials can be seen as a part of the self-teaching process." On the other hand, she noted that manuals are useful for specific tasks, such as learning to operate a printer. However, she contrasts using manuals to times when you do not have a "direct objective." She explained:

> I think that the difference between using a manual and being self-taught
> has to do with what you're trying to accomplish…When you want to try
> something out without a direct objective in mind, such as trying out a new
> software, that's more like "self-teaching" and you don't necessarily have
> guidelines to help you to achieve a particular goal. Basically, manuals are for
> when you want to know "How do I _(insert task here)_?" while self-teaching
> is for when you think to yourself, "Hm, I wonder how this works."

MirugaiSC's characterization of being self-taught evokes elite technical values that eschew what Perkel (2008) characterizes as forms of "copy and paste literacy." One might "lift" instructions from a manual or tutorial and metaphorically "paste" them into a particular situation, such as a work process. In copy and paste forms of online literacy, people reuse or remix materials, such as segments of HTML code, to obtain specific outcomes without necessarily achieving a comprehensive understanding of a system's underlying structure or overall functionality. What is at issue are interviewees' perceptions of the legitimacy of using such forms, and how they tie into ideologies of identity and learning.

Although some interviewees unambiguously associated socially encoded forms of knowledge such as manuals and tutorials as part of being self-taught, mirugaiSC introduces a further connotation. She associates it with more deep engagements and understanding of technologies. What is classified as being self-taught is not merely functional in her learning narrative. For mirugaiSC, being self-taught has cultural connotations that are associated with ideologies of appropriate use of computers; proper self-teaching is about in-depth engagement and learning how things "work." Still, her learning narrative indicates that some socially encoded forms of knowledge such as tutorials go "hand in hand" with being self-taught.

The narratives in the next two sections show the distinctions some interviewees made between being self-taught and using cultural artifacts such as manuals and tutorials. When the discussion turned to these forms, they used strategies such as disassociation and minimization to distance themselves from them, often in strong terms. Their disassociations suggest that usages of such forms were coded as negative identity practices that were not consistent with competent technical identities.

Disassociation

Fifteen-year-old Allison stated that she was self-taught. Further, she strongly rejected the idea that using a manual was useful for learning how to do "computer stuff." She strongly disassociates herself from using manuals. She expressed this view even for things that many people would say manuals are useful for, such as learning how to use a computer program.

> Patricia: Do you find yourself reading a lot of manuals to do the computer stuff?
>
> Allison: No. I must say I've never read a single manual for anything, even for like a computer program, like even Photoshop. I've never read a manual, unless we're in like graphic arts class where he's like we're required to read the manual, but I already know just about everything from figuring it out. It's not – I don't know – it's just, it's all easy.

Allison uses extreme terms to characterize her disassociation from using manuals to learn how to use computers. She notes that she has "never" read a "single manual" for "anything." These claims are very polarized with the extreme forms of "never" and not consulting even a "single" manual for any task. This characterization codes using a manual as a negative identity practice. She only uses one when "required" to do so, such as in a class. But prior to a class she "already" knows "just about everything" by "figuring it out." Through minimization, she characterizes classroom learning as negative identity markers in two ways. The first is by indicating that she does not need to read manuals, unless artificially required to do so in a classroom. The second is to say that even when she is required to read them, she appears to gain nothing from the exercise because she has already figured things out, since it is "all" just "easy."

Extreme forms of expression (such as "never" reading a manual) may invite ethnographic queries as to the claims' empirical realities. Although such verification is a legitimate research exercise, it is important to understand that in many contexts, it is someone's "perception of things that is of interest" (Agar 1980:225). As Agar (1980:225) observed long ago, asking only about the veracity of claims in ethnographic interviews is often an "inappropriate" question. The learning narrative, which may contain inconsistencies, is an idealistic form of autobiography in which the interviewee organizes experiences and implicitly provides analysis about the appropriateness of certain acts and how they relate to the self. By using such extreme terms, Allison makes visible a "hidden curriculum" in which *how* one learns is as important as *what* one learns.

Similarly, Wendy, a 16-year-old Asian girl from the east coast of the United States, disassociates herself from the practice of using online tutorials to learn to make videos. Wendy (a researcher-assigned pseudonym) participates regularly on YouTube, having first created a video for a class project. She joined in November 2005 before YouTube officially launched, which indexes her as an extremely early adopter of the site. She is an advanced amateur, who together with a group of friends made a series of sketch comedy videos. Chapter 4 details how she contributed her time to a volunteer organization for which she made a documentary video about problems with a run-down neighborhood park. Like Allison, and many of the boys in my study, Wendy characterized herself in her online chat interview as highly technical, and as "self-taught."

> *Patricia*:   How did you learn to make videos?
>
> *Wendy*:   I self taught myself basically, I'm a really fast learner and I'm a total computer geek, so eventually I learned how to do everything by myself with no manuals.
>
> *Patricia*:   Did you use computer tutorials like the kind you find on YouTube? Or video tutorials?
>
> *Wendy*:   Never, I have no patience for it...I end up getting much more confused than I was in the beginning.

Wendy associates being self-taught with being a "computer geek." Like Allison, she uses extreme phrasing. She is not just a geek, she is a "total" geek who learns not just some things but "everything" by herself. She rejects socially encoded forms of information such as manuals. Further, she rejects video tutorials on YouTube, saying she does not have the "patience" for them. This turn of phrase reverses characterizations associated with teacher's attitudes towards students. A good teacher is patient with slow students. Here, Wendy is impatient, implying that it is not the student, but the teaching that is slow paced or inadequate. She states that video tutorials "confuse" her more.

Wendy's assessment yields multiple interpretations. On the one hand, she could be criticizing the efficacy of the tutorials. It is not the genre itself that is the problem, but rather specific tutorials' ability to provide useful instruction. On the other hand, Wendy's comments appear within the context of rejecting socially encoded objects, such as manuals, that she distinguishes from being self-taught. In this sense, reliance on tutorials is a negative identity practice that is inconsistent with being a "total geek." Further research is necessary to understand why individual video makers accept or reject particular genres of instruction. Are they being rejected because individual instantiations are poorly executed from a functional point of view, or because as an entire genre they symbolically lie outside of acceptable, ideological parameters of being self-taught? Socially encoded forms of information were seen as generally unhelpful and thus did not present legitimate learning opportunities for the total geek.

Notably, both Allison and Wendy, who are female, present extremely polarized views that unhesitatingly reject socially encoded forms of information such as manuals. In so doing, they enact a new kind of "habitus" (Bourdieu 1977) within their technobiographies that opens a space for technologized personae among girls. Kearney (2006:12) explains:

> [Some] girls are helping to expand the experiences of contemporary girlhood and thus the spectrum of identities and activities in which all females can invest, for by engaging with the technologies and practices of media production, they are actively subverting the traditional sex/gender system that has kept female cultural practices confined to consumerism, beauty, and the domestic sphere for decades.

Kearney's point is important in that girls' reproduction of identities of being self-taught with respect to computers and media situate them in networked public spheres as highly technically competent. In my study, being self-taught aligned far less closely with whether a YouTuber was female or male, and more consistently with whether people perceived themselves as technical. People who saw themselves as a computer or video "geek" typically espoused an ideal of being self-taught, although the meanings of being self-taught varied across individuals.

Minimization

Both males and females in the study sometimes portrayed themselves as being self-taught by minimizing the contribution of social forms of instruction from peers, family members, or socially encoded forms of knowledge. A 13-year-old white girl who wished to be referred to by the pseudonym of Jordan acknowledged, but quickly minimized, parental assistance. Jordan's channel page indicates that she joined the site in January 2007, which makes her a relatively early adopter in the history of YouTube. Jordan makes videos with her three sisters, and with friends. She has a channel together with her sisters, as well as her own channel on YouTube.

During her online chat interview, Jordon mentioned that she is home schooled (but plans to attend a public high school). Her video page notes that church is very important to her. She told me that although many of her friends have computers, their parents are more "restrictive" than her own, and thus her friends do not participate online to the same extent that she does. Studies show that compared to boys, girls often experience more restrictive home access to computers (Holloway and Valentine 2003:61). Noting the effects of parental restrictions is an important observation that illustrates the variety of kids' experiences using computers. Such restrictive practices need to be ethnographically investigated to understand their potential impact on girls' informal learning. I have ethnographically observed that unfettered computer access can assist in the type of playing around that facilitates casual, informal learning.

Jordan posted 80 videos between 2007 and 2013. Her oeuvre includes diary video blogs, documentation of trips and special events, and slide show videos set to music. She also has videos in which she sings, puts on make-up, and participates in comedic vignettes. Her viewership varies widely. Many videos have a few hundred views or less, whereas her most viewed video, which includes a karaoke song performance, received over 50,000 views.

She describes her father but not her mother as capable with computers. She characterized herself and her sisters as "very good when it comes to computers and videos." Although her older sisters can edit video, she stated in her online chat interview that her younger sister depends on her for editing, although she was good at "directing."

> Patricia: How did you learn how to make videos, use a tripod, and do editing? Did your dad teach you?
>
> Jordan: Yes, my dad did, but I learned alot of it on my own
>
> Patricia: What is an example of something your dad taught you?
>
> Jordan: How to get into the [menu] on the camera, or how to hook it up to the tv.
>
> ...
>
> Patricia: And what is an example of something you taught yourself?
>
> Jordan: I taught myself what buttons were what and how to work the tripod.

Jordan became interested in video blogging when her dad and sister told her about YouTube. After seeing how much attention others received from making videos, she wanted to see if she too could become well known. Even these simple recollections offer two different socially based methods for learning about online participation. Her father and sister made her aware of YouTube, which opened up possibilities for accomplishing creative production and sharing her work. This digital literacy (that YouTube might be a good place to share her work) did not come from the self but rather from social sources. Further, she describes watching others and seeing which genres successfully garnered attention. Jordan engages in purposive viewing—to adapt Green's (2002) term of purposive musical listening—in which she learned about effective and popular genres on YouTube by watching other, successful video makers. These examples are social forms of learning that may or may not surface in learning narratives, especially those that aim to appear consistent with ideologies of being self-taught.

In her interview, I asked Jordan how she learned to make and edit videos, and whether she learned from her father or sister. In the first segment of her response, she acknowledges that her dad did teach her things about making videos. However, she quickly minimizes this fact and emphasizes being self-taught. In the same sentence, she follows the acknowledgement to her dad with the idea that she learned "a lot" of it on her own. Following targeted, direct inquiry, she produces specific examples of what her father taught her and what she learned on her own. But her initial response de-emphasizes her father's contribution and highlights the fact that she learned much about video making on her own.

Fred, the 18-year-old white male from the west coast of the United States who makes advanced-amateur videos with his friends as described in Chapter 2, similarly initially acknowledged social legacies and contributions. Fred (a researcher assigned pseudonym) mentioned that he began making videos because his dad had a camera. But during his learning narrative he emphasized being self-taught.

Patricia: So did your dad kind of teach you how to use the camera? What kind of camera was it?

Fred: It was – he just used an analog VHS camera at the time and he was kind of who taught me how to run that. And then eventually I moved on to using a digital camera. I'm mostly self-taught. I've pretty much figured out a lot of the editing and how to run the camera and just a lot of my resources and things I've just kind of figured them out myself.

Patricia: [Did] you end up teaching a lot about movie making to your brother Stuart?

Fred: Yeah, we kind of help each other through that. [We] both know just about all we need to know to get through the editing

process and all of that, but if one of us finds out a little trick or
something, we tell each other. I'd say we kind of figured it out
on our own. There wasn't a lot of learning between us. [We]
didn't both sit down and say, "Okay, now I'm going to show you
how to do this and this and that."

Initially, after a prompt in which he is asked about his dad, Fred
notes that it was his father who "kind of" taught him how to run it.
To "kind of" teach someone is a minimized form of teaching, which
occurred, incidentally on an older, analog, VHS camera. VHS stands
for video home system, a consumer video camera standard launched
in the 1970s. Fred quickly directs his learning narrative to focus on
how he eventually used a more advanced technology, a digital camera,
and how he is "mostly self-taught." He "figured out" how to do things
like "editing," and operating the camera. Fred's brief acknowledgement
minimizes the social contribution from his dad, and emphasizes the
fact that he was able to figure things out on his own.

Similarly, when queried about mentoring his 16-year old brother, Stuart,
who was also recognized by other members of their video-making group
as skilled, Fred initially acknowledges helping "each other" but once again
quickly minimized the sociality of their leaning trajectories. Learning narratives often simultaneously function as mentorship narratives. A mentorship narrative is an account of how people learn from or teach other people
to develop skills, adopt cultural attitudes with regard to executing tasks, or
accept particular literacies as important forms of knowledge. Autobiography of the kind prompted in an ethnographic interview typically contains
biographies of other people (Henwood et al. 2001). In this example, Fred
constructs himself and Stuart as similarly technically savvy.

Fred minimizes any "learning" by saying that both brothers "know just
about all [they] need to know." Even when he described potentially learning
or teaching his brother something, it is characterized in minimal ways such
as acquiring a "little trick or something" rather than learning something
more critical to the process of making videos. Fred states that "there wasn't
a lot of learning between us." Potentially influenced by his home-schooled
background, Fred seems to equate "learning" with more formal and institutional contexts. He describes learning as "[sitting] down" and deliberately
setting out to show someone specific things. His description evokes Drotner's (2008) characterization of formal learning, in which an encounter is
mutually recognized by all parties as an attempt to learn/teach something.
However, most of Fred's discourse minimizes "learning" in general.

Conflicting Narratives

Interviewees' frequent initial reaction to the question of how one learned was to emphasize how they were self-taught, with the aforementioned variety in what the term connoted functionally and ideologically. But as interviews progressed, it was often the case that additional details emerged about how one learned, and these details frequently involved social forms of information, from family, friends, and socially encoded artifacts. Learning narratives may be constructed in multiple ways, and are not limited to a specific ethnographic prompt.

In the example that follows, I spoke with Frank, a 15-year-old white male from the Midwestern United States. As described in Chapter 4, Frank (a researcher-chosen pseudonym) had a very eclectic oeuvre on YouTube. His work included soap opera parodies, discussions about video traffic, and video tips for YouTubers. He also posted video blogs that discussed important political issues such as net neutrality. A very early adopter of YouTube, Frank posted some 30 videos between February 2011 and YouTube's initial launch in December 2005. His most viewed video garnered some 2,000 views after being posted for three years, with his least viewed video receiving less than 100 after being posted for several months. At the time of our interview, Frank was very interested in YouTube and its participants. He posted video blogs indicating his concerns over how agonistic commentary was problematic, and how YouTube could become more of a community if people could get to know each other. During his interview, he acknowledged that over time YouTube might lose its "cool" factor, and that he was initially drawn to the site because it was not well known among the general, non-technical population. He enjoyed being on the leading-edge of new things online.

Frank characterized his parents, who are attorneys, as not particularly technical, but he mentioned having an older half-brother (in his thirties) who had obtained a film degree from a university. Early on in elementary school, Frank noted he had an interest in making videos and he credited his older brother with at least supporting that interest as they spoke about "movies and video stuff." In the following segment, Frank initially characterized his learning as "self-developed," but also recalled early interactions with his mother and a video camera.

Patricia: [How] about your parents? Did they teach you anything about video?

Frank: Not really. My parents aren't very tech savvy at all, so it's pretty much a self-developed interest on my part.

Patricia: Interesting. And when you first used a camera, do you remember, like, how old you were?

Frank: I know a lot – my mom, actually – she actually sort of knew how to work the camera, so she would record a lot of things, and then I would be in it. So I guess she did kind of teach me a little bit about it, because then I started using it to film some stuff. But I used to be in front of the camera, not behind it.

Patricia: Right. And when did you start getting behind it?

Frank: I slowly started doing more and more with it, and then I started definitely preferring being behind it probably fourth or fifth grade, cause I used to act in theater and stuff, but now I do crew and stuff. So I'm a behind the scenes kind of person now.

Initially Frank portrayed himself as having a "self-developed" interest and parents who are not "tech savvy at all." When the prompt moved away from "learning," he acknowledged more of his mother's contribution, including teaching him "a little bit about it." These remarks may initially seem contradictory. Again, learning a "little" from someone minimizes social learning. Plummer (2001) argues that recall memory, or how well one can recall personal details, is but one type of memory relevant to the analysis of life stories. Bruner (1987:31) asserts that life stories are less about detailed memory recall and more about offering insight into how an autobiographer "[structures] experience itself." Agar (1980:226-7) argues that the ethnographic interviewer should also focus on an interviewee's "perspective," defined as "an organization of concepts representing a guide for the analysis of different empirical instances."

Frank initially organizes empirical instances of his life trajectory in a way that emphasizes his "self-developed" interest in making videos. The biography of his parents as not technically savvy is compared to his tech-savvy persona, in which he had a self-developed interest in going "behind the camera" and pursuing technical aspects of video-making craft. His construction of a relational identity acknowledges yet initially minimizes his mother's contribution to his learning about videos. Portelli (1991) argues that what interviewees deliberately or inadvertently "hide" in oral narrative is just as important as what they tell. Even "wrong" statements are, in at least one sense, "psychologically true" to the interviewee's opinion of him- or herself (Portelli 1991:51). According to Portelli (1991:51), "The importance of oral testimony may lie not in its adherence to fact, but rather in its departure from it, as imagination, symbolism, and desire emerge."

Contradictions in the technobiographical learning narrative open an analytical space for understanding how interviewees wish to be portrayed in their own as well as in other people's eyes. In interviews expressly advertised as

investigating learning activities of "digital youth" on YouTube, interviewees' desire to be seen as technical may have motivated them to emphasize self-taught
aspects of their recollections of learning. For some interviewees, "learning" had
strong formal connotations that made informal learning encounters seem less
visible. Once they were prompted to provide other details about video-creation
and participation, additional information about their experiences emerged that
a researcher would likely label as part of informal learning.

Contradictions between the initial self-portrayal and eventual details
emerging in the learning narrative are well illustrated in an interview with
a 16-year-old white male from the Midwestern United States who asked to
be identified by his screen name of Carl. Wary of participating on YouTube,
his mediated, social center of gravity was located within the community of
first-generation video bloggers. This community of prominent early adopters included Jay Dedman, who co-founded the Yahoo! Video Blogging online
discussion list. This group believed that one should have one's own videoblogging webpage outside of YouTube. Many first-generation bloggers evangelized learning about video and believed that it was important to provide
support to other people who wished to learn about expressing the self through
video. Carl participated on the Yahoo! Video Blogging list in which people
asked questions and discussed the technical and social aspects of making and
sharing videos online.

Carl maintained his own video blog outside of YouTube, and with friends,
created several types of videos. His work included parodies of news broad-
casts done with friends, as well as other comedic sketches and video updates
about their work. Carl had not yet decided what he wanted to do professionally, but he said his parents believed he had a gift for making media, and he
was interested in practicing his skills to see where his efforts might lead.

Carl said that he considered his parents technical, and able to use computers. His mother is an accountant. He stated that he had three older sisters
who had completed college, were married, and had their own families. He
characterized two of the three sisters as "technical" with respect to "computers
and video." He noted that they taught him to use computers, and imparted
some tricks on making videos. But in his interview (conducted over Skype
in a voice-only call), he distanced himself from this social description, subse-
quently emphasizing that he "taught [himself] the rest."

> Carl: Well, [one of my sisters] taught me how to use computers and
>   how to, like, take care of it. And the other ones taught me some
>   of the tips on video and computer stuff. But I kind of taught
>   myself the rest.
>
> Patricia: Hmm. What kinds of things did you teach yourself?

Carl: How to install – my first one was how to install computer, or how to install programs on the computer, when I was, like, six. And then I've just – and video was something I just went on by myself. I just got a web cam and started from there.

Patricia: [How] did you teach yourself? Can you think of a few examples? You said you installed a program at six, but with regard to video?

Carl: Oh, video. Hmm. Well, I just read some stuff online and I just tried out, like, Windows Movie Maker and just experimented with it. So I just – I plunged in head first and just tried everything out.

Patricia: Mm hmm. You read ahead first and then tried everything out?

Carl: Well, no. I just plunged ahead and I tried it first, and if something didn't work, I would try something else or look for some tips online.

Initially Carl mentions that one of his sisters taught him "how to use computers," while his other sisters taught him "some of the tips on video and computer stuff." Carl quickly moves past this acknowledgment to state that he "kind of" taught himself the "rest." When prompted for examples of things he taught himself, he mentions installing computer programs which he began doing at the age of six. In terms of video, he started out with a web cam. He tried things out and if something "didn't work," he would "look for some tips online." What is interesting about this sequence is that Carl's narrative suggests crucial temporalities of learning. He only went online or sought tips when things did not work out. Such a sequential framing would suggest consistency with techno-cultural ideologies of learning that begin with one's own experimentation. Next, his narrative includes examples of things he learned from others when he became stuck.

Patricia: Do you remember any tips online that you got?

Carl: Yes. One tip was that – oh, yes. One tip I heard was keeping videos short online for people to be interested in them, and just – I actually got a video blogging book that's helped me. Do you want the name?...[Yeah,] it's *Video Blogging for Dummies*...It's been a – it's helped a lot.

Patricia: Oh, okay. What about the Yahoo! Video Blogging group? Do you get a lot of help from those guys?

Carl:	Yes. I got, like, help from, like, to use Quick Time from them. I just asked questions or just listen to discussions and I just got tips from there. And that's where I met [another video blogger]. I mean, as a video blogging friend, and we've been helping each other with videos.
Patricia:	Mm hmm. How do you help each other?
Carl:	Give ideas, test them out, or simply just give feedback and [that] has helped a lot.
Patricia:	Mm hmm. Can you think of a couple examples where you've helped each other on something specific?
Carl:	Oh, he was starting a new video series on his site, so we teamed up and had a video interview of it, and that – and really has helped increase the viewers of his show.
Patricia:	Hmm. And how has he helped you?
Carl:	He's helped me by giving me tips and he's actually just given me tips and given me feedback and also telling people about my site.

Over the course of his interview, Carl's learning narrative displays quite a range of social forms of assistance including family (his sisters), peers, and mentors in an online video blogging discussion forum. He also mentions socially encoded forms of information such as books and online discourse containing tips and tricks. The learning narrative is composed of comments not only following from a specific ethnographic prompt about learning, but also compiled over the course of the interview, as biographical details emerged during discussions about several subjects, including online participation. For instance, he used a book called *Video Blogging for Dummies*, which he said helped a lot. He also was a participant on the Yahoo! Video Blogging group. He mentions directly asking questions, or sometimes just observing discussions to gain tips and feedback.

Multiple interpretations may emerge from analyzing Carl's recollections. His learning narrative seems contradictory; he states that he taught himself yet he recalls drawing on a wide array of social forms of knowledge. One interpretation of these "contradictions" is that Carl is simply using the term "self-taught" to describe learning that exists outside of formal educational channels such as schools. In this sense, being self-taught is compatible with the range of sources he mentions such as reading books and asking questions in an online forum. Another interpretation is that being self-taught is a matter of degree. People can be introduced to things but can then teach themselves "the rest." They drive the process of learning something new by trying out and experimenting with a device, such as a web cam. In this sense, being self taught means being "self-directed," rather than responding to external pressure from parents or teachers to learn something specific. It is only when "something [doesn't] work" that Carl turns to online "tips." Carl emphasizes that the bulk of learning is on his own; it is only small "tips" that are needed.

An additional interpretation is that the contradictions yield, as Portelli (1991) suggests, a window into a "desired" technical persona of being self-taught. Maintaining a consistent portrayal of being self-taught becomes difficult when confronted with recollections of other forms of socially based learning that do not originate from "experimentation." Being self-taught is a truth, but it is also a narrative memory that functions to perform selective aspects of one's persona. Carl emphasizes those experiences which are compatible with being technical, and learning in the way that many elite technical cultures ideologically respect.

Narratives often have linear trajectories containing key temporalities in which things happen in particular sequences (Plummer 2001:400). Even when contradictions appear in learning narratives about how one eventually learned, detailed micro-sequences may emerge in which the initial impetus or interest in video is described as self-initiated and nurtured, and early learning is self-taught. Carl noted that he would just plunge ahead and try things first, and if something didn't work, his next move was to "try something else or look for some tips online." Trying things out on one's own before obtaining assistance is an important sequential aspect of a learning narrative that helps craft and performatively propose a technologically self-reliant persona.

Interrogating a Technologized Ideal

In describing how they learned to make videos and participate on YouTube, kids provide key information about the self that includes ideologies of learning and mentoring. Learning narratives discussed in this chapter reveal that being self-taught exhibits diverse connotations. For some kids, using socially encoded forms of media was acceptable, while for others, it was anathema. Being self-taught is part of many kids' realities, as they experiment and explore different kinds of video making and self-presentation skills. It is also a normative ideal, a concept deeply entwined with technical identities among kids and adults. Claiming to be self-taught echoes values exhibited in early computer cultures, which privileged trial and error as well as sharing and accessing arcane knowledge to achieve technical competence. Yet, not everyone adheres to this ideal in practice.

The processes of recognizing and handling learning opportunities are inseparable from people's self-conception of technical expertise. Ethnographic work reveals contradictions within learning narratives and provides a fuller picture of how kids learn and why they choose particular methods over others. Even highly technically oriented kids learn in social ways, though such forms are retrospectively minimized and coded as negative, technical identity associations.

"Learning" is a loaded word, and among technical groups it may have strong associations to culturally unacceptable types of formal classroom instruction. Even when socially encoded media are admitted as acceptable, temporalities of use are often crucial for establishing appropriate technical identities. In some cases, it is more acceptable to consult tutorials, manuals, and other media only as a last resort after intensive self-directed experimentation; in other contexts, socially encoded forms of knowledge must be consulted before approaching experts. In learning narratives that I gathered, one of the earliest ways to create learning opportunities was to give a child a camera. Passing on a material object often attitudinally codes it as worth using in daily life, and thus highlights its manipulation as a form of literacy. Kids' learning narratives often identified receiving a gift as the initial impetus that initiated a chain of experimentation and learning by having fun with a camera. Receiving a camera often meant receiving instruction about how to use it, even if these interactions were minimized in learning narratives.

Despite its symbolic loading, much can be gleaned when researchers ask directly about learning. Inconsistencies in learning narratives may appear as people recall the importance of mentorship encounters, yet casually minimize their personal impact. Researchers should not dismiss these inconsistencies nor focus only on reconciling them. Instead, ethnographers should explore them as desired aspirations of the technical self, and mine them for clues about people's learning dispositions. Future research projects might productively include both direct questioning about learning, and open-ended queries about creative production, interaction, and participation that do not carry the symbolically loaded term "learning." Resulting discrepancies may reveal considerable insight about personal aspirations as shaped through stances toward learning opportunities.

Even when being self-taught is understood in the same way (such as trial and error forms of learning), particular connotations of the term may be more efficient at different points in the phenomenological chain of learning about media. For example, trying things out on one's own might be more productive after a user has some basic knowledge of a task. Or, the opposite may be true; trial and error might be a better initial approach, and more complex, high-risk tasks or tasks with more severe consequences may require intensive mentorship. People's desired perceptions of their technical identities may prompt some individuals to avoid social forms or misrecognize rich, socially framed learning opportunities, even when these collaborative approaches may assist in improving digital literacies, especially at particular moments or within specific contexts.

Technically savvy peers do not always make good mentors. Parents have critiqued their children's "poor teaching" skills, especially when kids became frustrated with "their parents' slowness to pick things up" (Holloway and Valentine 2003:80). Children sometimes demonstrate feelings of "superiority and pleasure in the power that they hold" over their parents (Holloway and Valentine 2003:80). If learning on one's own is important for maintaining a technical identity, then having to teach others conflicts with a tacit, normative ideology of how one *should* learn.

An important implication of this research concerns skill assessment. Prior studies often cite parents' admiration as evidence of kids' technical prowess. But it is fair to ask, if some parents are supposedly far less technical than their children, how can they *know* that their children are technically competent? Supposedly atechnical parents can observe their kids solve technical problems or successfully execute tasks. Yet, additional assessment—perhaps emerging from outside of a kid's direct informal social network—may be required when evaluating complex tasks for which some observers may not be truly qualified to recognize mastery.

Many parents and kids now agree that to be a global citizen of the world, certain technical, self-presentation, and video-based participatory skills are necessary. As the debate rages on about whether to offer formal media courses in schools (Hobbs 1998), many kids have advanced their knowledge by taking advantage of their organic interests and calling upon networks of family, peers, and socially encoded artifacts for assistance in achieving new means of self-expression in a connected world. Perkel (2008) rightly argues that being able to call upon these social networks for assistance is an important literacy skill in and of itself.

However, not all kids may have access to networked opportunities, or find ready acceptance and help from their friends. If one's friends or acquaintances are not technically competent, adequate mentorship may be difficult to procure. Conversely, if one's highly technical peers espouse an ideal of being self-taught, then those without the "geeked out" interest or disposition to learn on their own may struggle to gain the expertise they need to craft personally expressive messages in a heavily mediated world. Kids who believe one should learn on one's own may not be particularly forthcoming with—or particularly capable of—providing adequate mentorship. Interventions may be required to address gaps in the socially constructed, informal learning spaces of kids' life worlds. Researchers need to push beyond the label of being "self-taught" and recognize how performing technical affiliation to this practice's complex connotations influences what is learned about mediated self-expression.

CHAPTER 8

‹‹‹ ◀ ■ ▶ ›››

Conclusion

Technical identities, digital literacies, and learning opportunities are intimately intertwined. It is hardly possible to talk to kids about what they learned about video and computers without understanding how they learned it and why they chose to learn it that way. Kids' learning opportunities are shaped in part by how they view themselves with respect to technological values and practices. Kids who see themselves as technical may not recognize mediated moments of learning or mentorship because they deeply espouse a techno-cultural value to learn on their own. Yet, as detailed across the prior chapters, most kids are not solely self-taught but rather rely on many social resources such as peers, family, tutorials, and socially encoded sources of information that help develop and negotiate what constitute digital literacies. Performing technical affiliation refers to displaying in words and actions certain beliefs, values, or practices that are assumed to be associated with particular techno-cultural groups. In the ethnographic study informing this book, kids often performed technical affiliation to being self-taught. In so doing, they often elided what they learned when growing up amid peers and families that provided techno-cultural values, equipment, knowledge, time, and emotional support so that kids can cultivate media skills and find new confidence in public self-expression.

Although most technically oriented participants espoused being self-taught, the term's meaning varied widely. To some interviewees, being self-taught was equated solely with tinkering and experimentation. For other participants, being self-taught meant being self-directed outside of classrooms, and included using tutorials, manuals, and social forums to improve. Yet things like tutorials are not simply neutral cultural artifacts found in the world; they are encoded by someone for someone else, and they identify appropriate digital literacies and technically inflected cultural values. Kids performed different degrees of affiliation toward socially encoded artifacts. Although some kids performed acceptance to socially encoded artifacts as commensurate with a technical identity, others roundly rejected them. Being self-taught is not a universally agreed upon category of analysis, and this term must be interrogated in more depth whenever it is used, especially in ethnographic interviews.

Learning opportunities were shaped in part by interpersonal dynamics. In some cases, making media with more technically oriented peers opened up new avenues for kids to learn about media and express the self. Participating in even ancillary roles in group video making helped kids learn how media is put together and how to craft visual messages. Kids reported discovering new technical knowledge or gaining self-expressive confidence by making videos with peers. Given the dearth of media programs in many schools (Buckingham 2003; Buckingham et al. 2000; Ito et al. 2010; Sefton-Green 2000), informal learning environments provide rich opportunities for gaining skills in manipulating and interpreting digital media.

Conversely, when kids exhibited highly asymmetrical knowledge, organic peer mentorship broke down. When kids did not share the basic technical vocabulary or interest in "geeky" topics, video making experts did not always exhibit the ability to bring others up to speed. Sometimes kids competed for higher position in micro-social hierarchies of technical ability and prowess; these competitions also shaped potential learning opportunities. One solution was to establish a space away from friends' critical eyes to develop new skills. Such competitions and jockeying for position show that negotiating identities requires more than just displaying the self online. Many scholarly works equate identity with online displays, yet these should more properly be analyzed as proposals or bids at particular identity characteristics. Successful ratification of technical personae depends on their negotiated uptake vis-à-vis other participants in technologized contexts.

Contrary to homogenizing discourses that portray "digital youth" as embracing all technologies equally, kids often displayed mediated dispositions in which they gravitated toward particular content, skills, and distribution preferences when they made YouTube videos. Even when they experimented with different genres or skills, kids' dispositions manifested in visible mediated centers of gravity as exhibited in their video oeuvres. Investigation of participants' accounts, rather than consideration of isolated videos, helps identify patterns in specialization and preferences. Of course, disposition may not always manifest in video catalogues; it is possible to prefer to do one genre, such as comedy, but feel the need to make tutorials to satisfy viewer interests. Researchers should investigate the alignment between disposition or preference and mediated output.

Although some degree of fluidity was observed among video making peers, in general people often exhibited consistent preferences with regard to the type of videos they made, the skills they contributed to group video making, and their choice of video making platforms and websites to showcase their work. As described in Chapter 2, some participants were content to specialize in more modest forms of messing around with a camera. Not everyone in the study expressed equal passion for making videos or appearing publicly in media, and when they did, kids tended to remain within particular roles—such as writing versus directing—that were suited to their personalities and mediated dispositions. Kids also observed wide gaps in technical ability not only vis-à-vis their non-video-making peers, but even within their own socio-economic, video making groups.

A key finding of this book is that digital divides extend beyond the traditional loci of investigation oriented toward gender, ethnicity, and class. Even if traditional divides are conquered (which seems highly unlikely), mediated dispositions, technical identity performance, concerns over public monitoring, and the dynamics of media peer groups will quite likely continue to influence how intensively kids gravitate toward making personally expressive media. Even though organic spaces of fun offer important skill-broadening opportunities, peer-based, video making dynamics may require interventions when learning gaps surface. Such interventions—whether emerging from classroom settings or informal environments—may be required to broaden access to media making when configurations of media-production and peer-to-peer mentoring fall short. Given that people have mediated centers of gravity that reflect and yield specializations, future interventions may be necessary to encourage skill development in areas in which a video maker is not inspired to strive for mastery.

Investigating informal learning in media environments requires broadened approaches. Despite the traditional emphasis on examining isolated media to understand online participation and digital literacies, much of the action occurs behind the scenes in micro-moments in everyday life. These subtle but crucial moves take place as Verdi noted (see Chapter 6) "all in and around and outside of" a particular video. Assessing informal learning dynamics also requires moving beyond the crude categorizations of production and viewership. Many steps occur at each moment within a chain of events in a video's creation. This book provides a phenomenological framework which advocates examining experiences of particular mediated moments in understanding how learning opportunities are recognized and handled. Such moments also have temporal inflections and influences. For example, the mediated moment of fun that one has when creating a video may not reveal improvement opportunities that become visible later on, at specific moments of viewership.

One may not notice a technical flaw or safety-related issue during the viewing of a video while editing, but may recognize the problem when viewing it after it has been posted, when seen in a different visual and cultural context. These varying contexts of viewership deserve consideration and are not productively collapsed under standard rubrics of "production" and "viewership."

Learning opportunities are shaped by different mediated moments of experience. Specific experiential pathways into digital spaces through video creation take on crucial salience for influencing how kids express the self through video. Studying spaces of play and media creation between peers remains vital to understand how social dynamics, individual dispositions, and technical affiliations interweave to influence the shape of learning opportunities in mediated contexts.

Pathways to Digital Literacies

Pathways to digital literacies were quite varied and were influenced in large measure by the interaction between individual identities and dispositions, and interactional dynamics. Peers and family provided crucial pathways into improving kids' digital media literacy skills by providing technical, financial, and emotional resources. Many case studies highlighted how participating with peers yielded new learning experiences. For example, the teenaged boys in Clubhouse Productions, discussed in Chapter 2, learned about video making fundamentals, technical processes, and visual story telling by participating with more technical, knowledgeable peers who were advanced amateurs working towards becoming media professionals. By participating in this group, teens reported learning many things, from technical facts such as camera positioning and lighting to finding acceptance with a mediated self.

In addition to making videos with friends, some very young children were introduced to media making as an accepted everyday activity and important life skill by their parents. Their pathway into creating videos began when parents gave them cameras, or encouraged them to find public self-expression through the medium of video, and by posting their work to online sites such as YouTube or to their own personal video blogs. Receiving a gift of a physical object such as a camera often provided the initial building block of a larger media infrastructure. Along with the camera came accompanying cultural values such as representational ideologies regarding using human images in personally expressive media. Sometimes families engaged in media skirmishes which, when posted publicly, saw potentially conflicting ideologies about how human images within families should be recorded and distributed. These interactions are also learning opportunities for families to see how interpretations and surrounding context are constructed by viewers.

As described in detail in Chapter 5, families with young children often make media together in ways that provide kids with media and representational ideologies. Through such things as testing technical devices, creating comedy sketches, and pranking, kids are introduced to aspects of technical culture that inform their future media practices. For example, in the case of Nick and his daughters, who are introduced in Chapter 5, images of girls describing cameras and other technical devices in the home reinforce the acceptability and appropriateness of kids having equipment that facilitates family fun, technical knowledge, and potential commercialization.

Through everyday forms of fun and humor, kids also learn about technocultural values espoused in technical groups. The discussion of Ted's prank (see Chapter 5) to drop in unannounced with his family to Malcolm, a fellow YouTuber whom he admired but had not yet met in person, is a prime example. The idea was to drop by Malcolm's house, meet him, and film the encounter for YouTube. Ted found Malcolm's contact information based on clues he gleaned on the Web. The video Ted's family recorded, which contained a technical hack, showed Malcolm and viewers how personal information is easily accessed online. The video prank is one example of the interrelationship between technical skills, humor, and hacking practices that are modeled to children as part of a techno-cultural identity that kids receive from family members as they grow up. Even if they do not perceive this everyday media making as learning, it is nevertheless part of kids' enculturation into appropriate participation in mediated milieus.

In learning narratives, or stories about how they learned, kids discussed the development of technical skills and access to physical resources that led to digital literacies. Yet, it is also important to recognize how emotional support can significantly help kids to gain appropriate levels of confidence when making media. As described in Chapter 3, Ashley's mother Lola was highly supportive and agreed to help her make YouTube videos in which they geek out and discuss reality TV shows. Stories of women and girls on YouTube show how females can use the medium of video to discuss subjects they enjoy and present a mediated, technologized identity of being a geek.

Despite the rhetoric of being self-taught that both mother and daughter promoted in interviews, it was quite clear that Ashley grew up in a media ecology that was highly conducive to self-actualizing through using technology and making personally expressive media. Not only did Ashley have access to computers and networks, the family also provided many knowledge resources. Lola had expertise in working with and fixing computers and Ashley had extended family members who were formally trained in filmmaking. Such transfers of institutional knowledge into informal settings of learning challenge the commonly held strict binary of knowledge sources that are said to divide professional and advanced-amateur media creators. In fact, professional filmmaking in the United States often begins as family affairs in which skills and job opportunities are passed down through social connections (Cole and Dale 1993:28; Kearney 2006:193). Studies argue that for girls, a mother figure is often crucial for increasing girls' confidence in using technology (Furger 1998). Ashley appreciated having the social and emotional infrastructure to be "self-taught." Lola helped create a socially shaped learning opportunity that gave her daughter Ashley an advantage in developing new media skills.

This dynamic contrasts to video making groups that exhibited difficulties in offering learning environments in which everyone had democratized access to making videos. Complicating factors included the time pressure of achieving results in an advanced amateur media context, and the fact that some members' mediated dispositions did not exhibit sufficient interest in learning the intricacies of video making. Some members were simply unable to push past their comfort zones. As discussed in Chapter 2, Max said that although he was recognized as the video specialist in his school, teaching most of his peers was difficult because they simply did not have the basic knowledge or vocabulary for him to bring them up to his level. Similarly, Frank stated in Chapter 4 that it was difficult to interest his peers at school about civic issues such as net neutrality because they were not interested in such "geeky" issues. Despite the fact that net neutrality has ramifications for everyone using the Internet, the informal learning process broke down when kids did not embrace the value of "geeky" topics.

Learning is an interactive process in which both the mentor and mentored presumably express desire to change the learner's state of knowledge. But not everyone exhibits pedagogical instincts or values. Technical individuals who strongly espouse the ideal that one should be self-taught are not inclined to help others. Tutorial makers have been observed to feel disdain for the users of their tutorials and to eschew using such materials themselves (Perkel and Herr-Stephenson 2008). As described in Chapter 7, not all interviewees in my study embraced tutorials as appropriate for being "self-taught." In addition, I found that geeking out on technology often makes a person feel special and maintaining a relative identity of being a geek can feel empowering. Some people may wish to strengthen rather than relax the barriers between geeks and non-geeks as a way to perform technical expertise. Technical affiliations and relative levels of expertise need to be studied as identity variables, to see how they affect interpersonal mentoring dynamics. Interventions may be necessary when peer mentorship is too asymmetrical or socially hierarchical to help kids learn about technologies and break through their initial dispositions.

In addition to peer dynamics, mediated dispositions that manifest in video specialization also impacted the crafting of technical identity and forms of learning. Consider the experiences of Anesha, an African American teen who specialized in editing. She also enjoyed the genre of making machinima videos. In a video exchange, a friend of hers on YouTube playfully challenged her status as an expert in editing. As discussed in Chapter 3, her editing skills gave her a relative, recognizable identity among her video making peers. The informal learning environment of YouTube enabled her to practice and develop her technical skills.

However, a legitimate question for educators and policy makers is whether specializations promote a broader suite of skills that includes verbal expression and writing as well as visual composition and technique. Even though Anesha specialized in editing and machinima, her video oeuvre did not contain the kind of civic discussion that was so well articulated in Chapter 4 by other kids on YouTube such as Frank (net neutrality), Wendy (neighborhood park improvement), Max (human rights and world peace), and the Field family (environmental concerns). Digital literacies include a wide range of interwoven skills and media. Having developed deep skills in a particular area such as editing or genres such as machinima does not guarantee achievement of skills in other areas such as rhetoric or civic engagement. A legitimate question for future research in informal learning in digital media is, Does specialization between peers encourage or complicate development of skills outside of areas of preferred expertise?

Although few in number, the selected case studies profiled in this book suggest that kids can accomplish civic engagement. Pathways into this skill may include, as it did for Wendy, volunteering media skills to community groups, or video blogging one's personal political concerns, as was the case for Frank. Children may also be introduced to civic mindsets through everyday family video blogging activities. As discussed in Chapter 4, the story of the Field family, who video blogged together in ways that helped form attachment to place, shows that civic engagement is being accomplished somewhat differently than in the past when participants oriented around issues. Pathways to digital literacies with regard to civic engagement are rather more diffuse. Many participants bond first through doing fun things together, such as making videos, and issues follow later. Participants often used media to reticulate or draw others into a social network that could lead to discussion around particular issues. A casual video blog about environmentally friendly buses emphasizes the family's and viewers' sociality, but it simultaneously raises awareness about environmental concerns. For some parents, the goal was not for their children to achieve stardom through video blogging, but rather to learn how to have a public voice in a global arena.

YouTubers also showed support of issues not only in terms of overt media content, but also with respect to the type of media or genre they chose to broadcast their message. For instance, Frank promoted net neutrality by making modest video blogs; he argued that the net should remain open for people of all economic levels and media preferences (including media with low production values such as diary forms of video blogs). In using a video with modest production values, Frank metaphenomenologically illustrated his arguments by using the very media approach he was trying to protect. If the phenomenological refers to how people experience the world, then an experience that normatively or proscriptively evaluates an experience is a metaphenomenological act. It is an experience that evaluates or assesses an experience. Making a modest video blog that supports net neutrality exhibits a kind of "meta" or observational quality about what constitutes appropriate media. By making the kind of media that one identifies as under threat, one illustrates the importance of using and protecting more modest media forms that may be jeopardized by fee structures that give more access and privilege to those who are able to pay.

Frank's video blogs provided a networked, peer-to-peer pathway for viewers to learn about an important political issue. Frank's video blog urged more democratized access to online expression of multiple voices. By providing information, opinion, and links, Frank's blog provided pathways for connecting others to gain insight and support net neutrality. People coming to the blog to hear Frank's point of view were thus reticulated into a civic discourse on net neutrality—even if they did not come looking for this topic in his diffuse video blogs.

The open space of online video offered an impressive variety of pathways into developing technical and self-expressive skills through exploration of organic interests. Although people tended to exhibit mediated dispositions, having a mediated center of gravity in one's oeuvre does not mean that one is incapable of developing digital skills in other areas. The completely open space of public sites may not serve all kids' interests to the same degree. Some people may benefit by finding places to learn in more safe and encouraging, perhaps semi-public learning environments, whether formal or informal. Kids' pathways to learning are complex and interactive, and not everyone may thrive when publicly performing technical affiliation to being self-taught.

The Ramifications of Being Self-Taught

Moving forward, scholars in informal learning should investigate why being self-taught is an important value, what is meant by this term, and under which circumstances being self-taught is productive. The concept of being "self-taught" brings forth an Americanized connotation of pulling oneself up by one's bootstraps and going it alone. Being self-taught is a techno-cultural value that intensifies when American kids are directly asked about their digital media practices and forms of learning. For many kids, to be technical is to be self-taught, even if this is never precisely how it works. Yet, how does one even know that it is important to be self-taught? Why is that important to emphasize in technical cultures? Somewhere along the line, kids were taught to be self-taught.

Investigating cherished values of being self-taught has important ramifications for understanding the landscape of informal learning. Peers are not always able to help others and tutor them in the way that they need. A solution may lie in what Ito (2012) calls "connected learning," which is "socially connected, interest-driven, and oriented towards educational or economic opportunity." The process calls for finding the right match of mentor to mentee to achieve successful learning exchanges. In classrooms, students might be teamed with peers who display strengths in contrasting skills so that everyone can push beyond their initial mediated dispositions. However, care should be taken to avoid surrendering tasks to specialists.

Another implication concerns what happens when kids internalize a value that is ultimately not beneficial for them in general, or in specific circumstances. What happens if kids think that culturally and proscriptively they *should* be self-taught because it is assumed that tinkering is the most beneficial way to understand fundamental technical structures, even though being self-taught does not address their individual learning needs? What problems might ensue for them, as digital divides based on dispositions and identity performances become ever wider? Being self-taught may be more appropriate for certain tasks, or during certain stages of the learning process. Yet, striving to maintain a respectable technical identity may make such socially driven learning opportunities difficult to identify or act upon. In striving to maintain an identity of being technical, people may eschew seeking help when they most need it, thus ironically self-sabotaging their technical progress. Educational programs may identify these discrepancies and address them. Sometimes online learning gaps are based on technical knowledge, but at other times, they result from people's dispositions or emotional readiness to show their work to a critical and unknown audience. Complications are likely to increase given governmental, parental, and corporate monitoring of everyone's publicly available online activity. Digital literacies include not only making media but developing the skills to know what to post, and to handle widespread and sometimes poorly articulated criticism. Emotional skills are also important for developing a mediated, public presence.

To question the role of the "self" in being self-taught is not a mere exercise in word play; it is crucial for understanding the social processes and effaced chains of learning that are crucial for achieving digital literacies. The use of socially encoded artifacts invites additional pedagogical and theoretical questions, such as: Why was certain information shared and other information excluded in these artifacts? Why are some techniques highlighted while others ignored in materials such as video tutorials? Why did participants choose to learn certain things and not others? Why and how did they come to accept certain information, ideologies, or practices (such as being self-taught) as important?

Focusing on being self-taught minimizes the recognition of the phenomenological chains of learning that are crucial for understanding how people develop digital skills and literacies. For example, consider Carl, the teen who was introduced in Chapter 7. Carl said he had been largely self-taught, but also gleaned numerous tips from people on the Yahoo! Videoblogging discussion list. Many of the participants on that list, which was started by Jay Dedman, were first-generation video bloggers and professional media makers in mass media industries who had considerable knowledge and expertise about new media and video blogging. For Carl, learning on one's "own" included finding tips and helpful advice from some of the most experienced, knowledgeable, and successful video bloggers in the world! These effacements need to be brought back into the light in order to create effective learning strategies.

Formal education often takes on a negative, staid, and less technical connotation for kids. Yet, trajectories of video making for some kids began when teachers assigned a media project, or encouraged students to create videos as part of a class assignment. The dynamic between playful spaces of learning and formal institutions need not be binary or unidirectional, but may be mutually-influencing. Kids may start by doing a class project, or having fun with media, and they may learn quite a bit by making videos together. In cases where gaps occur due to the particular shapes of learning environments that kids encounter, teachers and policy makers might assess and identify asymmetries in technical ability and confidence. Peers in informal learning environments do not always offer necessary levels of assessment that index mastery. Phenomenologies of learning may become more fluid within and outside of classrooms according to particular needs. Educators might discover individuals' mediated dispositions and craft learning opportunities that safely encourage participants to move outside of their mediated comfort zones.

Dialogic Emergence of Learning

When people use socially encoded forms of information or learn from peers, they effectively enter into a kind of dialogue and negotiation about what is important to know when making media. Anthropologists have long understood that language and culture are "dialogical," in that they are the "result of thousands of life-changing dialogues" (Attinasi and Friedrich 1995) that shape interactions. Indeed, "every interaction takes place within specific social, institutional, and historical coordinates, all of which color the interaction at the same time as they are reshaped, to greater or lesser extent, by that interaction" (Mannheim and Tedlock 1995:9). Similarly, learning interactions are dialogical. Any particular encounter is influenced by the many prior interactions, discourses, conversations, and cultural ideas about what constitutes appropriate digital literacies and learning in specific contexts.

The emergent outcome of learning opportunities may not be predicted from examining individual elements such as the people, technologies, and values that shape them. Yet, the interactional alchemy of these variables influences what kids learn about media. One cannot simply predict that a person will be an avid video maker, simply because they live in a computer-rich and networked ecology filled with technical and mentoring resources. In addition, gendered assumptions about technology use do not always bear out; as discussed throughout the book, girl geeks and moms are taking up the camera and expressing their technical identities through video making. Also, case studies of same-sex siblings in the same household sometimes show vastly different attitudes with regard to learning about technology and making videos. These examples demonstrate that technical identity variables should be studied in their own right, and that gender, class, and other traditional identity variables are not reliable predictors of technical identity and commensurate affiliations. People may encounter proscriptive ways of making videos, but various ideas may be taken up at different times, or according to participants' personalized uptake within the contours of a particular learning opportunity.

Learning opportunities may yield different outcomes according to the technical and social variables that go into the mix. During a mediated moment, interactions unfold according to the sequence of actions and choices participants make within a learning encounter. For instance, as described in Chapter 2, Ben and Clyde made videos together. But Ben had (jokingly?) said that he did not need Clyde to make videos and that he knew much more than Clyde did. Having a technical identity is relative; to be technical arguably means knowing more than someone else who is less—or not at all—technical. In an interview with me, Clyde said that he (jokingly?) set up a different, "secret" account that did not reveal his identity. His goal, he said, was to learn how to make better videos. When he achieved fame on YouTube through his amazing videos, he would reveal all to Ben, and demonstrate that Ben was wrong in his technical assessments of Clyde's abilities. Clyde continued to work with Ben and had fun making videos, yet he also created a separate space to create and experience learning opportunities with other friends. Technical identity performance within techno-social and techno-cultural configurations shaped Clyde's perceived learning opportunities.

This book focused on unpacking the dynamics and impact of the mediated moment on learning opportunities. Understanding and recognizing the phenomenologies of these events helps analyze how digital literacies are proposed, taken up, rejected, and negotiated. Not every piece of advice or information that is posted on one's videos on YouTube, for example, is taken up and read as useful or is ratified as a digital literacy. New media studies suggest that circulating one's work to a wide viewing public has been extremely fruitful for learning how to improve. Yet, while some advice may be well intentioned, not all of it is taken up and ratified as providing an appropriate path to improvement.

Participants may or may not collude (McDermott and Tylbor 1995) with their interlocutors and ratify proposed digital literacies, or submit to how a learning opportunity plays out. Note that Clyde did not fully ratify the way in which Ben had characterized their video making dynamic and relative levels of expertise. In many circumstances, a dialogic interaction occurs in which the mentored considers whether or not advice or interpersonal learning dynamics will be applicable or useful to their circumstances.

Learning opportunities emerge in the dialogic interaction between video makers and viewers. Recall from Chapter 2 the case of Therapix, the YouTuber from Spain in his 20s who was popular for his video tutorials. His very identity shows his position as a person providing "picture therapy" consultations to YouTubers. Therapix created tutorials to teach YouTubers to incorporate special effects into their videos. He became popular for these tutorials as viewers responded positively to learning about the techniques he demonstrated, such as adding a special-effects "light saber" to their videos. In the mediated moments of distribution and viewership, what was perhaps not anticipated was that the process helped Therapix to improve the quality of his tutorials. He learned that he had to make them easy to follow and compelling. His experience of making videos tutorials improved through dialogic interaction with viewers. He not only helped others learn a special effects technique; he interactively discovered what made a good tutorial, a genre with its own requirements. The mediated moment of learning for viewers (to learn about how to add special effects in videos) became a learning opportunity for the video creator (to improve the quality and legibility of his tutorials).

Notably, however, not all advice that one receives within a particular learning opportunity is taken up by a media maker. It may not even be recognized as relevant to improving digital literacies; some commentary is about facilitating a viewer's personal tastes and desires. The case of Eric and Liam, the young teens who fled YouTube, illustrates this dynamic. They greatly decreased their engagement with YouTube after receiving odd comments from a viewer who complimented them on their "hot bodies." Similarly, Wendy, who created comedy videos, lip-synched videos, and a documentary about underserved neighborhood parks said that she received comments from so-called "haters." Negative comments included being told she was "ugly" or "not funny." She neutralized these comments by perceiving them as "funny" time wasters. Wendy told me that she never let them deter her from making and posting more videos.

Comments about revealing young bodies or changing the comedic direction of their videos were not received as ways to improve digital literacies. They rightly were rejected as unhelpful. Although these types of comments are easily dismissed by the video makers, other comments, intended to improve the technical and communicative aspect of videos may be incorporated into a maker's repertoire. However, not all comments are so neatly compartmentalized; some comments may be received in ambivalent or contradictory ways.

Future research in media learning opportunities outside of classrooms should attend to how advice is taken up, rejected, or ambivalently evaluated by those seeking to improve. Given that "literacies" are typically negotiated according to context, it is not surprising to see certain suggestions fall into gray areas or be rejected. Future studies should document and analyze, in an interactive and phenomenological way, the dialogical uptake or rejections that occur when a person or socially encoded artifact proposes an idea, skill, practice, or value that is said to improve the quality of a video making process.

An area that is often highly dialogical in terms of appropriate video making includes ethics. In many cultural groups in the United States, media has become integrated into expressions of affection and love. To record someone in a loving, respectful way is to transmit the message that the person or that moment is worth preserving in video. The *act* of recording becomes just as or even more important than looking at the images later. A common trope in films includes a child at the big game or recital who searches in vain for their parents in the audience. The absent paparazzo-parent and the lack of commensurate footage of their big moment index a broken or uncaring relationship between child and parent in these films.

Yet, not all kids or parents agree on what constitutes ethical video making in an era in which images tend to exist in perpetuity or be appropriated in unanticipated ways. In this context, ethics have an emergent quality that depends upon the layers of context in which media is produced and circulated. Sometimes it is through media skirmishes—in which people disagree on how or whether media subjects will be recorded—that ethics are interactionally and dialogically established between parties in a media making encounter. Representational ideologies are revealed in these skirmishes, and if they are ratified they may become accepted digital literacies of video creation.

Mediated disappointment among families is not relegated to poignant vignettes depicted in fictional films. Not all parents have the disposition or desire to intensively record their children's lives. People growing up without video may be disappointed at their dearth of personal media histories. Michael Ambs, a member of the first-generation video blogging community who asked that I refer to him by his real name, expressed such disappointment. Although he had photographs, little video of him was recorded when he was a small child.

> *Mike:* My parents didn't give me any video or anything like that. We never really had like a camera in the house when I was growing up, which sucks 'cause it seems like everybody I know has video of them running around as a kid and I don't. I have like all of two minutes of me as a toddler of what I've seen.
>
> *Patricia:* Are you disappointed about that?
>
> *Mike:* Yeah. It sucks because it's crazy to see yourself as a kid. My uncle was like – my dad's twin brother, he has some video of me running around and it was so surreal to see it. I want more of it. That's all there is.
>
> *Patricia:* If you had kids would you take video of them?
>
> *Mike:* Oh yeah. I'm gonna have so many videos and stuff and pictures of my kids.

Kids may feel regret when they grow up if there are no images of them as kids, but the mediated moment of recording may present challenges if a person does not feel like being recorded at a particular moment, and a resulting altercation ensues.

Media skirmishes refer to those encounters in which people hold different ideas about the appropriateness of a particular recording or its distribution. By working through these skirmishes dialogically, appropriate boundaries and digital literacies are created and articulated. It is often lamented that media online receives criticism because the commenters have no "context" for understanding the circumstances under which media is recorded and shared. However, as described in Chapter 6, a home video of a seemingly resistant teenaged daughter in the Verdi family that was posted online (after a family negotiation not revealed on camera) ushered in a passionate debate from viewers about video blogging ethics. The Verdi case study suggests that even after layers of context about the video's creation were provided in comments and a response video, it was nevertheless perceived as controversial by certain individuals from within their community of video bloggers.

The moral contradiction to the contextual lament suggests that even when people are provided with context about a video's creation, it may not be interpreted as relevant if viewers hold dissimilar moral views to those of media creators. Such viewers will not likely accept or agree that knowing more "context" will shed additional light on the issue. Scholars have observed a human tendency to ignore context that does not fit with a person's original moral assessment of a situation (Gellner 1970 [1962]). In the Verdi example, each text commenter brought to the mediated court of public opinion the contextual arguments that justified their views. In the phenomenology of the mediated moment of recording, father and daughter might have engaged in a media skirmish, but in the mediated moment of editing and creating the video, they might have had a good laugh and agreed that it was appropriate to share, thus ratifying a particular representational ideology of human-image recording and distribution. Their story suggests that for some viewers, the mediated moment of recording may hold different interpretive ethics than those exhibited in the mediated moment of distribution; for other viewers, subsequent interpretations during editing do not challenge their original interpretations of events during recording.

This book sought not to adjudicate such ethical issues, but rather to be a co-productive text that invites readers to consider their own practices, and reflect on how they engage in chains of learning about what constitutes ethical media making practices. Such a process is ongoing and ever changing, and requires concentrated attentiveness on the part of all media makers and viewers to ensure sensitivity to mediated participants and creators. The phenomenology of the mediated moment may assume different tones; a playful moment of video creation could reveal subsequent problems that are revealed in the mediated moments of viewership. Such revelations might prompt creators to take action and reconsider their video making practices. Digital literacies are negotiated in an ongoing way between creators and viewers, whose opinions may change over time.

Dialogic aspects of learning are important to understand, so that interventions may be designed to push past obstacles created by kids' mediated dispositions and technical identity performances. As kids learn outside of classrooms, and as schools become more porous by incorporating online sources through networked learning, more fluid learning environments with various shapes will offer a broadened—and unpredictable—array of learning experiences. By watching kids on YouTube, we may all learn how to become self-actualized contributors to our mediated world.

APPENDIX

《《《◀ ■ ▶ 》》》

Studying YouTube: An Ethnographic Approach

This book draws heavily from an ethnographic study that I undertook between 2006 and 2008. The goal of the study was to understand how kids aged 10 to 18 used YouTube in everyday life in the United States. Funded by the John D. and Catherine T. MacArthur Foundation, the objective was to investigate, in an open-ended, ethnographic way, what kids did when they hung out on YouTube. Key questions included: How and why did kids make videos? What kinds of videos did they make? How did kids learn about videos and computers? What did kids learn by making their own videos or cooperating in other people's media?

The study combined new forms of digital ethnography with classical methodological approaches. New forms of ethnography included observing mediated interaction, participating online, posting open video field notes, and studying dispersed interaction online and in person. Although YouTube was a point of departure as an online "field site," research was conducted at gatherings and through media as interaction occurred.

Contemporary ethnography often calls for participation in mediated, digital milieu. To that end, I maintained my own video blog called *Anthro Vlog* (for anthropology video blog) to understand the video blogging experience. I maintained one version of this blog on YouTube, and a similar one outside of YouTube, using WordPress, a blogging platform. Publicly posting interviews and field work stands in stark contrast to traditional models, in which anthropologists arrive in the field alone, collect data, and release only the final ethnographies for public review.

Similar to traditional ethnographies, the study combined 1) an intensive two-year investigation; 2) a multi-method, comparative analysis; and 3) a deeply detailed and descriptive approach to understanding video-making practices, online video sharing, and YouTube participation. The study also combined analyses of interviews, artifacts, and first-hand participation. No-

Patricia G. Lange, "Studying YouTube: An Ethnographic Approach" in *Kids on YouTube: Technical Identities and Digital Literacies*, pp. 231-236. © 2014 Left Coast Press, Inc. All rights reserved.

tably, artifacts included not only videos, but also surrounding discourse such as video makers' text descriptions of their videos and viewers' text comments posted to the videos.

The study benefited from a comparative approach that analyzed You-Tubers as well as a group that I refer to as first-generation video bloggers. Although many kids maintained YouTube accounts, not everyone's mediated center of gravity was focused on the site. Fiercely espousing a democratization of the lens, first-generation video bloggers began exchanging ideas, compressing video files, and uploading videos to their own websites at least as early as 2004, before YouTube was launched. Compression refers to transforming a large video file to a format that reduces the file size for transmission online, yet provides acceptable levels of quality. Such techniques made it feasible to post video on more personalized rather than institutionally sponsored websites.

Comparing practices on and off of YouTube yielded many interesting observations that might otherwise be elided through the study of one, albeit vastly popular, video-sharing site. Posting to YouTube is a choice from among other video-sharing options, each of which has ramifications on public negotiation of technical affiliations and identity associations. Video bloggers were often perceived as more technical if they had worked out compression techniques to post to their site before YouTube even opened. Although many scholars speak of all online videos as "YouTube videos," the stories of kids and families among first-generation bloggers reveals numerous cultural choices, affiliations, and identifications that are often elided in discourses about online vernacular video sharing.

First-generation video bloggers also influenced some YouTubers. Mark Day, a popular YouTube comedian who later became a Comedy Content Manger for YouTube, said he was in part influenced by Ze Frank, who began adding video to his websites before YouTube opened (Buechner 2005). Ze Frank maintained a wildly popular video show from 2006 to 2007. In a video called *Greetings from VidCon*, posted on July 10, 2010, Day, a highly recognized YouTube participant, describes how Ze Frank's fast editing and provocative, comedic style was influential to him. Such video blogging influences coming from outside of, yet impacting, YouTube are often missed in mass-media coverage of the site.

Data

The ethnography combined analyses of more than 200 videos, interviews from 150 participants, numerous text comments posted to videos, and observation of behavior both on and off of the site. The study began in the 2006-2008 timeframe, about six months after YouTube opened to the public. Research continues as of this writing, as additional data are analyzed to understand video-sharing practices. Notably, most of the participants interviewed were early adopters of the site. It is thus not surprising that most of the kids in the study considered themselves to be technical in terms of using computers and making videos. Knowing that YouTube existed before it became a mainstream site of video sharing was one way of demonstrating a technologized identity.

The study was conducted in an open-ended way with regard to the types of videos chosen for analysis. However, video blogs and comedy sketches were popular with young people and facilitated potential identification for study recruitment. It was easier to guess that video makers might be children if they put themselves in their videos. Video blogs were also of personal interest to me, and thus this genre is well represented in the research. From its inception, YouTube focused on video blogging, although in recent years it has trended toward more commercialized fare. YouTube's first test video, entitled *Me at the zoo*, was uploaded on April 23, 2005. The video depicted Jawed Karim, one of YouTube's founders, commenting on an elephant exhibit. Other genres—including comedy sketch, everyday hanging out, events, machinima, prank videos, and many others—were also analyzed. The ethnography did not target a particular genre, but rather analyzed what study participants chose to do with video.

The study analyzed interactive moves, rather than simply examining media as isolated artifacts. When kids posted a video that communicated a message, and others responded by posting response videos or text comments, such moves resulted in *interactions*. The study considered how such public interactions provided insight into how kids shaped learning opportunities and how they crafted technical identities.

Interviewees

The ethnography uses the term "kids" instead of "children"; it is an emic term used by kids to refer to themselves. To some young people, the term "children" holds an adult-centric, disempowering connotation of their work, education, and lives. The term "kids" was used to display respect for their self-portrayal and media experiences.

Kids were recruited based on videos they had posted online, and through my social networks of colleagues who had age-appropriate acquaintances. Kids also suggested friends or peers for the study. A few kids were interviewed in the San Francisco Bay Area, or in the Los Angeles area near where I lived and worked at the University of Southern California, although an effort was made to interview kids from different areas of the United States.

In all but one case, participants posted at least one video to YouTube. Most kids were interviewed using a voice-only Skype service, which resembles making a telephone call over the Internet. A few kids were interviewed using online chat, and a few kids and families were interviewed in person in their homes.

I interviewed 40 young people who participated on YouTube. These included: 22 kids (aged 9-17) and 18 youth (aged 18-26). In addition I interviewed 110 adult participants. I had the opportunity to interview some of the parents of the youth who participated in the study, as well as parents of very small children (younger than 10 years old). In addition, I interviewed adult YouTubers whom kids greatly admired. Interviewees were mostly from the United States, as it was the focus of the study, although influential participants from Europe, Australia, and Canada were also interviewed.

Semi-structured interviews included questions about perceptions of learning, technical identity, and video-making. Sample questions included 1) How did you begin making videos? 2) How and why did you begin posting videos to YouTube? 3) Do you consider yourself technical with regards to using computers and making videos? Why or why not? 4) How did you learn to make videos? 5) How do you make videos? and 6) What makes a video "good" or "bad"? As is the case with many ethnographic studies, participants exhibited a rich variety of experiences, and interviewees were also given an open-ended opportunity to talk about personally important issues.

Participation

Although the website of YouTube was the study's point of departure, it became apparent that many kids, adults, and families on YouTube were making offline connections to other participants. Some met in person at private gatherings or at large-scale meet-ups that attracted YouTubers from around the world. I attend several public meet-ups in New York City; Los Angeles; San Diego; San Francisco; Marietta, Georgia; Minneapolis; Santa Monica; Philadelphia; and Toronto, Canada. I also attended special events. For instance, I was invited to attend the Hollywood DVD release party for the popular YouTube channel called *Ask a Ninja*. About 75 video-recorded interviews with adult participants were conducted at the meet-ups that I attended.

At gatherings, people mostly socialized, made videos, and explored local sites together. At a meet-up in Philadelphia, for example, I joined YouTubers at the restaurant and gaming facility called Dave & Busters. I also attended gatherings and events popular with first-generation video bloggers. For example, I served as a curator for Pixelodeon, the first independent video blogging festival, which was held at the American Film Institute in Los Angeles in 2007.

Participant observation also included posting my own videos online. Having two video blogs—one on YouTube and one on a WordPress video blogging site—facilitated a comparative analysis. Although I posted similar and sometimes the same videos on both blogs, I varied my intensity of engagement across sites. Whereas I was very active on YouTube, on the WordPress video blog I maintained a relatively quiet online presence. Perhaps not surprisingly, I received far more attention on YouTube for the same videos that I posted to both publicly available online sites.

The videos posted to *Anthro Vlog* on YouTube received a combined total of more than one million views. One of the videos, *What Defines a Community?*, in which I queried participants about the possibilities and limits for community on the site, was chosen to be featured for one week on YouTube's home page in October 2007. Anthropologists generally believe that one should participate in activities along with members of cultural groups whom they study. In accordance with study participants' video blogging standards, I posted one video per week for a one-year period—a grinding pace that gave me a deep appreciation for the effort that goes into consistently recording, editing, and crafting videos for global scrutiny.

Maintaining my own account revealed insights that are not always possible to glean from observation alone. For example, through my participation, I observed that YouTube changed its policies and practices, sometimes without warning. I could leave the site for a few days and come back to find confusing layout and feature changes, favorite videos deleted by YouTube or removed by uploaders, and new policies suddenly instated. These moments of personal insight might not have surfaced had I not maintained my own account over time. Such observations also provided a wealth of productive interview topics.

Scholars interested in mediated interaction should catalogue how new online sites change, sometimes on a daily basis. These changes should be carefully recorded so that interactions may be analyzed with deeper appreciation for the infrastructural options and parameters within which people are communicating at a particular moment in time. For example, it would be wrong to assume that all YouTubers who have an advertisement posted to a video are eager to make money. I once had the experience of returning to YouTube to find an advertisement posted—without my knowledge or permission—on one of my videos. I was never told why it appeared. I surmise that the advertisement was added because I had included music from YouTube's pre-approved music catalogue in the video, yet that song was later removed from the catalogue. Understanding a site's infrastructural parameters is important for evaluating and analyzing participatory options and choices.

Names, Screen Names, and Pseudonyms

In accordance with the human subjects protocol established for the study, kids and adults were usually referred to by pseudonyms. Children were given an option to provide their own pseudonym; they were also permitted to use their screen name, as indicated in children's and parents' human subjects forms. Children were not allowed to use their real names in the research.

Adults were also referred to by pseudonyms. If adults so desired, they could use their screen name or they could indicate on their human subjects form that they wished to be referred to by their real names in the research. Some video bloggers preferred using their real names in order to receive public attribution for the contributions they made to the study. In cases where participants did not supply a preferred pseudonym, a pseudonym was chosen from a random name generator of common names in the United States.

Information was also collected on adults and kids who were public figures, such as the YouTube comedian Nalts, David of the popular *David After Dentist* videos, and Michael Verdi's daughter Dylan, who was profiled by a global news organization. These individuals were referred to by their real names. Study participants' and sometimes their families' identities became increasingly difficult to pseudonymize, given that they had posted volumes of personal information, comments, and images of themselves in online blogs, videos, websites, and social media. Such practices are severely challenging conceptions of what is meant by being a "public figure."

REFERENCES
<<<◄ ■ ►>>>

Acquisti, Alessandro, and Ralph Gross
2009   Predicting Social Security Numbers from Public Data. *PNAS* 106(27):10975–10980.

Agar, Michael
1980   Stories, Background Knowledge and Themes: Problems in the Analysis of Life History Narrative. *American Ethnologist* 7(2):223–239.

Anderson, Benedict
1985   *Imagined Communities*. London: Verso.

Andrejevic, Mark
2004   *Reality TV: The Work of Being Watched*. Lanham: Rowman & Littlefield Publishers, Inc.

Arnstein, Sherry R.
1969   A Ladder of Citizen Participation. *Journal of the American Institute of Planners* 35(4):216–224.

Associated Press
2007   Video of Drunk David Hasselhoff Taken by Teen Daughters. Fox News. May 4. http://www.foxnews.com/story/0,2933,269917,00.html, accessed March 21, 2011.

Attinasi, John, and Paul Friedrich
1995   Dialogic Breakthrough: Catalysis and Synthesis in Life–Changing Dialogue. In *The Dialogic Emergence of Culture*. Dennis Tedlock and Bruce Mannheim, eds., pp. 33–53. Chicago: University of Illinois Press.

Aufderheide, Patricia, and Charles M. Firestone
1993   Media Literacy: A Report of the National Leadership Conference on Media Literacy, the Aspen Institute Wye Center, Queenstown Maryland. Washington, D.C.: Communications and Society Program, the Aspen Institute.

Bakardjieva, Maria
2005   *Internet Society: The Internet in Everyday Life.* London: Sage Publications.

Bakhtin, Mikhail M.
1994   [1965] Carnival Ambivalence. In *The Bakhtin Reader.* Pam Morris, ed., pp. 194–244. London: Oxford University Press.

Banet-Weiser, Sarah
2007   *Kids Rule Nikelodeon and Consumer Citizenship.* Durham, North Carolina: Duke University Press.
2011   Branding the Post-Feminist Self: Girls' Video Production and YouTube. In *Mediated Girlhoods.* Mary Celeste Kearney, ed., pp. 277–294. New York: Peter Lang Publishing, Inc.

Baron, Naomi
2008   *Always On: Language in an Online and Mobile World.* Oxford: Oxford University Press.

Battaglia, Debbora
1995   Problematizing the Self: A Thematic Introduction. In *Rhetorics of Self-Making.* Debbora Battalia, ed., pp. 1–15. Berkeley: University of California Press.

Bauman, Richard
1977   *Verbal Art as Performance.* Prospect Heights, Illinois: Waveland Press, Inc.

Becker, Dave
1997   Lilith Computer Club? It's A Girl Thing. No Boys Allowed. In This Club, Born Of A Vision Of Better Training For Girls. *The Wisconsin State Journal.* October 4. http://journaltimes.com/ news/girls-only-computer-clubs-trying-to-break-the-silicon-ceiling/article_d955c38d-6940-559d-b5b3-956baed36ebb.html, accessed August 5, 2013.

Becker, Ernest
1973   *The Denial of Death.* New York: Free Press Paperbacks.

Becker, Howard S.
1982   *Art Worlds.* Berkeley: University of California Press.

Benkler, Yochai
2006   *The Wealth of Networks: How Social Production Transforms Markets and Freedom.* New Haven: Yale University Press.

Bennett, W. Lance, Chris Wells, and Deen Freelon
2011   Communicating Civic Engagement: Contrasting Models of Citizenship in the Youth Web Sphere. *Journal of Communication* 61(5):835–856.

Bloustein, Gerry
2003   *Girl Making: A Cross-Cultural Ethnography on the Processes of Growing Up Female*. New York and Oxford, UK: Berghahn Books.

Blum, Lenore, and Carol Frieze
2005   The Evolving Culture of Computing: Similarity is the Difference. *Frontiers: A Journal of Women Studies* 26(1):110–125.

Bordwell, David, and Kristin Thompson
1997   *Film Art: An Introduction*, Fifth Edition. New York: The McGraw-Hill Companies, Inc.

Borrelli, Christopher
2012   Funny Or Die's Adam McKay on His Site's Comedy Influence after Five Years. Chicago Tribune, April 28. http://articles.chicagotribune .com/2012-04-28/entertainment/ct-ent-0430-funny-or-die-main -20120427_1_dot-comedy-chicago-comedy-scene-short-videos, accessed August 3, 2013.

Bortree, Denise Sevick
2010   Talking Pink and Green: Exploring Teen Girls' Online Discussions of Environmental Issues. In *Girl Wide Web 2.0: Revisiting Girls, the Internet, and the Negotiations of Identity*. Sharon R. Mazzarella, ed., pp. 245–262. New York: Peter Lang.

Bourdieu, Pierre
1977   *Outline of a Theory of Practice*. Cambridge, UK: Cambridge University Press.

Brake, David R.
2009   As if Nobody's Reading?': The Imagined Audience and Socio-Technical Biases in Personal Blogging Practice in the UK. Ph.D. dissertation, Department of Media and Communications, London School of Economics.

Brenner, Joanna
2013   Pew Internet: Social Networking. February 14. http://pewinternet .org/Commentary/2012/March/Pew-Internet-Social-Networking- full-detail.aspx, accessed July 17, 2013.

Brubaker, Rogers, and Frederick Cooper
2000   Beyond Identity. *Theory and Society* 29:1–47.

Bruner, Jerome
1987   Life as Narrative. *Social Research* 54(1):11–32.

Bruns, Axel, Jason A. Wilson, and Barry J. Saunders
2008   Building Spaces for Hyperlocal Citizen Journalism. In *Proceedings of the Association of Internet Researchers* 2008: Internet Research 9.0: Rethinking Community, Rethinking Place. Copenhagen, October 15–18. http://eprints.qut.edu.au/15115/, accessed December 7, 2013.

Bryan, Hobson
1979   Conflict in the Great Outdoors. *Sociological Study* Number 4. Birmingham: Birmingham Publishing Company.
2000   Recreation Specialization Revisited. *Journal of Leisure Research* 32(1):18–21.

Bucholtz, Mary
1998   Geek the Girl: Language, Femininity, and Female Nerds. In *Gender and Belief Systems: Proceedings of the Fourth Berkeley Women and Language Conference*. Natasha Warner, Jocelyn Ahlers, Leela Bilmes, Monica Oliver, Suzanne Wertheim, and Melinda Chen, eds., pp. 119–131. Berkeley: Berkeley Women and Language Group.
1999   Why be Normal? Language and Identity Practice in a Community of Nerd Girls. *Language in Society* 28:203–223.
2002   Geek Feminism. In *Gendered Practices in Language*. Sarah Benor, Mary Rose, Devyani Sharma, Julie Sweetland, and Qing Zhang, eds., pp. 277–307. Stanford: Center for the Study of Language and Information Publications.

Buckingham, David
2003   *Media Education: Literacy, Learning and Contemporary Culture.* Cambridge, UK: Polity Press.
2008   Introducing Identity. In *Youth, Identity, and Digital Media*. David Buckingham, ed., pp. 1–22. Cambridge, MA: The MIT Press.

Buckingham, David, Pete Fraser, and Julian Sefton-Green
2000   Making the Grade: Evaluating Student Production in Media Studies. In *Evaluating Creativity: Making and Learning by Young People*. Julian Sefton-Green and Rebecca Sinker, eds., pp. 129–53. London: Routledge.

Buckingham, David, Maria Pini, and Rebekah Willett
2007   'Take Back the Tube!': The Discursive Construction of Amateur Film and Video Making. *Journal of Media Practice* 8(2):183–201.

Buckingham, David, Rebekah Willett, and Maria Pini
2011   *Home Truths? Video Production and Domestic Life*. Ann Arbor, MI: University of Michigan Press.

Buechner, Maryanne Murray
2005   50 Coolest Websites 2005: Arts and Entertainment. *Time*. June 20. http://www.time.com/time/business/article/0,8599,1073316,00.html, accessed August 1, 2013.

Burgess, Jean, and Joshua Green
2009a   *YouTube: Online Video and Participatory Culture*. Cambridge, UK: Polity.
2009b   The Entrepreneurial Vlogger: Participatory Culture Beyond the Professional-Amateur Divide. In *The YouTube Reader*. Pelle Snickars and Patrick Vonderau, eds., pp. 89–107. Stockholm: National Library of Sweden.

Bury, Rhiannon
2011   She's Geeky: The Performance of Identity among Women Working in IT. *International Journal of Gender, Science and Technology* 3(1):33–53.

Camper, Fred
1986   Some Notes on the Home Movie. *Journal of Film and Video* 38(3–4):9–14.

Castells, Manuel
2002   *The Internet Galaxy: Reflections on the Internet, Business, and Society*. Oxford: Oxford University Press.

Chalfen, Richard
1987   *Snapshot Versions of Life*. Bowling Green: Bowling Green State University Press.

Citron, Michele
1999   *Home Movies and Other Necessary Fictions*. Minneapolis: University of Minnesota Press.

Clawson, Mary Ann
1999   *Masculinity and Skill Acquisition in the Adolescent Rock Band. Popular Music* 18(1):99–114.

Clayburn, Thomas
2009   Social Security Number Prediction Makes Identity Theft Easy. *Information Week*. July 7. http://www.informationweek.com/news/security/privacy/showArticle.jhtml?articleID=218400854, accessed February 23, 2011.

Cohen, Julie
2000   "Examined Lives: Informational Privacy and the Subject as Object."
        Stanford Law Review 52:1373–1437.

Cole, Janis, and Holly Dale, eds.
1993   *Calling the Shots: Profiles of Women Filmmakers.* Kingston, Ontario:
        Quarry Press.

Coleman, E. Gabriella
2013   *Coding Freedom: The Ethics and Aesthetics of Hacking.* Princeton:
        Princeton University Press.

Coleman, Stephen
2008   "Doing IT for Themselves: Management versus Autonomy in Youth
        E-Citizenship." In *Civic Life Online: Learning How Digital Media Can
        Engage Youth.* W. Lance Bennett, pp. 189–206. Cambridge, MA: The
        MIT Press.

Corsaro, William A.
2005   *The Sociology of Childhood.* Thousand Oaks, CA: Pine Forge Press.

Currie, Dawn H., Deirdre M. Kelly, and Shauna Pomerantz
2006   "'The Geeks Shall Inherit the Earth': Girls' Agency, Subjectivity, and
        Empowerment." *Journal of Youth Studies* 9(4):419–436.

Darrah, Charles N., James M. Freeman, and J.A. English-Lueck
2007   *Busier Than Ever! Why American Families Can't Slow Down.* Stan-
        ford: Stanford University Press.

Davies, Lynn
2005   "Teaching About Conflict Through Citizenship Education." *Interna-
        tional Journal of Citizenship and Teacher Education* 1(2):17–34.

Davis, Dennis K., and Stanley J. Baran
1981   *Mass Communication and Everyday Life.* Belmont, CA: Wadsworth
        Publishing Company.

Dedman, Jay, and Joshua Paul
2006   *Videoblogging.* Indianapolis: Wiley Publishing, Inc.

Delli Carpini, Michael X.
2000   "Gen.com: Youth, Civic Engagement, and the New Information
        Environment." *Political Communication* 17:341–349.

de Moraes, Lisa
2103   "Comedy Central boasts about 'Daily Show,' 'Colbert Report' ratings
        in 18-to-49-year-old category." *Washington Post.* April 4. http://www.
        washingtonpost.com/blogs/tvcolumn/post/comedy-central-boasts-

about-daily-show-colbert-report-ratings-in-18-to-49-year-olds/2
013/04/04/4602109a-9d77-11e2-9a79-eb5280c81c63_blog.html,
accessed July22, 2013.

Denner, Jill, and Shannon Campe
2008   *What Games Made by Girls Can Tell Us. In Beyond Barbie® and*
         Mortal Kombat: New Perspectives on Gender and Gaming. Yasmin
         B. Kafai, Carrie Heeter, Jill Denner, and Jennifer Y. Sun, eds., pp.
         129–144. Cambridge, MA: MIT Press.

Denner, Jill, and Jacob Martinez
2010   "Whyville versus MySpace: How Girls Negotiate Identities Online."
         In *Girl Wide Web 2.0*, Sharon R. Mazzarella, ed., pp. 203–221. New
         York: Peter Lang.

Derrida, Jacques
1972   *Limited Inc.* Evanston: Northwestern University Press.

de Vreese, Claes H.
2007   "Digital Renaissance: Young Consumer and Citizen?" *The ANNALS of*
         the American Academy of Political and Social Science 611(1):207–216.

Donnelly, Matt
2010   "Britney Spears on 'Glee': the 10 Best Moments." *LA Times.* Septem-
         ber 29. http://latimesblogs.latimes.com/gossip/2010/09/britney-
         spears-on-glee-recap.html, accessed March 22, 2011.

Drotner, Kirsten
2008   "Informal Learning and Digital Media: Perceptions, Practices and
         Perspectives." In *Informal Learning and Digital Media.* Kirsten Drot-
         ner, Hans Siggaard Jensen, and Kim Christian Schrøder, eds., pp.
         10–28. Newcastle, UK: Cambridge Scholars Publishing.

Ede, Lisa, and Andrea Lunsford
1984   "Audience Addressed/Audience Invoked: The Role of Audience in
         Composition Theory and Pedagogy." *College Composition and Com-*
         munication 35(2):155–171.

Edwards, Richard L., and Chuck Tryon
2009   "Political Video Mashups as Allegories of Citizen Empowerment."
         First Monday 14 (10). http://firstmonday.org/ojs/index.php/fm/
         article/view/2617/2305, accessed August 5, 2013.

English-Lueck, J. A., and Andrea Saveri
2000   "Silicon Missionaries and Identity Evangelists." Paper presented at
         the Annual Meeting of The American Anthropological Association,
         San Francisco, November 17.

Erens, Patricia
1986   Home Movies in Commercial Narrative Film. *Journal of Film and Video* 38(3–4):99–101.

Eriksen, Thomas H.
2001   *Tyranny of the Moment: Fast and Slow Time in the Information Age.* London: Pluto Press.

Feuer, Alan, and Jason George
2005   Internet Fame is Cruel Mistress for Dancer of the Numa Numa. *The New York Times.* February 26. http://www.nytimes.com/2005/02/26/ nyregion/26video.html, accessed March 21, 2011.

Fine, Gary Alan
2004   *Everyday Genius: Self-Taught Art and the Culture of Authenticity.* Chicago: The University of Chicago Press.

Fisch, A. L.
1972   The Trigger Film Technique. *Improving College and University Teaching* 20(4):286–289.

Fishman, Jessica M.
2003   News Norms and Emotions: Pictures of Pain and Metaphors of Distress. In *Image Ethics in the Digital Age.* Larry P. Gross, John Stuart Katz, and Jay Ruby, eds., pp. 53–70. Minneapolis: University of Minnesota Press.

Fiske, John
1992   Cultural Economy of Fandom. In *The Adoring Audience.* Lisa A. Lewis, ed., pp. 30–49. London: Routledge.

Flanagan, Constance
2003   Developmental Roots of Political Engagement. *PS: Political Science and Politics* 36 (2):257–261.

Flanagan, Constance A., and Nakesha Faison
2001   Youth Civic Development: Implications of Research for Social Policy and Programs. *Social Policy Report* 15 (1):3–15.

Freelon, Deen G.
2010   Analyzing Online Political Discussion Using Three Models of Demo- cratic Communication. *New Media & Society* 12(7):1172–1190.

Furger, Roberta
1998   *Does Jane Compute?: Preserving Our Daughters' Place in the Cyber Revolution.* New York: Warner Books.

Gayle, Damien
2012   YouTube Cancels Billions of Music Industry Video Views after Finding They Were Fake or 'Dead.' *Daily Mail UK*. December 28. http://
www.dailymail.co.uk/sciencetech/article-2254181/YouTube-wipes-
billions-video-views-finding-faked-music-industry.html, accessed
July 19, 2013.

Garcés-Conejos Blitvich, Pilar
2010   The YouTubification of Politics, Impoliteness and Polarization. In
*Handbook of Research on Discourse Behavior and Digital Communi-
cation: Language Structures and Social Interaction*. Rotimi Taiwo, ed.,
pp. 540–563. Hershey, PA: ICI Global.

Gee, James Paul
2000   New People in New Worlds: Networks, the New Capitalism and
Schools. In *Multiliteracies: Literacy Learning and the Design of Social
Futures*. Bill Cope and Mary Kalantzis, eds., pp. 43–68. London:
Routledge & Keegan Paul.

Gellner, Ernest
1970   [1962] Concepts and Society. In *Sociological Theory and Philosophical Analysis*. Dorothy M. Emmet and Alasdair MacIntyre, eds., pp.
115–149. London: Macmillan.

Gershon, Ilana
2010a   *The Breakup 2.0: Disconnecting Over New Media*. Ithaca: Cornell
University Press.
2010b   Media Ideologies: An Introduction. *Journal of Linguistic Anthropology* 20(2):283–293.

Giddens, Anthony
1991   *Modernity and Self-Identity: Self and Society in the Late Modern Age*.
Stanford: Stanford University Press.

Gillis, Stacy, Gillian Howie, and Rebecca Munford, eds.
2004   *Third Wave Feminism: A Critical Exploration*. New York: Palgrave
Macmillan.

Gmelch, George
2000   Rules and Respect, Pranks and Performance: The Culture of Professional Baseball. *Anthropology of Work Review* 20(2):25–34.

Goffman, Erving
1959   *The Performance of Self in Everyday Life*. New York: Doubleday.

Goldhaber, Michael H.
1996   The Attention Economy and the Net. *First Monday* 2(4–7). http://
        firstmonday.org/htbin/cgiwrap/bin/ojs/index.php/fm/article/
        view/519/440, accessed February 23, 2011.

Golombek, Silvia Blitzer
2006   Children as Citizens. *Journal of Community Practice* 14(1/2):11–30.

Goodwin, Jeff, James M. Jasper, and Francesca Polletta
2001   Why Emotions Matter. In P*assionate Politics: Emotions and Social
        Movements.* Jeff Goodwin, James M. Jasper, and Francesca Polletta,
        eds., pp. 1–24. Chicago: University of Chicago.

Graham, Sandy, and Celine Latulipe
2003   CS Girls Rock: Sparking Interest in Computer Science and Debunk-
        ing the Stereotypes. *SIGCSE'03*, February 19–23, 2003, pp. 322–326.
        Reno, Nevada, USA.

Green, Lucy
2002   *How Popular Musicians Learn: A Way Ahead for Music Education.*
        Aldershot: Ashgate.

Gross, Larry, John Stuart Katz, and Jay Ruby
1988   *Image Ethics: The Moral Rights of Subjects in Photographs, Film, and
        Television.* New York: Oxford University Press.
2003   *Image Ethics in the Digital Age.* Minneapolis: University of Minne-
        sota Press.

Gubrium, Aline, and Krista Harper
2013   *Participatory Visual and Digital Methods.* Walnut Creek, California:
        Left Coast Press, Inc.

Harris, Anita
2004   *Future Girl: Young Women in the Twenty-First Century.* New York:
        Routledge.

Hayes, Elisabeth R., and Elizabeth M. King
2009   Not Just a Dollhouse: What the Sims2 Can Teach Us about Women's
        IT Learning. *On the Horizon* 17(1):60–69.

Heath, Shirley Brice
1983   *Ways with Words.* Cambridge, UK: Cambridge University Press.

Henwood, Flis, Gwyneth Hughes, Helen Kennedy, Nod Miller, and Sally Wyatt
2001   Cyborg Lives in Context: Writing Women's Technobiographies.
        In *Cyborg Lives? Women's Technobiographies.* Flis Henwood, Helen
        Kennedy, and Nod Miller, eds., pp. 11–34. York: Raw Nerve Press.

Herring, Susan C.

1996   Posting in a Different Voice: Gender and Ethics in Computer-Mediated Communication. In *Philosophical Perspectives in Computer-Mediated Communication*. Charles Ess, ed., pp. 115–145. New York: State University of New York Press.

2008   Questioning the Generational Divide. In *Youth, Identity, and Digital Media*. David Buckingham, ed., pp. 71–92. Cambridge, MA: The MIT Press.

Herring, Susan, Deborah A. Johnson, and Tamra DiBenedetto

1995   This Discussion is Going Too Far! Male Resistance to Female Participation on the Internet. In *Gender Articulated: Language and the Socially Constructed Self.* Kira Hall and Mary Bucholtz, eds., pp. 67–96. New York: Routledge.

Hess, Aaron

2009   Resistance Up in Smoke: Analyzing the Limitations of Deliberation on YouTube. *Critical Studies in Media Communication* 26(5):411–434.

Hobbs, Renee

1998   The Seven Great Debates in the Media Literacy Movement. *Journal of Communication* 48(1):16–32.

Hoffman, Donna L., and Thomas P. Novak

2000   The Growing Digital Divide: Implications for an Open Research Agenda. In *Understanding the Digital Economy: Data, Tools and Research*. Erik Brynjolfsson and Brian Kahin, eds., pp. 245–260. Cambridge, MA: The MIT Press.

Holland, Patricia

1991   Introduction: History, Memory and the Family Album. In *Family Snaps: The Meanings of Domestic Photography*. Jo Spence and Patricia Holland, eds., pp. 1–14. London: Virago.

Holloway, Sarah L., and Gill Valentine

2003   *Cyberkids: Children in the Information Age*. London: RoutledgeFalmer.

Hopkins, Jim

2006   Surprise, There's a Third YouTube Co-Founder. *USA Today*. October 11. http://usatoday30.usatoday.com/tech/news/2006-10-11-youtube-karim_x.htm, accessed October 5, 2013.

Horowitz, Etan

2010   Family Cashing in on 'David After Dentist.' *CNN Tech*. March 18. http://www.cnn.com/2010/TECH/03/18/david.after.dentist.video/, accessed February 15, 2011.

Huizinga, Johan
1949   *Homo Ludens: A Study of the Play-Element in Culture.* New York: Routledge.

Hull, Glynda, and Kathy Schultz, eds.
2002   *School's Out! Bridging Out-of-School Literacies with Classroom Practice.* New York: Teachers College Press.

Irvine, Judith
1989   When Talk Isn't Cheap: Language and Political Economy. *American Ethnologist* 16:248–267.

Ito, Mizuko
2012   Connected Learning. Mimi Ito Web Log, March 1. http://www.itofisher.com/mito/weblog/2012/03/connected_learning.html, accessed January 9, 2013.

Ito, Mizuko, Sonja Baumer, Matteo Bittanti, danah boyd, Rachel Cody, Becky Herr, Heather A. Horst, Patricia G. Lange, et al.
2010   *Hanging Out, Messing Around and Geeking Out: Kids Living and Learning with New Media.* Cambridge, MA: The MIT Press.

Ito, Mizuko, and Matteo Bittani
2010   *Gaming. In Hanging Out, Messing Around and Geeking Out: Kids Living and Learning with New Media.* Mizuko Ito et al., pp. 195–242. Cambridge, MA: The MIT Press.

Jacoby, Sally, and Patrick Gonzales
1991   The Constitution of Expert-Novice in Scientific Discourse. *Issues in Applied Linguistics* 2(2):149–181.

James, Carrie
2009   *Young People, Ethics, and the New Digital Media: A Synthesis from the GoodPlay Project.* Cambridge, MA: The MIT Press.

Jans, Marc
2004   Children as Citizens: Towards a Contemporary Notion of Child Participation. *Childhood* 11(1):27–44.

Jenkins, Henry
1992   *Textual Poachers: Television Fans & Participatory Culture.* New York: Routledge.

Jenkins, Henry, Katie Clinton, Ravi Purushotma, Alice J. Robison, and Margaret Weigel
2006   Confronting the Challenges of Participatory Culture: Media Education for the 21st Century. http://www.projectnml.org/files/working/NMLWhitePaper.pdf, accessed July 8, 2013.

Jennings, M. Kent, and Vicki Zeitner
2003   Internet Use and Civic Engagement: A Longitudinal Analysis. *Public Opinion Quarterly* 67:311–334.

Johnson, Beth
1995.   A Fan's Fatal Obsession. *Entertainment Weekly*. July 14. http://www .ew.com/ew/article/0,,297902,00.html, accessed February 25, 2011.

Jones, Michael Owen
2001   The Aesthetics of Everyday Life. In *Self-Taught Art: The Culture and Aesthetics of American Vernacular Art*. Charles Russell, ed., pp. 47–67. Jackson: University Press of Mississippi.

Jorgensen, Marilyn
1984   A Social-Interactional Analysis of Phone Pranks. *Western Folklore* 43(2):104–116.

Kahne, Joseph, Ellen Middaugh, Nam-Jin Lee, and Jessica Timpany Freezell
2010   Youth Online Activity and Exposure to Diverse Perspectives. DML-central Working Paper. http://dmlcentral.net/resources/4428, accessed February 27, 2011.

Kahne, Joseph, Nam-Jin Lee, and Jessica Timpany Freezell
2011   Digital Media Literacy Education and Online Civic and Political Participation. DMLcentral Working Paper. http://ypp.dmlcentral. net/content/digital-media-literacy- education-and-online-civic-and-political, accessed March 2, 2011.

Katz, James, and Philip Aspden
1997   Motivations for and Barriers to Internet Usage: Results of a National Public Opinion Survey. Paper presented at the 24th Annual Tele-communications Policy Research Conference, Solomons, Maryland, October 6.

Keane, Webb
2003   Semiotics and the Social Analysis of Material Things. *Language & Communication* 23:409–425.

Kearney, Mary Celeste
1998   Producing Girls: Rethinking the Study of Female Youth Culture. In *Delinquents and Debutantes: Twentieth Century American Girls' Cultures*. Sherrie A. Inness, ed., pp. 283–310. New York: New York University Press.
2006   *Girls Make Media*. New York: Routledge.

Kearney, Mary Celeste, ed.
2011   *Mediated Girlhoods*. New York: Peter Lang.

Kelly, Dierdre M., Shauna Pomerantz, and Dawn H. Currie
2006   'No Boundaries'? Girls' Interactive, Online Learning About Femininities. *Youth & Society* 38(1):3–28.

Kendall, Lori
2002   *Hanging Out in the Virtual Pub: Masculinities and Relationships Online.* Berkeley: University of California Press.

Kinney, David. A.
1993   From Nerds to Normals: The Recovery of Identity among Adolescents from Middle School to High School. *Sociology of Education* 66(1):21–40.

Kitzmann, Andreas
2004   *Saved From Oblivion: Documenting the Daily from Diaries to Web Cams.* New York: Peter Lang.

Klein, Naomi
2000   *No Logo: No Space, No Choice, No Jobs.* New York: Picador.

Knight, Mark
2012   U.S. Presidential Race and the Social Media Battle. *The Huffington Post.* September 18. http://www.huffingtonpost.com/mark-knight/us-presidential-race-socialmedia_b_1889883.html, accessed July 8, 2013.

Kohut, Andrew
2008   Social Networking and Online Videos Take Off: Internet's Broader Role in Campaign 2008, Washington, D.C.: Pew Research Center. Pew Internet and American Life Project. http://www.pewinternet.org/~/media//Files/Reports/2008/Pew_MediaSources_jan08.pdf.pdf, accessed March 2, 2011.

Kuhn, Annette
1995   *Family Secrets: Acts of Memory and Imagination.* New York: Verso.

Kuttab, Daoud
1993   Palestinian Diaries: Grass Roots TV Production in the Occupied Territories. In *Channels of Resistance.* Tony Dowmunt, ed., pp. 138–145. London: BFI.

Lacan, Jacques
1949   The Mirror Stage as Formative of the Function of the I as Revealed in Psychoanalytic Experience. Paper presented at the 16th International Congress of Psychoanalysis, Zurich, Switzerland, July 17.

Lange, Patricia G.

2003   Virtual Trouble: Negotiating Access in Online Communities. Ph.D. dissertation, Department of Anthropology, University of Michigan.

2006   Covert Mentoring on the Internet: Methods for Confirming Status in Imagined Technical Communities. *Anthropology of Work Review* 26(2):21–24.

2007a   Publicly Private and Privately Public: Social Networking on YouTube. *Journal of Computer-Mediated Communication* 13(1), October 2007. http://jcmc.indiana.edu/vol13/issue1/lange.html, accessed August 3, 2013.

2007b   The Vulnerable Video Blogger: Promoting Social Change through Intimacy. *The Scholar and Feminist Online* 5(2). http://www.barnard .edu/sfonline/blogs/lange_01.htm, accessed August 3, 2013.

2007c   Searching for the 'You' in 'YouTube': An Analysis of Online Response Ability. National Association of Practicing Anthropology Proceedings of the Ethnographic Praxis in *Industry Conference 2007*, pp. 31–45. Berkeley CA: University of California Press.

2007d   Fostering Friendship through Video Production: How Youth Use YouTube to Enrich Local Interaction. Paper presented at the International Communication Association Conference, San Francisco, May 27.

2007e   Commenting on Comments: Investigating Responses to Antagonism on YouTube. Paper presented at the Society for Applied Anthropology Annual Conference, Tampa, March 31. http:// sfaapodcasts.files.wordpress.com/2007/04/update-apr-17-lange-sfaa-paper-2007.pdf, accessed August 3, 2013.

2008a   (Mis)Conceptions about YouTube. In *Video Vortex Reader: Responses to YouTube*. Geert Lovink and Sabine Niederer, eds., pp. 87–100. Amsterdam: Institute of Network Cultures. http:// networkcultures. org/wpmu/portal/files /2008/10/vv_reader_small.pdf, accessed August 3, 2013.

2008b   Living in YouTubia: Bordering on Civility. Proceedings of the Southwestern Anthropological Association Conference 2008, April 10–12, Volume 2, pp. 98–106. http://www.patriciaglange.org/assets/Lange SWAA08.pdf, accessed August 3, 2013.

2009   Videos of Affinity on YouTube. In *The YouTube Reader*. Pelle Snickars and Patrick Vonderau, eds., pp. 228–247. Stockholm: National Library of Sweden.

2010   Achieving Creative Integrity on YouTube: Reciprocities and Tensions, Enculturation. http://enculturation.gmu.edu/achieving -creative-integrity, accessed July 8, 2013.

2011   Video-Mediated Nostalgia and the Aesthetics of Technical Compe-
        tencies. *Visual Communication* 10(1):25–44.
2012   Rhetoricizing Visual Literacies. Paper presented at the International
        Communication Association Conference, Phoenix, Arizona, May
        25. http://www.patriciaglange.org/page4/assets/Lange%20ICA%20
        2012%20Final%20Paper.pdf, accessed January 9, 2014.

Lareau, Annette
2003   *Unequal Childhoods: Class, Race, and Family Life.* Berkeley: Univer-
        sity of California Press.

Lave, Jean, and Etienne Wenger
1991   *Situated Learning: Legitimate Peripheral Participation.* Cambridge,
        UK and New York: Cambridge University Press.

Lawrence, Sandra M., and Beverly Daniel Tatum
1997   White Educators as Allies: Moving from Awareness to Action. In
        Offwhite: Readings on Race, Power, and Society. Michelle Fine, Lois
        Weis, Linda C. Powell, and L. Mun Wong, eds., pp. 333–342. New
        York: Routledge.

Leavitt, Lydia
2011   Facebook to Release Phone Numbers, Addresses, to Third-Party De-
        velopers. *TG Daily.* March 1. http://www.tgdaily.com/business-and-
        law-features/54400-facebook-to-release-phone-numbers-addresses-
        to-third-party-developer, accessed March 2, 2011.

Levine, Peter
2008   A Public Voice for Youth: The Audience Problem in Digital Media
        and Civic Education. In *Civic Life Online: Learning How Digital
        Media Can Engage Youth.* W. Lance Bennett, ed., pp. 119–138. Cam-
        bridge, MA: The MIT Press.

Levy, Stephen
1984   *Hackers: Heroes of the Computer Revolution.* New York: Penguin Books.

Lim, Merlyna and Mark E. Kann
2008   Politics: Deliberation, Mobilliation, and Networked Practices of
        Agitation. In *Networked Publics.* Kazys Varnelis, ed., pp. 77–108. The
        MIT Press.

Lim, Sun Sun, and Jemima Ooi
2011   Girls Talk Tech: Exploring Singaporean Girls' Perceptions and Uses
        of Information and Communication Technologies. In *Mediated
        Girlhoods.* Mary Celeste Kearney, ed., pp. 243–260. New York: Peter
        Lang Publishing, Inc.

Livingstone, Sonia
2009   *Children and the Internet.* Cambridge, UK: Polity Press.

Lowery, Shearon, and Melvin L. DeFleur
1995   *Milestones in Mass Communication Research*, Third Edition. White Plains, NY: Longman Publishers.

Lutkehaus, Nancy, and Jenny Cool
1999   Paradigms Lost and Found: The "Crisis of Representation and Visual Anthropology." In *Collecting Visible Evidence*. James M. Gaines and Michael Renov, eds., pp. 116–139. Minneapolis: University of Minnesota Press.

Madden, Mary
2007   Online Video. Pew Internet & American Life Project. Washington, D.C.: Pew Research Center. http://www.pewinternet.org/~/media//Files/Reports/2007/PIP_Online_Video_2007.pdf.pdf, accessed July 17.

Madigan, Elinor M., Marianne Goodfellow, and Jeffrey A. Stone
2007   Gender, Perceptions, and Reality: Technological Literacy Among First-Year Students. *SIGCSE'07* March 7–10, pp. 410–414, Covington, Kentucky.

Mahiri, Jabari
2004   New Literacies in a New Century. In *What They Don't Learn in School: Literacy in the Lives of Urban Youth*. Jabari Mahiri, ed., pp. 1–18. New York: Peter Lang.

Malinowski, Bronislaw
1972   [1923] *Phatic Communication. In Communication in Face to Face Interaction*. John Laver and Sandy Hutcheson, eds., pp. 146–152

Mannheim, Bruce, and Dennis Tedlock
1995   Introduction. In *The Dialogic Emergence of Culture*. Dennis Tedlock and Bruce Mannheim, eds., pp. 1–32. Chicago: University of Illinois Press.

Margolis, Jane, and Allan Fisher
2002   *Unlocking the Clubhouse: Women in Computing*. Cambridge, MA: The MIT Press.

Marwick, Alice E., and danah boyd
2011   *I Tweet Honestly, I Tweet Passionately: Twitter Users, Context Collapse, and the Imagined Audience*. New Media & Society 13(1):114–133.

Mayer-Schönberger, Viktor
2009   *Delete: The Virtue of Forgetting in the Digital Age.* Princeton:
        Princeton University Press.

Mazzarella, Sharon R., ed.
2010   *Girl Wide Web 2.0.* New York: Peter Lang Publishing.

McArthur, J. A.
2009   Digital Subculture: A Geek Meaning of Style. *Journal of Communi-
        cation Inquiry* 33(1):58–70.

McDermott, R. P., and Henry Tylbor
1995   On the Necessity of Collusion in Conversation. In *The Dialogic
        Emergence of Culture.* Dennis Tedlock and Bruce Mannheim, eds.,
        pp. 218–236. Chicago: University of Illinois Press.

McRobbie, Angela
1981   Just like a Jackie Story. In *Feminism for Girls: An Adventure Story.*
        Angela McRobbie and Trisha McCabe, eds., pp. 113–128. London:
        Routledge & Kegan Paul.
2000   *Feminism and Youth Culture.* Second Edition. New York: Routledge.

MeFeedia Blog
2007   State of the Vlogosphere, Vol. 2: Trends in Online Video. July 30.
        http://blog.mefeedia.com/state-of-the-vlogosphere-vol-2---trends-
        in-online-video, accessed April 4, 2012.

Miller, Paul D.
2004   *Rhythm Science.* Cambridge, MA: Mediawork/The MIT Press.

Milner, Murray Jr.
2004   *Freaks, Geeks, and Cool Kids.* New York: Routledge.

Montgomery, Kathryn C.
2008   Youth and Digital Democracy: Intersections of Practice, Policy, and
        the Marketplace. In *Civic Life Online: Learning How Digital Media
        Can Engage Youth.* W. Lance Bennett, ed., pp. 25–49. Cambridge,
        MA: The MIT Press.

Moore, Jo Ellen, and Mary Sue Love
2004   An Examination of Prestigious Stigma: The Case of the Technol-
        ogy Geek. ACM SIGMIS CPR Conference, April 22–24, 2004, pp.
        103–123, Tucson, Arizona.

Moran, James M.
2002   *There's No Place Like Home Video.* University of Minnesota Press.

Moy, Patricia, Edith Manosevitch, Keith Stamm, and Kate Dunsmore
2005   Linking Dimensions of Internet Use and Civic Engagement. *Journalism & Mass Communication Quarterly* 82(3):571–586.

Müller, Eggo
2009   Where Quality Matters: Discourses on the Art of Making a YouTube Video. In *The YouTube Reader*. Pelle Snickars and Patrick Vonderau, eds., pp. 126–139. Stockholm: National Library of Sweden.

N.A.
2006   And the Vloggies Winners are… PodTech. November 6. http://www.podtech.net/home/1441/and-the-vloggies-winners-are, accessed March 23, 2011.

Nissenbaum, Helen
2004   Privacy as Contextual Integrity.*Washington Law Review* 79(1):10–158.

O'Brien, Chris
2013   Apple in PR mode for Pro X." *The Los Angeles Times*. March 28. http://articles.latimes.com/2013/mar/28/business/la-fi-apple-final-cut-20130328, accessed August 7, 2013.

Oreskovic, Alexei
2012   Exclusive: YouTube Hits 4 Billion Daily Video Views. *Reuters*, January 23. http://www.reuters.com/article/2012/01/23/us-google-youtube-idUSTRE80M0TS20120123, accessed July 17, 2013.

Palfrey, John, and Urs Gasser
2008   *Born Digital: Understanding the First Generation of Digital Natives*. New York: Basic Books.

Parpis, Elefteria
2009   Geico Gecko Dances with 'Numa Numa.' *AdWeek*. March 24. http://www.adweek.com/aw/content_display/creative/news/e3ie7d1eee3b5e787af53d590084d20aebf, accessed March 21, 2011.

Patriquin, Alex
2008   Online Video: 2007 Year in Review. Compete.com. January 16. http://blog.compete.com/2008/01/16/online-video-share-december-2007-year-in-review/, accessed April 4, 2012.

Pauwels, Luc
2008   A Private Visual Practice Going Public? Social Functions and Sociological Research Opportunities of Web-based Family Photography. *Visual Studies* 23(1):34–49.

Peirce, Kate
1990   A Feminist Theoretical Perspective on the Socialization of Teenage Girls Through Seventeen Magazine. *Sex Roles* 23(9/10):491–500.

Pelletier, Caroline
2008   Gaming in Context: How Young People Construct their Gendered Identities in Playing and Making Games. In *Beyond Barbie® and Mortal Kombat: New Perspectives on Gender and Gaming*. Yasmin B. Kafai, Carrie Heeter, Jill Denner, and Jennifer Y. Sun, eds., pp. 145–159. Cambridge, MA: MIT Press.

Perkel, Dan
2008   Copy and Paste Literacy? Literacy Practices in the Production of a MySpace Profile. In *Informal Learning and Digital Media*. Kristen Drotner, Hans Siggaard, and Kim Christian Schroder, eds., pp. 203–224. Newcastle, United Kingdom: Cambridge Scholars Publishing.

Perkel, Dan, and Becky Herr-Stephenson
2008   Peer Pedagogy in an Interest-Driven Community: The Practices and Problems of Online Tutorials. Presented at MEDIA@LSE Fifth Anniversary Conference, September 21–23, 2008, pp. 1–30. London, UK.

Peters, John Durham
2001   Witnessing. *Media, Culture & Society* 23:707–723.

Peterson, T. F.
2003   *Night Work: A History of Hacks and Pranks at MIT*. Cambridge, MA: The MIT Press.

Pham, Alex
2010   YouTube Turns 5, Can't Wait to Grow Up. *The Los Angeles Times*. May 17. http://www.webcitation.org/5y6MI3hAC, accessed October 5, 2013.

Pini, Maria
2009   Inside the Home Mode. In *Video Cultures: Media Technology and Everyday Creativity*. David Buckingham and Rebekah Willett, eds., pp. 71–92. London: Palgrave Macmillan.

Plato
1973   [411–404 B.C.E.] *Phaedrus and Letters VII and VIII*. London: Penguin Books.

Plummer, Ken
2001   The Call of Life Stories in Ethnographic Research. In *Handbook of Ethnographic Research*. Paul Atkinson, Amanda Coffey, Sara Delamont, John Lofland, and Lyn Lofland, eds., pp. 395–406. London: Sage.

Portelli, Alessandro
1991   *The Death of Luigi Trastulli and Other Stories: Form and Meaning in Oral History.* Albany, NY: State University of New York Press.

Portelli, John P.
1993   Exposing the Hidden Curriculum. *Journal of Curriculum Studies* 25(4):343–358.

Prensky, Marc
2001   Digital Natives, Digital Immigrants. On the Horizon 9(5). http://www.marcprensky.com/writing/Prensky%20-%20Digital%20 Natives,%20Digital%20Immigrants%20-%20Part1.pdf, accessed April 19, 2010.
2006   *Don't Bother Me Mom—I'm Learning.* St. Paul, Minnesota: Paragon House.

PR Newswire
2013   comScore Releases April 2013 U.S. Online Video Rankings. May 22. http://www. prnewswire.com/news-releases/comscore-releases-april-2013-us-online-video-rankings-208523851.html, accessed July 10, 2013.

Purcell, Kristen
2010   The State of Online Video. Pew Internet & American Life Project. Washington, D.C.: Pew Research Center. http://www.pewinternet .org/Reports/2010/State-of-Online-Video.aspx, accessed February 23, 2011.

Raymond, Eric S.
1996   *The Hacker's Dictionary.* Cambridge, MA: The MIT Press.

Rheingold, Howard
1993   *The Virtual Community: Homesteading on the Electronic Frontier.* Reading, MA: Addison Wesley.
2008   Using Participatory Media and Public Voice to Encourage Civic Engagement. In *Civic Life Online: Learning How Digital Media Can Engage Youth.* W. Lance Bennett, ed., pp. 97–118. Cambridge, MA: The MIT Press.

Rotman, Dana, and Jennifer Preece
2010   The 'WeTube' in YouTube—Creating an Online Community Through Video Sharing. *International Journal of Web Based Communities* 6(3):317–333.

Rotundo, E. Anthony
1998   Boy Culture. In *The Children's Culture Reader.* Henry Jenkins, ed., pp. 337–362. New York: New York University Press.

Ruby, Jay

1991   Speaking for, Speaking About, Speaking with, or Speaking Along-
        side—An Anthropological and Documentary Dilemma. *Visual
        Anthropology Review* 7(2):50–67.
2000   *Picturing Culture: Explorations of Film & Anthropology.* Chicago:
        University of Chicago Press.

Scammell, Margaret

2000   The Internet and Civic Engagement: The Age of the Citizen-Con-
        sumer. *Political Communication* 17:351–355.

Schutz, Alfred

1967   *The Phenomenology of the Social World.* Evanston: Northwestern
        University Press.

Schwab, Nikki

2008   In Obama-McCain Race, YouTube Became a Serious Battleground
        for Presidential Politics. *US News & World Report.* November 7.
        http://www.usnews.com/news/campaign-2008/articles/2008/11/07/
        in-obama-mccain-race-youtube-became-a-serious-battleground-
        for-presidential-politics, accessed October 5, 2013.

Scodari, Christine

2005   You're Sixteen, You're Dutiful, You're Online. In *Girl Wide Web*. Sha-
        ron R. Mazzarella, ed., pp. 105–120. New York: Peter Lang.

Scott, David, and Geoffrey Godbey

1994   Recreation Specialization in the Social World of Contract Bridge.
        Journal of Leisure Research 26(3):275–295.

Scott, David, and C. Scott Shafer

2001   Recreation Specialization: A Critical Look at the Construct. *Journal
        of Leisure Research* 33(3):319–343.

Sefton-Green, Julian

2000   Introduction: Evaluating Creativity. In *Evaluating Creativity: Making
        and Learning by Young People.* Julian Sefton-Green and Rebecca
        Sinker, eds., pp. 1–15. London: Routledge.

Selwyn, Neil

2007   Hi-tech = Guy-tech? An Exploration of Undergraduate Students'
        Gendered Perceptions of Information and Communication Tech-
        nologies. *Sex Roles* 56:525–536.

Senft, Theresa M.

2008   *Camgirls: Celebrity and Community in the Age of Social Networks.*
        New York: Peter Lang.

Shantz, Carolyn Uhlinger
1987   Conflicts between Children. *Child Development* 58:283–305.

Shah, Dhavan, Michael Schmierbach, Joshua Hawkins, Rodolfo Espino, and Janet Donovan
2002   Nonrecursive Models of Internet Use and Community Engagement: Questioning Whether Time Spent Online Erodes Social Capital. *Journalism & Mass Communication Quarterly* 79(4):964–987.

Sherman, Tom
2008   Vernacular Video. In *Video Vortex Reader: Responses to YouTube.* Geert Lovink and Sabine Niederer, eds., pp. 161–168. Amsterdam: Institute of Network Cultures.

Silverstein, Michael
1979   Language Structure and Linguistic Ideology. In *The Elements: A Parasession on Linguistic Units and Levels.* Paul R. Clyne, William F. Hanks, and Charles L. Hofbauer, eds., pp. 193–247. Chicago: Chicago Linguistic Society.

Smith, Aaron
2008   The Internet's Role in Campaign 2008. Pew Internet and American Life Project. Washington, D.C.: Pew Research Center. http://www.pewinternet.org/Reports/2009/6--The-Internets-Role-in-Campaign-2008.aspx, accessed August 6, 2013.

Snow, David A., and Robert Benford
1988   Ideology, Frame Resonance, and Participant Mobilization. *International Social Movement Research* 1:197–217.

Snyder, Benson R.
1970   *The Hidden Curriculum.* Cambridge: The MIT Press.

Sobchack, Vivian
1999   Toward a Phenomenology of Nonfictional Film Experience. In *Collecting Visible Evidence.* Jane M. Gaines and Michael Renov, eds., pp. 241–254. Minneapolis: University of Minnesota Press.

Sontag, Susan
1977   *On Photography.* New York: Anchor Books Doubleday.
2003   *Regarding the Pain of Others.* New York: Picador.

Stebbins, Robert A.
1977   The Amateur: Two Sociological Definitions. *Pacific Sociological Review* 20(4):582–606.
1980   'Amateur' and 'Hobbyist' as Concepts for the Study of Leisure Problems. *Social Problems* 27(4):413–417.

1992   *Amateurs, Professionals, and Serious Leisure.* Montreal: McGill-
          Queen's University Press.

Stern, Susannah
1999   Adolescent Girls' Expression on Web Home Pages: Spirited, Sombre
          and Self-Conscious Sites. *Convergence* 5(4):22–41.
2008   Producing Sites, Exploring Identities: Youth Online Authorship.
          In *Youth, Identity, and Digital Media.* David Buckingham, ed., pp.
          95–118. Cambridge, MA: The MIT Press.

Strangelove, Michael
2010   *Watching YouTube: Extraordinary Videos by Ordinary People.* Toronto:
          University of Toronto Press.

Street, Brian V.
1993   Introduction: The New Literacy Studies. In *Cross-Cultural Approach-
          es to Literacy.* Brian V. Street, ed., pp. 1–21. New York: Cambridge,
          UK University Press.

Sugarbaker, Mike
1998   What is a Geek? Gazebo: The Journal of Geek Culture. http://www.
          gibberish.com/gazebo/articles/geek3.html, accessed December 11,
          2005.

Sunstein, Cass R.
2006   *Infotopia: How Many Minds Produce Knowledge.* Oxford: Oxford
          University Press.

Sutton, Laurel
1994   Using Usenet: Gender, Power, and Silence in Electronic Discourse.
          *Proceedings of th 20th Annual Meeting of the Berkeley Linguistics
          Society*, pp. 506–520. Berkeley: Berkeley Linguistics Society.

Szwed, John F.
1981   The Ethnography of Literacy. In *Writing: The Nature, Development,
          and Teaching of Written Communication, Part 1.* Marcia Farr White-
          man, ed., pp. 13–23. Hillsdale, NJ: Erlbaum.

Tannen, Deborah
1998   *The Argument Culture: Stopping America's War of Words.* New York:
          Ballentine Books.

Tapscott, Don
2009   *Grown Up Digital: How the Net Generation is Changing Your World.*
          New York:McGraw–Hill.

Thomas, Douglas
2002 *Hacker Culture*. Minneapolis: University of Minnesota Press.

Toffler, Alvin
1980 *The Third Wave*. New York: Bantam.

Torney-Purta, Judith, Carole L. Hahn, and Jo-Ann M. Amadeo
2001 Principles of Subject-Specific Instruction in Education for Citizen-ship. In *Subject-Specific Instructional Methods and Activities, Vol. 8*. Jere Brophy, ed., pp. 373–410. New York: JAI Press, Elsevier Science.

Torney-Purta, Judith, Rainer Lehmann, Hans Oswald, and Wolfram Schulz
2001 Citizenship and Education in Twenty Eight Countries. Amsterdam, The Netherlands: The International Association for the Evaluation of Educational Achievement. http://terpconnect.umd.edu/~jtpurta/interreport.htm, accessed September 27, 2010.

Urban Dictionary
2005. Nub. May 20. http://www.urbandictionary.com/define. php?term=nub, accessed July 22, 2013.

van Dijck, José
2007 Television 2.0: YouTube and the Emergence of Homecasting. Paper presented at Media in Transition 5, April 27–29, Cambridge, Mas-sachusetts. http://web.mit.edu/comm-forum/mit5/papers/van Dijck_Television2.0.article. MiT5.pdf, accessed July 8, 2013.

Vargas, Elizabeth
2004 People of the Year: Bloggers. ABC News. December 30. http://abcnews.go.com/WNT/PersonOfWeek/ story?id=372266&page=1, accessed August 2, 2013.

Varma, Roli
2007 Women in Computing: The Role of Geek Culture. *Science as Culture* 16(4):359–376.

Varnelis, Kazys, ed.
2008 *Networked Publics*. Cambridge, MA: The MIT Press.

Verba, Sydney, Kay Lehman Schlozman, and Henry E. Brady
1995 *Voice and Equality: Civic Volunteerism in American Politics*. Cam-bridge, MA: Harvard University Press.

Verdi, Michael, and Ryanne Hodson
2006 *Secrets of Videoblogging: Videoblogging for the Masses*. Berkeley: Peachpit Press.

Walkerdine, Valerie
1984   Some Day My Prince Will Come. In *Gender and Generation*. Angela McRobbie and Mica Nava, eds., pp. 162–184. Great Britain: Macmillan Publishers.

Warman, Matt
2013   YouTube at 8: 100 hours uploaded every minute. *The Telegraph*. May 13. http://www.telegraph.co.uk/technology/news/10068258/ YouTube -at-8-100-hours-uploaded-every-minute.html, accessed July 29, 2013.

Warner, Michael
2002   Publics and Counterpublics. *Public Culture* 14(1):49–90.

Wenger, Etienne
1998   *Communities of Practice: Learning, Meaning, and Identity*. Cambridge, UK: Cambridge University Press.

Wesch, Michael
2009   YouTube and You: Experiences of Self-Awareness in the Context Collapse of the Recording Webcam. *Explorations in Media Ecology* 8(2):19–34.

Weston, Kath
1992   The Politics of Gay Families. In *Rethinking the Family: Some Feminist Questions*. Barrie Thorne and Marilyn Yalom, eds., pp. 119–139. Boston: Northeastern University Press.

Wheelock, Jane
1992   Personal Computers, Gender, and an Institutional Model of the Household. In *Consuming Technologies: Media and Information in Domestic Spaces*. Roger Silverstone and Eric Hirsch, eds., pp. 97–112. London: Routledge.

Willett, Rebekah
2009   Parodic Practices: Amateur Spoofs on Video-Sharing Sites. In *Video Cultures: Media Technology and Everyday Creativity*. David Buckingham and Rebekah Willett, eds., pp. 115–132. London: Palgrave Macmillan.

Woolard, Kathryn
1998   Introduction: Language Ideology as a Field of Inquiry. In *Language Ideologies: Practice and Theory*. Bambi Schieffelin, Kathryn A. Woolard, and Paul V. Kroskrity, eds., pp. 3–50. Oxford: Oxford University Press.

Wortham, Jenna

2012 Campaigns Use Social Media to Lure Younger Voters. *The New York Times*. October 7. http://www.nytimes.com/2012/10/08/tech nology/campaigns-use-social-media-to-lure-younger-voters.html, accessed July 8, 2013.

Zimmerman, Patricia R.

1995 *Reel Families: A Social History of Amateur Film*. Bloomington: Indiana University Press.

INDEX

《《◀ ■ ▶ 》》

Note: Italicized page numbers indicate illustrations.

ABOUT THE AUTHOR
《《◀ ■ ▶》》

Patricia G. Lange is an Assistant Professor of Critical Studies at California College of the Arts in San Francisco, California. As an anthropologist, Lange studies technical identities, mediated communication, and use of video to express the self and accomplish civic engagement. For over a decade, Lange has investigated how technical experts and enthusiasts propose and negotiate technical identities through media. She also studies expressions of emotion online, and how culturally contested genres of argumentation and criticism—such as "flaming" and "hating"—are used strategically.

Recognized as an expert on YouTube and new media, she has been published in a wide variety of journals and contributed to the first edited volumes on YouTube including *The YouTube Reader* (2009) and *Video Vortex: Responses to YouTube* (2008). She is a co-author of *Hanging Out, Messing Around, and Geeking Out: Kids Living and Learning with New Media* (2010), and *Living and Learning with New Media: Summary of Findings from the Digital Youth Project* (2009). She has also released an ethnographic film entitled *Hey Watch This! Sharing the Self Through Media* (2013), which is a diachronic investigation of YouTube as a social media site.

Lange is the inaugural Editor-in-Chief of The CASTAC Blog, which is the official blog of the American Anthropological Association's Committee on the Anthropology of Science, Technology, and Computing. Currently, she is studying the genre of video rants, and how they expose social problems. She studies ranters' exploration of how the parameters of online, vernacular expression are being culturally and infrastructurally constructed. Additional details about Lange's research and publications may be found on her website at patriciaglange.org.